Across Generations

Across Generations

Immigrant Families in America

EDITED BY

Nancy Foner

NEW YORK UNIVERSITY PRESS

NEW YORK AND LONDON

NEW YORK UNIVERSITY PRESS
New York and London
www.nyupress.org

Library of Congress Cataloging-in-Publication Data

Foner, Nancy, 1945–
Across generations : immigrant families in America / Nancy Foner.
p. cm.
Includes bibliographical references and index.
ISBN-13: 978–0–8147–2770–6 (cl : alk. paper)
ISBN-10: 0–8147–2770–0 (cl : alk. paper)
ISBN-13: 978–0–8147–2771–3 (pb : alk. paper)
ISBN-10: 0–8147–2771–9 (pb : alk. paper)
1. Family—United States. 2. Immigrant families—United States—Social
conditions. 3. United States—Emigration and immigration. I. Title.
HQ536.F656   2009
306.85086'9120973—dc22   2008050313

New York University Press books are printed on acid-free paper, and
their binding materials are chosen for strength and durability. We strive
to use environmentally responsible suppliers and materials to the
greatest extent possible in publishing our books.

Manufactured in the United States of America

c   10 9 8 7 6 5 4 3 2 1
p   10 9 8 7 6 5 4 3 2 1

Contents

Acknowledgments

In editing this volume, I have been fortunate in being able to bring together the work of an outstanding group of scholars whose rich ethnographic research helps to illuminate the complex nature of relations among different generations in immigrant families. I would like to thank all of the authors for their commitment to the book, their responsiveness, and the quality of their contributions.

At New York University Press, Ilene Kalish has been a wonderful editor. This is the second book project on which I have worked with Ilene, and, once again, it has been a great pleasure. I have benefited enormously from her enthusiasm, efficiency, and valuable suggestions. I am also grateful to editorial assistant Aiden Amos and managing editor Despina Papazoglou Gimbel, who helped in numerous ways in the publication process, and to Eric Zinner, editor-in-chief of the press, for his support of my work. Thanks as well to the two anonymous reviewers for their suggestions, which have, I believe, made this a better book.

In my own family, I owe a debt across generations: to my mother, Anne Foner, a sociologist of aging, for her many helpful comments along the way; to my daughter, Alexis Swerdloff, who continues to remind me of the strong bonds tying the generations together (as well as, on occasion, the inevitable tensions); and to my husband, Peter Swerdloff, for his unfailing good humor and wise advice.

III

Introduction

Intergenerational Relations in Immigrant Families

Nancy Foner

Immigration is one of the most pressing issues in the United States. The foreign-born now represent about 13 percent of the nation's population. Together with their American-born children, this group constitutes nearly a quarter of the United States—more than 65 million people. This is an astonishing figure. If today's foreign-born and their children were to form a country, it would have approximately twice the population of Canada and slightly more than that of France or Italy.

The numbers are critical, but their implications are even more significant. Much has been written about immigrants in the labor market, in the educational system, and in neighborhoods in the United States. Much less scholarly attention has been paid to what happens in the privacy of their families, although understanding family dynamics is essential for appreciating the first- and second-generation immigrant experience. This volume puts the spotlight on a key aspect of immigrant family life: intergenerational relations. The primary concern is relations between immigrant parents and their children, many of whom were born or largely raised in the United States, although relations between immigrant grandparents and their grandchildren are also investigated. Intergenerational relations—so central in immigrant families—are characterized by an intricate tangle of attachments and divisions. Intergenerational dynamics in immigrant families help shape the contours and trajectories of individual lives and also affect involvements outside the confines of the family.

It has become a cliché to talk about immigrant children in pitched battles against tradition-bound parents from the old country, but the essays in this book offer a more nuanced and complex view of intergenerational relations. As one might expect, one major theme is the sources of tensions and conflicts—for example, about parental discipline, children's marriage choices, and educational and occupational expectations for children. But intergenerational relations are not just about strife and strain. The essays also point to the ties that bond and bind immigrants and their children, and the way they work out accommodations and compromises.

Immigrants often leave children behind in the home country when they head for the United States, and a central theme of several of the chapters is relations in transnational families—when parents and children are apart, when they see each other on visits, and when, as happens in many cases, they reunite in the United States. Even when children are not left behind, intergenerational relationships, as many of the chapters make clear, are often embedded in transnational extended-family networks. Indeed, in some cases, separation involves parents or grandparents who return to the country or community of origin while children or grandchildren remain in the United States.

While the essays are concerned with intergenerational relations as they develop and play out within immigrants' families and households, these relations have an impact well beyond the household and family arena. Among other things, family intergenerational dynamics can affect how the children of immigrants fare at school and at work and their experiences in a host of other institutional settings. By the same token, what goes on at work, at school, and in the wider immigrant community—and in the home country—can have consequences for relations within the immigrant family in the United States. As several of the authors emphasize, U.S. immigration policy also affects family dynamics, particularly as it determines whether—and how—immigrants can establish authorized or legal status. Moreover, U.S. policies with regard to welfare benefits provide economic and other resources that can affect intergenerational relations. The immigrant family, in short, cannot be viewed in isolation.

In exploring these themes, the eight chapters in this volume draw on in-depth ethnographic research that captures the complexities of interactions between immigrant parents and their children and gives a flavor for the everyday lives of immigrant families. The broad range of national-origin groups represented—Latin American (Mexicans, Guatemalans, and Salvadorans), Asian (Bangladeshis, Chinese, and Filipinos), African (Sierra Leoneans), and Caribbean (Dominicans and West Indians)—provides a window into the dynamics of intergenerational relations in immigrant families from different regions, countries, and cultures. Moreover, the studies are based on research in a variety of settings in the United States, from New York City and Washington, DC, to Los Angeles and Phoenix.

The inclusion of chapters on diverse immigrant populations under-scores the role of home-country cultural and social patterns—and migration pathways of national-origin groups—in shaping intergenerational relations. Within an immigrant group, as the case studies show, gender, class, race, and legal status also have an important impact. Moreover, intergenerational relations are not fixed or static; they undergo shifts over time, as parents and children move through the life course into new life stages and as family and household arrangements—and in some cases the very country of residence—change.

The book begins with chapters primarily focused on intergenerational relations among family members living in the United States (Zhou, Espiritu, Waters and Sykes), continues with cases that look at the impact of transnational ties and orientations on intergenerational relations (Kibria, D'Alisera, Gilbertson), and concludes with analyses that explore parent–child relations across borders when migration leads to the separation of parents and children and relations must be managed from a distance (Menjívar and Abrego, Dreby).

In general, the chapters use "generation" in two interrelated ways. One meaning refers to genealogical rank in a kinship system—for example, the relationship of individuals to persons in the generation before or children in the generation after. Generation also is used as a measure of distance from the country of origin, so that people who move to the United States from another society as adults are often referred to as "first-generation" immigrants, their American-born children as the "second generation," and their children in turn as the "third generation."[1] Also implicit throughout is a distinction between household and family; the household is a residential unit made up of kin and sometimes non-kin, whereas the family is a kinship grouping, including people related by blood and marriage, that may not be tied to a residential unit.

Intergenerational Strains and Conflicts

The tale of the conflict between immigrant parents steeped in old-country traditions and values and their children who have grown up in the American social and cultural world is an old one.[2] Indeed, it forms the basis for many novels and memoirs about contemporary immigrants, typically from the point of view of aggrieved children.[3]

Intergenerational conflict, of course, is not unique to immigrant families. Adolescents in American society typically seek greater independence and autonomy while parents seek to assert their authority. Young people adopt styles of dress, decoration, music, and dance that their parents do not understand—and often cannot stand. Yet the strains resulting from "normal" teenage rebelliousness or lifestyles often become intensified when the parents come from another country and culture and are unfamiliar with or disapprove of dominant American values and practices. The parents may even hold up an idealized version of traditional values and customs as a model for their children, even though these values and traditions have undergone considerable change since they left their home country.[4] The key point is that rebelliousness among American adolescents represents a conflict between an adolescent world and an adult world, whereas the children of immigrants, as Min Zhou notes, also have to struggle to make sense of the inconsistencies between *two* adult worlds: that of the immigrant community or family and that of the larger society.[5] Intergenerational conflicts may be especially acute in groups whose cultural patterns and practices differ radically from those of the broader American culture.

As the essays in this book demonstrate, intergenerational conflicts in immigrant families have many sources. One is issues of discipline and respect. In many immigrant cultures children are supposed to show parents and their elders a level of respect and deference far greater than expected in American families—and parents are permitted, even encouraged, to discipline their children in ways that Americans, and the American legal system, deem abusive. In their chapter, Mary Waters and Jennifer Sykes discuss how corporal punishment was an accepted—indeed, taken-for-granted—aspect of child-rearing in the West Indies, and cultural attitudes about parenting techniques rooted there continue to have a strong impact when West Indians move to the United States. West Indian immigrant parents believe that sparing the rod is a recipe for disaster, leading to behavioral problems and delinquency. They are outraged that if they discipline children the way they think best, they can be reported to the police or state agencies for child abuse.[6] Just how common such reports are is an open question, yet even the possibility that children might appeal to U.S. legal authorities can be a flashpoint for tensions between the generations in many immigrant groups, giving children added leverage in relations with their parents and bringing to the fore the conflict between U.S. and home-country behavioral norms.

For their part, members of the second generation, reared in an America culture where early independence for children is encouraged and child-rearing norms are generally more permissive than in the country of origin, often view their parents as authoritarian and domineering. The parents, with their (sometimes idealized) old world standards, often think their children are rude and disrespectful. Chinese immigrant parents, as Min Zhou reports in her essay, feel that their children owe them filial piety and are horrified when their Americanized children are disrespectful and disobey.[7] Grandparents, too, as Greta Gilbertson indicates in her study of a Dominican extended family, may have similar complaints. She cites one older Dominican woman who objects that her grandchildren in New York call her by her nickname instead of *abuela* (grandmother). When parents feel frustrated and threatened by the new values and behaviors to which their children are exposed, they may attempt to tighten the reins, which, in turn, heightens children's resentment and desire to flout parental controls.

Sexual relations are often a source of conflict, particularly when it comes to daughters. Immigrants from cultures where dating is frowned upon or forbidden can be frightened and appalled by their daughters' desire to go out on dates and "hang out" with their friends. One of the second-generation West Indian women in Waters and Sykes's chapter said her parents restricted her dating until she was twenty-two. In general, immigrant parents are stricter with daughters than sons, seeking to keep daughters home or close to home and heavily monitoring and controlling their social activities. In Filipino families, as Yen Le Espiritu reports, parental control over daughters' movements and actions begins the moment they are perceived as young adults and sexually vulnerable. The parents Espiritu interviewed seldom allowed their daughters to date, to stay out late, to spend the night at friends' houses, or to take out-of-town trips. Daughters railed against parents' constant surveillance, which placed greater restrictions on them than on their brothers—a key source of frustration and even intense anger. "I always had to fight long, drawn-out arguments with my parents just to move two feet from the house," one daughter complained. Espiritu argues that Filipino immigrant parents' emotional hold over their daughters strengthens the parents' power as they attempt to regulate daughters' independent choices by branding disobedient young women as "nonethnic" or "untraditional," thereby striking at the children's sense of ethnic identity.

A further source of conflict is parental pressure to marry within the ethnic group, which second-generation young people may resent—and resist.[8] Additional problems arise in immigrant groups where arranged marriage is commonly practiced. Arranged marriages, needless to say, conflict sharply with the emphasis on romantic love in American culture. Indeed, American society—and, in some cases, its legal institutions—may encourage young people to reject traditional arranged marriages. Increasingly, young people in these families are given some element of choice; for example, they may have veto power over parental choices, or, in a "semi-arranged marriage," they may be introduced to acceptable partners and then allowed a brief courtship in which they decide whether or not they wish to marry. Even with these changes, many second-generation youth bristle at parental pressure, as Nazli Kibria's chapter on Bangladeshis indicates. Bangladeshis born and raised in the United States were opposed to the idea of arranged marriages and, to a lesser degree, semi-arranged marriages, as well as their parents' desire to see them marry someone of Bangali origin.

Intense, and often high, parental expectations for children are also a point of contention, as the chapters on Chinese and Filipino immigrants emphasize. "We did it for the children," is a common refrain among Filipino immigrants, who feel that their children's educational and occupational success will validate their move to the United States and the sacrifices they have made along the way. Young people in Filipino and Chinese families are under tremendous pressure from their parents to get good grades, to graduate from college, and to pursue "practical" careers such as law, medicine, or engineering.[9] Zhou describes the Chinese immigrant family as a pressure cooker in which parents are demanding and unyielding about their children's educational achievements. If their children work hard, they believe, they can get A's; those who fail to achieve bring shame to the family. The result, she says, is that children often find themselves working at least twice as hard as their American peers while feeling that their parents never think they work hard enough. As Espiritu points out, in the case of Filipinos, this is aggravated by the fact that parents who are overburdened by demanding work schedules and unfamiliar with the requirements of American schools are unable to offer their children much assistance.

Parents who don't speak English often depend on their children to translate, mediate, and interpret, which can also cause difficulties. As Zhou indicates in her chapter, this reversal of roles can give children power over their parents, which may exacerbate conflict and accentuate the gulfs between them. Parents understandably feel frustrated by having to depend on children for translating government documents and other material and for communicating with English-speaking officials, professionals, and merchants. Parents may worry, in fact, that their children are not translating correctly—and a number of studies note instances where children deliberately mistranslate reports from teachers, saying that a grade of *F* means "fine," for example. For their part, young people may be embarrassed by their parents' inability to fill out forms, make appointments, or conduct business on their own, be annoyed by this encroachment on their time, and feel uncomfortable about learning family secrets—or intervening and mediating—in the process of translating in medical, legal, and other social settings.[10]

Two additional sources of tension between the generations are highlighted in the chapters by D'Alisera and Kibria: different relations and reactions to the homeland. Many Sierra Leonean children in JoAnn D'Alisera's study, influenced by mainstream American values and images of Africa, felt ashamed of their parents' home country and the customs practiced there; sometimes they held up their parents to ridicule, causing distress to parents who were trying to connect the children to the homeland culture. Trips to the country of origin can also create strains. Bangladeshi parents were eager for their children to become acquainted with family in Bangladesh and establish a sense of connection there, but the children were often reluctant and uneasy about going to visit, complaining, for example, about the heat, the food, and the poverty.

Gender clearly affects tensions and conflicts between the generations in a powerful way, if only because daughters nearly always experience greater strictures on their freedom outside the household than sons. Class, race, and ethnicity figure in as well. Zhou observes, for example, that middle-class Chinese immigrant parents are more willing to accept "American" behavior and are less strict with their children. In the West African case, negative images of Africa that affect Sierra Leonean children are related to long-held racial constructions in the United States. Espiritu suggests that one reason Filipino parents have such a strong emotional hold on their daughters is that accusations that children are "not Filipina enough" have a bitter sting when children are trying to establish a positive ethnic identity in the U.S. context. Legal status also needs to be considered, and Cecilia Menjívar and Leisy Abrego indicate that the advantages of American-born children over their unauthorized siblings—when it comes, for example, to access to health care or easier ability to travel to the home community—can lead to resentments that impinge on relations with parents.

Although the immigrant family can become a battlefield between the generations,[11] this characterization is too sharp and one-sided. Relations between the generations are filled with inconsistencies and contradictions and shift in different contexts and over time. In many, probably most, cases, conflict is mixed with cooperation and caring, and rejection of some parental standards and practices is coupled with acceptance of others.

As is evident in this volume's case studies, even when young people chafe under parental constraints and obligations, the vast majority feel deep affection for and loyalty to their parents and grandparents and recognize the importance of family and the need to assist and support family members. Families create strong emotional ties that bond members together. Moreover, parents and children often work out compromises as a way to get along. Far from being inflexible traditionalists, many immigrant parents adapt and change in the new context. This can mean giving children more say in marriage arrangements, for example, extending the evening curfew hour, or permitting dating earlier than some parents would like.[12] Although Waters and Sykes emphasize the persistence of old-country parenting practices among West Indian immigrants, they note that some parents are trying to learn new ways to discipline their children; some are learning new techniques from their children, who explain how American or Americanized friends are disciplined. Alejandro Portes and Ruben Rumbaut suggest that when parents and children acculturate at the same time—what they call 'consonant acculturation'—children are less prone to feel embarrassed by their parents and more willing to accept parental guidance, thereby reducing the likelihood of intergenerational conflict.[13]

As for the children of immigrants, they are not inevitably rebels, nor do they necessarily reject or entirely abandon their parents' ways. Not all Sierra Leonean young people are ashamed of their parents' homeland; many, D'Alisera points out, develop a sense of cultural pride and a link to Sierra Leone and try their best to "accommodate their parents' desire for them to stay connected to a place they have never seen." Bangladeshi young people may not want to go "home" to visit and may reject the notion of arranged marriage, but they understand their parents' desire to see them married endogamously to other Muslims and Bangalis. As Waters and Sykes report, many West Indian teenagers defend their parents' disciplinary practices and said that when they had children they would try to combine West Indian strictness with American freedoms and openness. Whatever young people think about their parents' standards, they often try to conceal their behavior from parents in order to avoid clashes, and they may simply go along with parental expectations to keep the peace.

Transnational Dynamics

Intergenerational relations in immigrant families are not just about what happens among those living in the United States. Many of the chapters demonstrate the critical significance of transnational ties and obligations: immigrants and their children and grandchildren in the United States often maintain active and ongoing involvements with close relatives in the home country and are part of what have been conceptualized as transnational families.[14] Intergenerational relations that span national borders are, as one would expect, complicated by the realities and difficulties of physical separation.

This comes out dramatically in the chapters by Joanna Dreby and Menjívar and Abrego, who discuss the dynamics in Mexican, Guatemalan, and Salvadoran families when parents leave their children with relatives in the home community—or in some cases send them back—when they go to the United States to work. Parent–child separations, as both chapters show, are linked to the demands of labor migration for those facing limited opportunities in their home countries and restrictive U.S. policies that, among other things, have recently made border crossing more difficult, dangerous, and expensive. It is an old, familiar immigrant story for fathers to migrate without wives and children. What is new, as Dreby emphasizes, is the growing number of mothers from poorer countries who are leaving their children to work abroad, a phenomenon that has been called transnational motherhood.[15]

Whatever the reason for leaving children in the home community, the separation takes a toll on the children—and their parents—and obviously affects their relations. "When parents and children do not live in the same country," Dreby writes, "share in the same routines, or experience similar opportunities and constraints, intergenerational relations are constantly in flux. During periods of separation, parents and children must constantly adapt to each other's changing needs. They do so based on the little information they can glean through weekly conversations, second-hand accounts from caregivers, and neighbors' gossip. Lack of contact increases insecurity and intensifies emotions. The effects of changes in family composition are harder to adjust to." The Mexican mothers and fathers in Dreby's study struggled to exert authority from a distance over children who were dubious and at times resentful of their parents' decisions to migrate. Mothers and fathers often felt jealous of their children's primary caregivers in Mexico. Further complications ensued when children in Mexico had to share their parents, especially mothers, with siblings who were born and lived with parents abroad and thus were in competition for parents' love, attention, and resources.

The burden of separation in Mexican as well as Guatemalan and Salvadoran families fell more heavily on mothers than fathers since mothers were expected to provide more emotional care. Menjívar and Abrego report that children used more emotional language and expressed greater suffering when it was their mother who migrated. Although both parents of one teenage boy in El Salvador lived in the United States, he directed his anger and resentment only toward his mother, saying that "the man can do as he pleases." Mexican fathers, as Dreby notes, were evaluated as family providers, and their economic support was enough to demonstrate love; mothers were expected to show greater concern and devotion. As a result of this gendered double standard, mothers felt much guiltier than fathers when they left children behind—and the children judged them more harshly for having gone. Many mothers she interviewed said they cried for months when they arrived in the United States; the fathers were relatively guilt-free, feeling that they were fulfilling their paternal responsibilities by working and sending money home.

When children are reunited with their parents in the United States, different sets of problems arise. The reunions, as Menjívar and Abrego put it, can be bittersweet, leading to great joy and renewed intimacy as well as tension and disappointment. Among other things, parents and children must become reacquainted and get used to living together again in a situation in which both may have unrealistic expectations of each other. The children's separation from grandmothers or other close kin who cared for them in the home community for much of their childhood is often wrenching. Not only do children have to adjust to new living arrangements in an unfamiliar country, but also new schools and a new cultural, social, and physical environment. In some cases, they also have to adjust to a new step-parent and new siblings as well.[16] That parents are often working long hours and have little time to spend with their children adds difficulties.

For their part, parents may be disappointed if their children are confused, resentful, or withdrawn instead of grateful for the reunion, which usually entailed great financial sacrifices. Trying to establish discipline over children they have spent little time with or may not have seen for several years poses another frustrating challenge. Still, as Menjívar and Abrego remind us, reunifications in the United States also offer new opportunities for parents and children to recognize each other's sacrifices and to build closer relationships with each other.

In unusual instances, it is parents who stay behind while their children migrate to the United States—as Zhou describes in her discussion of "parachute kids," the term used for young people, from the age of about eight to seventeen, who are sent to California to attend school (so they will gain entry to prestigious colleges and jobs) while their parents remain in Taiwan, Hong Kong, or mainland China. Usually, these children see their parents only two or three times a year, leading to emotional distance and greater independence from them and their controls.

Another transnational permutation occurs when parents or grandparents return to the home community while maintaining close relations with their children or grandchildren in the United States through visits, phone calls, and other means of communication. In portraying the complex dynamics of the Castillo's extended family, Gilbertson indicates that family members who have remained in or returned to the Dominican Republic are still often pivotal figures for those who reside in the United States and continue to interject their opinions in the affairs of their children and grandchildren there.[17] When older women go back to the Dominican Republic, this may give their adult daughters more scope in being able to assume leadership positions in the extended family in the United States, but it can create problems in that the daughters cannot rely on the older women for day-to-day support the way they did when their mothers were always around. On return to the Dominican Republic, the older women may also seek to pull back some of their children and grandchildren to join them, which obviously influences the shape of intergenerational relations and no doubt, on occasion, sparks tensions and conflicts.

A study of Mexican New Yorkers indicates that many second-generation adult Mexican women sent their pre-school-aged children back to rural Mexico to be cared for by grandmothers who had gone home to retire, thereby forging and fortifying relations between three generations

in a transnational field. Second-generation Mexican teenagers were sometimes sent back, too, often because parents felt they showed signs of trouble in the United States.[18] In my research on Jamaican migrants in New
York, parents often tried to keep wayward teenagers in line by threaten-
ing to send them to Jamaica; such threats sometimes heightened intergenerational conflicts—although, if carried out, the separation itself might
eventually heal the breach. Whether teenagers are sent home as punishment, protection from the dangers of American urban life, or in response
to changing family needs and dynamics, a large-scale survey of second-
generation New Yorkers found that a surprising number of West Indians
and Latinos were sent back home to live with relatives at some point in
their teen years.[19] This back-and-forth movement among young people—
as well as among their parents and grandparents—often reflects and has
reverberations for intergenerational relations in immigrant families.

Intergenerational Relations: Beyond the Family and Household

Families and households do not exist in isolation. An analysis of intergenerational relations within immigrant families must inevitably take
into account broader social, economic, political, and cultural institutions
and practices. State policies, for instance, have an impact on how relations develop between immigrant parents and their children and grandchildren because, as the chapters by Gilbertson and Menjívar and Abrego
highlight, they shape, among other things, people's ability to move to
and remain legally in the United States as well as access to social welfare
benefits. What happens at school has implications for family dynamics at
home. To give just one example, when children are struggling or get into
difficulties at school this can lead to conflicts with immigrant parents and,
in some cases as just mentioned, sending children to grandparents in the
home country. In her chapter, Espiritu points to another dynamic, argu-
ing that the pervasive sexualization of Filipinas and other Asian women
in the United States helps explain why Filipino immigrants have such inflexible expectations of their daughters' chastity—a common cause of intergenerational clashes in Filipino families.

Work life also influences intergenerational relations because it affects
the economic resources available to family members and creates strains
that can carry over into the family. When the children of immigrants
spend time working in a family business, the boundaries between family

and work are blurred and other tensions arise. A recent study of Korean American and Chinese American children of entrepreneurial immigrants describes the anger and resentment of adolescents who had to work in the family business, which, they felt, robbed them of a "normal" childhood. Role reversals were magnified since the young people found themselves translating and mediating, often in times of stress, with customers on a daily basis as well as with professionals such as lawyers on vital business matters.[20]

Involvement in the ethnic community may also have consequences for intergenerational relations in the family, in some cases serving to reduce tensions and conflicts. Zhou argues that Chinese language schools help the second generation deal with the pressures they face and provide a socially acceptable setting where they can let off steam. When they socialize with young people like themselves in the Chinese language schools and other ethnic institutions catering to Chinese American adolescents, they come to understand that the problems they have with their parents are common to other Chinese families. In the Chinese language schools, they can commiserate with their peers, share their feelings, and develop strategies to cope with parental constraints. At the same time, ethnic institutions reinforce parental norms and values regarding the importance of schooling, showing respect to parents, and feeling proud of Chinese culture and being Chinese. In a variation on the same theme, Sierra Leonean parents described by D'Alisera try to counter negative images of African cultural practices that many children have imbibed in America by seeking to instill a sense of pride and involvement in culture and traditions through various community activities and organizations (such as naming ceremonies, weddings, and fundraising events), although how successful such efforts are is unclear.

As these comments suggest, various institutions and organizations outside the family are influenced by the contours of intergenerational dynamics within it. In the Sierra Leonean case, parents consciously shaped community events to convey positive sentiments about the home country to children who were ashamed of their parents' culture. Chinese language schools were designed for educational purposes, but as a result of intergenerational strains they also ended up as places where young people could vent their frustrations.

Resentments that build up in the family spill over into other arenas as well, school being especially noteworthy in this regard. Troubles at home may lead to trouble at school. When children and grandchildren are sent back and forth between the home community and the United States, their educational progress may suffer.[21] Not that this is inevitable; indeed, some members of the second generation in a large-scale New York study who had been sent home and gone to school there were in a better position than their cousins who remained in the New York City public schools in terms of getting into U.S. colleges and being hired for U.S. jobs.[22] With regard to gender, second-generation daughters may resent that they face greater restrictions than their brothers on their freedom of movement, yet, paradoxically, their more highly structured and monitored lives can have positive effects on their educational achievement because they are kept closer to home and away from the temptations of the street.[23] Less happily, the double standard for daughters can lead immigrant families to cut short daughters' educational pursuits or pressure them to attend less prestigious institutions closer to home.[24]

Young people's activities in religious institutions and politics may also be affected by, or at least parallel, the generational divide in immigrant families. Studies indicate that members of the second generation may segregate themselves from the immigrant generation in religious con-gregations because they feel estranged from the ethnic ambience there, and sometimes they complain that the religious services are too rigid or old-fashioned.[25] In political organizations and community groups, the second generation may have a different perspective on ethnic group iden-tity as well as a different style of political expression from those whose early political experience was in another country.[26] For example, a study of Dominican activists in New York shows that the American civil rights movement had a far greater influence on the style and substance of po-litical expression among the second generation, whose members were more willing to work closely with African Americans and other Latinos.[27] Among Asian Americans, there is a greater panethnic consciousness of "Asian" (as opposed to Chinese, Korean, or Vietnamese) identity among the second than the first generation.[28]

Conclusion: Looking Ahead

Most of the chapters in this volume explore relations between children in adolescence or young adulthood and their middle-aged immigrant parents. However, relations change as both children and their parents grow older. Children form families of their own—and become parents themselves. Parents become grandparents. Members of both generations often shift residences within or outside the United States. At the same time, the societies in which families and households are embedded also change. Individuals respond to a multiplicity of changing social, economic, and political conditions, all of which affect the shape and form of families and the relations within them.

Gilbertson's twelve-year longitudinal study of the Castillo extended family brings out many of these dynamics, as she shows how relations among family members continually took new twists and turns and tensions rose and fell. There were moves back and forth between the Dominican Republic and New York, or to other parts of the United States; marriages split up and new unions were constituted; children went from being toddlers to teenagers or from teenagers to young adults; and middle-aged women turned into grandmothers.

While relations between the generations in immigrant families may be severely strained at one point in the children's, and parents', life course, later on they may become less conflictual. A theme in many novels and memoirs is how members of the second generation who were deeply divided from and involved in intense conflicts with parents in their youth work out rapprochements when they become adults and strike out on their own. An ethnographic study by Lisa Park describes how the anger and resentment that Chinese American and Korean American daughters felt toward parents in their teenage years when they worked in the family business tended to subside when they moved away from home for college.[29] In another study, Vivian Louie notes that second-generation Chinese American college students who balked at parental pressure when they were younger thought during their college years that it stimulated them to do well in school.[30] In many cases, when daughters become mothers, a new closeness develops between them as they turn to their own mothers for advice and support. They may also reevaluate their own earlier critical approaches in light of their experiences as parents.

As members of the second generation grow older and establish families of their own, they may end up acting more like their own parents than they would ever have imagined and sharing many of their parents' attitudes toward child-rearing. The young adult second-generation West Indians described by Waters and Sykes often said they resented their parents' harsh parenting styles when they were young, but now attributed their success to their parents' strict control and discipline. Many saw corporal punishment as a positive way to keep their own children in line—and like their parents, complained about interventions from state agencies. At the same time, cultural innovation was taking place as many sought to combine the best of West Indian and American methods and said they would try to communicate more with their children than their parents had with them.

If the passage of time, and movement through the life course, have the potential to reduce strains between immigrant parents and their children, by the same token, new sources of conflict can emerge—or old ones may, at times, be heightened. Adult children, for example, who have been significantly upwardly mobile may be embarrassed by their poorer, less educated, and old-fashioned immigrant parents. To the extent that adult children adopt middle-class American ideas and parenting practices, there may be tensions with immigrant parents about these practices or other household matters. Gilbertson describes how older Dominican women criticized their Americanized daughters and daughters-in-law for insufficient dedication to their children and their family—for buying meals from restaurants or stores rather than cooking at home or paying strangers to care for their children.

Because most members of the contemporary second generation are still young children, teenagers, or young adults, we have little research on the dynamics of their relations with their immigrant parents or third-generation children when they set up households and families of their own or, in some cases, continue as adults to live with parents in extended family households.[31] Relations between immigrant grandparents and their American-born grandchildren are also still largely unexplored. Among the many intriguing questions is how members of the third generation will relate to their immigrant heritage and their grandparents' countries of origin. Kibria brings up another issue in her chapter regarding changes over time in the Bangladeshi community. At the time of her research, the Bangladeshi community was a relatively new one in the United States, with most immigrants having arrived in the last ten or fifteen years. The second generation, she notes, therefore generally grew up in the context of a "sparse transnational sphere," and the question arises as to whether and how transnational connections—and family relations—among the second generation will change as the Bangladeshi community becomes larger, more settled, and older.

Whether considering transnational links and obligations or U.S.-based institutions and practices, the case studies in this volume provide rich and detailed analyses of the intricate relations between the generations in immigrant families, including the factors that shape these relations as well as their consequences. Because immigrants and their descendants live out a good part of their lives and often develop their most meaningful relationships in families, what happens in the family arena has enormous significance. Indeed, in analyzing the complexities of family life, the chapters that follow offer insights and raise questions that go beyond the family and household to enrich our general understanding of the immigrant and second-generation experience. It is hoped that they will inspire additional research that will lead to further advances in appreciating the complex and multifaceted dynamics of intergenerational relations in immigrant families.

NOTES

1. Foner and Kasinitz 2007: 270.

2. This section on intergenerational strains and conflicts draws on Foner and Kasinitz 2007.

3. To name just a few: Diaz 2007; Fong-Torres 1994; Lahiri 2003; Lee 2007; Mar 2000; Ng 1994.

4. Foner 1997.

5. Zhou 2001: 214.

6. See also Kibria 1993; Pessar 2003; Stepick and Stepick 2003; and Suarez-Orozco and Suarez-Orozco 2001.

7. Also see Zhou and Bankston 1998 on the high value on parental authority and respect for parents and elders.

8. In a large-scale study of the second generation in New York, a majority in almost every group rejected the notion that it was important to marry someone in the same ethnic group, a view that was not often shared by their parents (Kasinitz et al. 2008).

9. See, for example, Kim 2004 and Min 1998 on similar pressures in Korean immigrant families.

10. See also Valenzuela 1999; Menjívar 2000: 214–16.

11. Lessinger 1995: 97.

12. Lessinger 1995; Zephir 2001.

13. Portes and Rumbaut 2001.

14. On transnational families, see, for example, Foner 2005; Gardner and Grillo 2002; Levitt and Glick Schiller 2004; Parreñas 2005; and Schmalzbauer 2008.

15. Hondagneu-Sotelo and Avila 1997.

16. See Levitt 2001: 79–80; Suarez-Orozco et al. 2008: 63–67.

17. The notion that older relatives in the home country can be a source of support comes out in Junot Diaz's (2007) recent novel, *The Brief Wondrous Life of Oscar Wao*, in which the American-born Oscar and his sister return for lengthy stays with their grandmother (who never left the Dominican Republic) when they are experiencing serious difficulties in the United States.

18. Smith 2006: 196–202.

19. Kasinitz et al. 2002.

20. Park 2005.

21. Levitt 2001: 79–80.

22. Kasinitz et al. 2002: 115.

23. See Lopez 2003; Smith 2006.

24. See Wolf 1997.

25. Ebaugh and Chafetz 2000: 129–33.

26. Foner and Kasinitz 2007.

27. Marwell 2004. I am grateful to Philip Kasinitz for bringing this point to my attention.

28. Espiritu 1992.

29. Park 2005: 58–60.

30. Louie 2004: 42–47.

31. More than one in five children of immigrants aged twenty-eight to thirty-two in the New York second-generation study were still living with a parent (Kasinitz et al. 2008: 212–19).

REFERENCES

Diaz, Junot. 2007. *The Brief Wondrous Life of Oscar Wao.* New York: Riverhead.

Ebaugh, Helen Rose, and Janet Saltzman Chafetz. 2000. *Religion and the New Immigrants.* Walnut Creek, CA: Altamira Press.

Espiritu, Yen Le. 1992. *Asian American Panethnicity.* Philadelphia: Temple University Press.

Foner, Nancy. 1997. "The Immigrant Family: Cultural Legacies and Cultural Changes." *International Migration Review* 31: 961–74.

———. 2005. *In a New Land: A Comparative View of Immigration.* New York: New York University Press.

Foner, Nancy, and Philip Kasinitz. 2007. "The Second Generation." Pp. 270–82 in Mary Waters and Reed Ueda (eds.), *The New Americans: A Guide to Immigration since 1965.* Cambridge: Harvard University Press.

Fong-Torres, Ben. 1994. *The Rice Room: Growing Up Chinese-American—From Number Two Son to Rock 'N Roll.* New York: Hyperion.

Gardner, Katy, and Ralph Grillo. 2002. "Transnational Households and Ritual: An Overview." *Global Networks* 2: 179–90.

Hondagneu-Sotelo, Pierrette, and Ernestine Avila. 1997. "I'm Here But I'm There: The Meanings of Latina Transnational Motherhood." *Gender & Society* 11: 548–71.

Kasinitz, Philip, et al. 2002. "Transnationalism and the Children of Immigrants in Contemporary New York." Pp. 96–122 in Peggy Levitt and Mary C. Waters (eds.), *The Changing Face of Home: The Transnational Lives of the Second Generation*. New York: Russell Sage Foundation.

Kasinitz, Philip, John Mollenkopf, Mary Waters, and Jennifer Holdaway. 2008. *Inheriting the City: The Children of Immigrants Come of Age*. Cambridge: Harvard University Press.

Kibria, Nazli. 1993. *Family Tightrope: The Changing Lives of Vietnamese Americans*. Princeton: Princeton University Press.

Kim, Dae Young. 2004. "Leaving the Ethnic Economy: The Rapid Integration of Second-Generation Korean Americans in New York." Pp. 154–88 in Philip Kasinitz, John H. Mollenkopf, and Mary C. Waters (eds.), *Becoming New Yorkers: Ethnographies of the New Second Generation*. New York: Russell Sage Foundation.

Lahiri, Jhumpa. 2003. *The Namesake*. Boston: Houghton Mifflin.

Lee, Min Jin. 2007. *Free Food for Millionaires*. New York: Warner Books.

Lessinger, Johanna. 1995. *From the Ganges to the Hudson*. Boston: Allyn and Bacon.

Levitt, Peggy. 2001. *The Transnational Villagers*. Berkeley: University of California Press.

Levitt, Peggy, and Nina Glick Schiller. 2004. "Conceptualizing Simultaneity: A Transnational Social Field Perspective on Society." *International Migration Review* 38: 1002–39.

Lopez, Nancy C. 2003. *Hopeful Girls, Troubled Boys: Race and Gender Disparity in Urban Education*. New York: Routledge.

Louie, Vivian. 2004. *Compelled to Excel: Immigration, Education, and Opportunity among Chinese Americans*. Stanford: Stanford University Press.

Mar, M. Elaine. 2000. *Paper Daughter: A Memoir*. New York: Harper Perennial.

Marwell, Nicole. 2004. "Ethnic and Postethnic Politics in New York City: The Dominican Second Generation." Pp. 227–56 in Philip Kasinitz, John H. Mollenkopf, and Mary C. Waters (eds.), *Becoming New Yorkers: Ethnographies of the New Second Generation*. New York: Russell Sage Foundation.

Menjívar, Cecilia. 2000. *Fragmented Ties: Salvadoran Immigrant Networks in America*. Berkeley: University of California Press.

Min, Pyong Gap. 1998. *Changes and Conflicts: Korean Immigrant Families in New York*. Boston: Allyn and Bacon.

Ng, Fae. 1994. *Bone*. New York: Harper.

Orleck, Annelise. 1999. *The Soviet Jewish Americans*. Westport, CT: Greenwood Press.

Park, Lisa Sun-Hee. 2005. *Consuming Citizenship: Children of Asian Immigrant Entrepreneurs.* Stanford: Stanford University Press.

Parreñas, Rhacel Salazar. 2005. *Children of Global Migration: Transnational Families and Gendered Woes.* Stanford: Stanford University Press.

Pessar, Patricia. 2003. "Anthropology and the Engendering of Migration Studies." Pp. 75–98 in Nancy Foner (ed.), *American Arrivals: Anthropology Engages the New Immigration.* Santa Fe, NM: SAR Press.

Portes, Alejandro, and Ruben Rumbaut. 2001. *Legacies: The Story of the Immigrant Second Generation.* Berkeley: University of California Press.

Schmalzbauer, Leah. 2008. "Family Divided: The Class Formation of Honduran Transnational Families." *Global Networks* 8: 329–46.

Smith, Robert C. 2006. *Mexican New York: Transnational Lives of New Immigrants.* Berkeley: University of California Press.

Stepick, Alex, and Carol Dutton Stepick. 2003. "Becoming American: Immigration, Identity, Intergenerational Relations, and Academic Orientation." Pp. 129–62 in Nancy Foner (ed.), *American Arrivals: Anthropology Engages the New Immigration.* Santa Fe, NM: SAR Press.

Suarez-Orozco, Carola, and Marcelo Suarez-Orozco. 2001. *Children of Immigration.* Cambridge: Harvard University Press.

Suarez-Orozco, Carola, Marcelo Suarez-Orozco, and Irina Todorova. 2008. *Learning in a New Land: Immigrant Students in American Society.* Cambridge: Harvard University Press.

Valenzuela, Abel. 1999. "Gender Roles and Settlement Activities among Children and Their Immigrant Families." *American Behavioral Scientist* 42: 720–42.

Waters, Mary C. 1999. *Black Identities: West Indian Immigrant Dreams and American Realities.* Cambridge: Harvard University Press.

Wolf, Diane. 1997. "Family Secrets: Transnational Struggles among Children of Filipino Immigrants." *Sociological Perspectives* 40: 457–82.

Zephir, Flore. 2001. *Trends in Ethnic Identification among Second Generation Haitian Immigrants in New York City.* Westport, CT: Bergin and Garvey.

Zhou, Min. 2001. "Straddling Different Worlds: The Acculturation of Vietnamese Refugee Children." Pp. 187–227 in Ruben Rumbaut and Alejandro Portes (eds.), *Ethnicities: Children of Immigrants in America.* Berkeley: University of California Press.

Zhou, Min, and Carl Bankston, 1998. *Growing Up American: How Vietnamese Children Adapt to Life in the United States.* New York: Russell Sage Foundation.

1

|||||||||||||||||||||||||||||||||||||||||||||||||||||||

Conflict, Coping, and Reconciliation
Intergenerational Relations in Chinese Immigrant Families

Min Zhou

Relations between parents and children in Chinese immigrant families are characterized by intense bicultural and intergenerational conflicts.[1] In the United States, most children of Chinese immigrants live in two-parent, nuclear families, with a smaller number in extended or transnational families. In these various immigrant households, a modified version of Confucian values emphasizing filial piety, education, hard work, and discipline serve as normative behavioral standards for socializing the younger generation. Many immigrant parents feel they have sacrificed for their children's better future in America. They have clearly articulated expectations that their children will attain the highest levels of educational and occupational achievement possible, help elevate the family to middle-class status, and, most importantly, take care of parents when they are old and frail. Deviation from these expectations is considered a family shame or failure and is thus negatively sanctioned by the family and the ethnic community.

It is not easy, however, for immigrant parents to enforce these behavioral standards and guarantee that familial expectations are met owing to vulnerabilities associated with the parents' foreign birth, bicultural and intergenerational conflicts, and the different pace of acculturation between parents and children. Often times, children regard their immigrant parents as *lao-wan-gu* (old sticks-in-the-mud or stubborn heads from the old world) and parental ways as feudal or old-fashioned—and a rebellion against tradition almost inevitably results. Parents are convinced that their own ways are the best recipe for success, and they constantly worry that their children are becoming too Americanized too soon.

Yet these strains rarely break families apart, even when they are manifested in young people's rebellious behavior. Other studies have pointed to factors that lead to conciliation, including children's bonds of affection, loyalty, and obligation to parents.[2] These studies have tended to stress dynamics within immigrant families. My emphasis is different. I argue that involvement in the institutional environment in the ethnic community plays an important role in reducing tension in Chinese immigrant families. Not only do ethnic social and cultural institutions reinforce parental standards, but they also provide socially acceptable places where young people can meet and interact—and commiserate and let off steam.

While the bulk of this chapter focuses on conflict, coping, and conciliation when parents and children live together, I also consider intergenerational relations in the context of an altogether new type of living arrangement that has arisen in the Chinese immigrant community: "parachute kids." These are children who have come to the United States on their own, usually in their early teens, for a better education and are therefore separated from their parents in the key adolescent years. I draw on a combination of U.S. census data and my own qualitative fieldwork data collected in the Chinese immigrant communities in Los Angeles and New York between 1996 and 2002.

Chinese Immigration in the Post-1965 Era

Chinese Americans are by far the oldest and largest ethnic group of Asian ancestry in the United States. Their long history of migration and settlement dates back to the late 1840s, including some sixty years of legal exclusion. With the lifting of legal barriers to Chinese immigration during World War II and especially following the 1965 Hart-Celler Act, which abolished the national-origins quota system and emphasized family reunification and the importation of skilled labor, the Chinese American community increased dramatically—from 237,000 in 1960 to more than three million (including half a million mixed-race persons) in 2005. Much of this extraordinary growth is due to immigration. Between 1961 and 2005, more than 1.8 million immigrants were admitted to the United States as permanent residents from China, Hong Kong, and Taiwan.[3] The foreign born accounted for more than two-thirds of the ethnic Chinese population in the United States. Today's second generation is still very young and has not yet come of age in significant numbers.[4] The 2000 Current Population Survey indicates that 44 percent of the U.S.-born Chinese are under the age of eighteen and another 10 percent are between eighteen and twenty-four.[5]

After 1965, the Chinese American community was transformed from a bachelors' society to a family community. There have been other significant changes as well. Unlike earlier Chinese immigrants, post-1965 Chinese arrivals have come not only from mainland China, but also from the greater Chinese Diaspora—Hong Kong, Taiwan, Vietnam, Cambodia, Malaysia, and the Americas. Diverse national origins entail diverse cultural patterns. Linguistically, for example, Chinese immigrants come from a much wider variety of dialect groups than in the past. While all Chinese share a single ancestral written language, they speak numerous regional dialects—Cantonese, Mandarin, Minnanese, Hakkaese, Chaozhounese, and Shanghainese.

Post-1965 Chinese immigrants also have diverse socioeconomic backgrounds. Like those in the past, some arrive in the United States with little money, minimum education, few job skills, and from rural areas, but a significant number now come with considerable family savings, education, and skills far above the levels of average Americans. The 2004 American Community Survey reports that 50 percent of adult Chinese Americans (age twenty-five or older) in the United States have attained four or more years of college education, compared to 30 percent of non-Hispanic whites. Immigrants from Taiwan displayed the highest levels of educational attainment, with nearly two-thirds completing at least four years of college, followed by those from Hong Kong (just shy of half) and from mainland China (about a third). Professional occupations were also more common among Chinese American workers (age sixteen or older) than non-Hispanic white workers (52 percent versus 38 percent). The annual median household income for Chinese Americans was $57,000 in 2003 dollars, compared to $49,000 for non-Hispanic whites. While major socioeconomic indicators are above the national average and above those for non-Hispanic whites, the poverty rate for Chinese Americans was also higher (13 percent) than for non-Hispanic whites (9 percent), and the homeownership rate was lower (63 percent) than for non-Hispanic whites (74 percent).[6]

In terms of settlement patterns, Chinese Americans have continued to concentrate in the western United States and in urban areas. California alone accounts for nearly 40 percent of all Chinese Americans (1.1 million); New York comes in second with 16 percent, followed by Hawaii with 6 percent. At the same time, other states that historically received few Chinese immigrants, such as Texas, New Jersey, Massachusetts, Illinois, Washington, Florida, Maryland, and Pennsylvania, have now witnessed phenomenal growth. Traditional urban enclaves, such as Chinatowns in San Francisco, New York, Los Angeles, Chicago, and Boston, still receive new immigrants, but they are no longer the primary centers of initial settlement now that many new immigrants, especially the affluent and highly skilled, go straight to the suburbs on arrival. Currently, only 2 percent of the Chinese in Los Angeles, 8 percent in San Francisco, and 14 percent in New York City live in old Chinatowns. Half of all Chinese Americans live in suburbs. A good number live in the new multiethnic, immigrant-dominant suburban municipalities, often referred to as "ethnoburbs," that have appeared since the 1980s.[7] In 2000, there were eleven cities in the United States—all in California and all but San Francisco in the suburbs—in which Chinese Americans made up more than 20 percent of the population.

These demographic changes in the Chinese American community have created multiple contexts in which the new second generation (the U.S.-born or -raised children of post-1965 Chinese immigrants) is coming of age. Three main neighborhood contexts—the traditional ethnic enclaves such as inner-city Chinatowns, the ethnoburbs, and the white middle-class suburbs—are particularly important in understanding the challenges confronting new Chinese immigrant families.

Community Transformations and Contexts

During the era of legal exclusion, most Chinese immigrants were isolated in inner-city ethnic enclaves that were characterized as bachelors' societies. Many Chinatown "bachelor" workers were actually married but had left their wives, children, and parents behind in their villages in China. The few "normal" families in the bachelors' society often were those of merchants or workers who, for immigration purposes, claimed to be partners of merchants. In old Chinatowns, individuals and families were enmeshed in and highly dependent upon the ethnic community for social,

economic, and emotional support, while also subject to its control. Chinatown children grew up in an extended family environment surrounded by
and under the watchful eyes of many "grandpas" and "uncles" who were
not actually related by blood but were part of an intricate system of family, kin or parental friendship associations.

The behavior of both children and parents in old Chinatowns was carefully monitored by a closely knit ethnic community. Children were either
"good" kids—loyal, *guai* (obedient), and *you-chu-xi* (promising)—or "bad"
kids, disrespectful, *bai-jia-zi* (family failure), and *mei-chu-xi* (good-for-
nothing). They grew up speaking fluent Chinese, mostly in local dialects,
going to Chinese schools, working in Chinese-owned businesses in the
community, and interacting intimately with other Chinese in the ethnic
enclave. Many wished to become like other American children but faced
resistance from the larger society as well as from their own families. The
larger society looked down on the Chinese and set barriers to keep them
apart, such as segregation in schools and workplaces. The Chinese family tied children to Chinatown and its ethnic institutions, Chinese school
being the most important, to shield them from overt discrimination. Despite considerable adolescent rebellion and generational conflict within
the family, the children often found themselves dependent on ethnic networks without much scope to break free.

Whereas members of the old second generation grew up in ethnic enclaves isolated from middle-class America, those of the new second generation come from more diverse socioeconomic backgrounds and have
settled in a wider range of neighborhoods. Those who reside in inner-city
Chinatowns are generally from low-income families who have recently arrived. Like the old second generation, they speak Chinese fluently, interact
primarily with people in a Chinese-speaking environment, and participate
in various cultural and social institutions in the ethnic community. However, they no longer live in a hostile environment that socially and legally
excludes the Chinese. Even though they may go to neighborhood schools
with mostly immigrant Chinese and other minority children, they have
more opportunities to interact with non-coethnic children and adults and
a wider range of occupational choices.

Members of the new second generation who reside in multiethnic ethnoburbs are mainly from upper- and middle-income families. They generally go to higher-quality suburban public schools. They also have access to ethnic institutions unavailable, or less available, in old Chinatown,
such as after-school tutoring (*buxiban*), academic enrichment, sports, and

music programs offered by Chinese-owned private businesses. Although they speak Chinese fluently, interact with other Chinese, and are involved with things "Chinese," including food, music, and customs, they also interact regularly with people of diverse racial/ethnic backgrounds.

The children of Chinese immigrants in suburban white middle-class neighborhoods tend to have parents who have achieved high levels of education, occupation, income, and English proficiency and who are bicultural, transnational, cosmopolitan, and highly assimilated. These children attend schools where white students are in the majority and have few primary contacts with coethnic peers. Many grow up speaking only English at home and have mostly white friends.

Overall, compared to the old, pre-1965, second generation, members of the new second generation are growing up in a more open society. They do not face the kinds of legal barriers to educational and occupational attainment that blocked the mobility of the old second generation. They tend to live in family neighborhoods and have more sources of social support beyond the ethnic community. They also have much more freedom to "become American" and more leverage to rebel against their parents if they choose. They can even report their parents to government authorities if they feel they have been "abused" at home, because social institutions and the legal system in the larger society provide support. And to take another extreme measure, should they decide to run away from home, they have more options to get by. In today's more open society, immigrant parents often find it harder than in the isolated enclave to raise children "the Chinese way" because of the more intense conflicts between the parents' social world and the mainstream society.

Challenges Confronting the Chinese Immigrant Family

Post-1965 Chinese immigrants confront profound challenges when they move to America. One such challenge has to do with structural changes in the immigrant family. In Taiwan, Hong Kong, and the mainland, Chinese families are often extended in form, with grandparents or other relatives living in the home or in close contact. When family members arrive in the United States, their extended kin and friendship networks, and the associated support and control mechanisms, are disrupted. When immigrant families locate first in ethnic enclaves or ethnoburbs, they may be able to reconnect to, or rebuild, ethnic networks, but these new ethnic networks tend to be composed of coethnic "strangers" rather than close kin and friends and tend to be more instrumental than emotionally intimate. Those who go to white middle-class suburbs are more detached from the existing ethnic community and have a harder time rebuilding social networks based on common origins and a common cultural heritage. Even though affluent Chinese immigrant families may have less need of ethnic networks and ethnic resources than their working-class counterparts, many find them comforting and, at times, helpful in enforcing traditional Chinese values to which they are still closely attached.

A second challenge is the change in roles within the immigrant family. In most Chinese immigrant families, both parents work full time, and some hold several jobs on different shifts. Because of the disadvantages associated with immigrant status, many Chinese immigrant men experience downward mobility and have difficulty obtaining jobs that enable them to be the main breadwinners. Women have to work outside the home, and many contribute equally, if not more, to the family income while also assuming the principal responsibility for child-rearing. That women work outside the home often creates difficulties for children in the family. Without the help of grandparents, relatives, and other close friends, many of them become latch-key children, staying home alone after school hours. Immigration affects parent-child roles in another way, particularly in families where the parents have low levels of education and job skills and speak little or no English. Often, these parents have to depend on their children as translators and brokers between home and the outside world, which typically diminishes parental authority.

A third challenge is the generation gap between parents and children, which is exacerbated by a cultural divide between the immigrant family and the larger society. There is a pronounced discrepancy in goal orientation—and views of the means of achieving goals—between immigrant parents and their U.S.-born or -raised children. Most immigrants structure their lives primarily around three goals—as one Chinese immigrant put it, "to live in your own house, to be your own boss, and to send your children to the Ivy League." They try to acculturate or assimilate into American society, but only in ways that facilitate the attainment of these goals. The children, in contrast, want more. They aspire to be fully American. In the words of a U.S.-born high school student in Los Angeles's Chinatown, ". . .Looking cool, going to the ball games, eating hamburgers and french fries, taking family vacations, having fun . . . feeling free to do whatever you like rather than what your parents tell you to."

This cultural gap sets the parents and children apart and increases what are often already-strained parent–child relations. Children frequently view their immigrant parents as *lao-wan-gu* and consciously rebel against familial traditions. The parents, aside from juggling work and household responsibilities that devour most of their waking hours, are worried that their children have too much freedom, too little respect for authority, and too many unfavorable stimuli in school, on the street, and on the television screen at home. They are horrified when their children are openly disrespectful, for example, or aggressively disobey their orders. Intergenerational strains are further intensified because parents have difficulty communicating with their Americanized children. To make matters worse, the parents' customary ways of exercising authority or disciplining children—physical punishment by beating, for example—which were considered normative and acceptable in the old world, have suddenly become obsolete and even illegal, further eroding parental power in parent-child relations.

Immigrant children who arrive in the United States as teenagers have additional problems that affect relations with their parents. They have spent their formative years in a different society, were schooled in a different language, and were immersed in a different youth culture than that of the United States. In their homeland, they played a leading role in defining what was *in*, what was cool, and what was trendy, and many were average students in their schools. However, once in the United States, they find themselves standing out the wrong way, becoming the objects of mockery and ridicule and being referred to derogatively as "FOB" (fresh-off-boat) by their U.S.-born or raised coethnic peers. They also experience problems in school. Because of language difficulties, many are unable to express themselves and are misunderstood by their teachers and fellow students; they are often teased, mocked, or harassed by other students because of their different look, accent, and dress; and they worry that if they bring up these problems at home their parents will get upset or blame them. When their problems are unaddressed by schools or parents, the youth become discouraged. This discouragement is sometimes followed by loss of interest in school and plunging grades, and some eventually drop out and join gangs.

Sensitive Pressure Points

The generation gap between parents and children that I have described is particularly acute in Chinese immigrant families because Chinese cultural norms are so different from those that dominate in the United States and because Chinese parents are often afraid of losing their children to Americanization. Second-generation Chinese, born and raised in the United States, find themselves straddling two social-cultural worlds—Chinese and American—which is at the core of head-on intergenerational conflicts within the Chinese immigrant family. Lacking meaningful connections to their parents' countries of origin, they rarely consider the homeland as a point of reference and generally evaluate themselves against and adopt American standards and values.[8]

This is clearly different for immigrant parents who remain oriented to the homeland and, especially relevant here, to Chinese notions of filial piety. In the Chinese cultural context, filial piety is at the core of parent-child relationships. In its ideal form, the child's filial responsibility is the debt of life owed to parents; a child is expected to suppress his or her own self-interests to satisfy parental needs, whether or not these needs are appropriate or rational.[9] Related to filial piety is the notion of unconditional obedience, or submission, to authority—to the parent, the elder, and the superior. The parent is the authority in the home, as is the teacher in the school. The parent, often the father, is not supposed to show too much affection to his children, to play with them, or treat them as equals. This stone-faced, authoritative image often inhibits children from questioning, much less challenging, their parents. Furthermore, in the traditional Chinese family, there is little room for individualism. All family members are tied to one another, and every act of individual members is considered to bring honor or shame to the whole family. Thus, Chinese parents are expected to bring up their children in ways that honor the family.

Asymmetric filial piety, unconditional submission to authority, and face-saving override other familial values in the traditional Chinese family. Even though modernization has brought changes to the family in China, these traditional influences still loom large among Chinese immigrants. The problem is that in the American context, these practices and values are frowned upon, and children and parents are expected to be independent individuals on equal terms.

The immigrant Chinese family is often referred to by the children as a "pressure cooker," where intense intergenerational conflicts accumulate and sometimes boil to the point of explosion. Issues related to education, work ethic, consumption behavior, and dating, among others, are sensitive pressure points that can create potentially intense conflicts. For example, a young Chinese American who returned to college to complete her associate degree recalled:

> I never felt I was good enough to live up to my parents' expectations. So I fought them non-stop through high school. A war broke out when I got accepted into a few UC [University of California] schools but decided not to enroll in any one of them. I got kicked out of home. I moved in with my white boyfriend and started to work to support myself. I felt that the only way to get back at my parents was to make them feel ashamed. With a rebellious daughter, they had nothing to brag about and they lost the war. It may seem silly now, but at that time I really liked what I did.

Chinese parents who were raised in the Confucian tradition tend to be particularly demanding and unyielding about their children's educational achievement. While education is generally considered a primary means to upward social mobility in all American families, it is emphasized in some unique ways in the immigrant Chinese family. First and foremost, the children's success in school is tied to face-saving for the family. Parents consistently remind their children that achievement is a duty and an obligation to the family goal, and that if they fail they will bring shame to the family. Not surprisingly, children are under tremendous pressure to succeed.

Immigrant parents also have a pragmatic view of education. They see education as not only the most effective means to achieve success in society but also the *only* means. The parents are keenly aware of their own limitations as immigrants and the structural constraints blocking their own mobility—for example, limited family wealth even among middle-income immigrants, lack of access to social networks connecting them to the mainstream economy and various social and political institutions, and entry barriers to certain occupations because of racial stereotyping and discrimination. Their own experience tells them that a good education in certain fields will allow their children to get good jobs in the future. These fields include science, math, engineering, medicine, and, to a lesser extent, business and law. Parents are more concerned with their children's academic coursework, grades, and majors in these preferred fields than with a well-rounded learning experience and extracurricular activities. They actively discourage their children from pursuing interests in history, literature, music, dance, sports, or any subject that they consider unlikely to lead to well-paid, stable jobs. Involvement in these academic fields and extracurricular activities is only encouraged to the extent that it will improve their children's chances of getting into an Ivy League college. The children are often frustrated—sometimes deeply resentful—that their parents choose the type of education they are to pursue and make decisions for their future. At college, many Chinese American students pursue double majors, one in science or engineering for their parents and the other in history, literature, or Asian American studies for themselves.

Another sensitive issue is the work ethic. Immigrant Chinese parents believe that hard work, rather than natural ability or innate intelligence, is the key to educational success. Regardless of socioeconomic background, they tend to think that their children can get A's on all their exams if they just work hard, and if the children get lower grades they will be scolded for not working hard enough. The parents also believe that by working twice as hard it is possible to overcome structural disadvantages associated with immigrant and/or racial minority status. They tend to ignore the fact that not everybody learns English, catches up with school work, and establishes productive relationships with teachers and fellow students at the same rate. As a result, the children often find themselves working at least twice as hard as their American peers and simultaneously feeling that their parents never think that they work hard enough.

A third sensitive issue is related to the value of thrift.[10] Immigrant Chinese parents emphasize savings as a means of effectively deploying available family resources. They often bluntly reject their children's desire for material possessions and view spending money on name-brand clothes, stylish accessories, and fashionable hairstyles as a sign of corruption, or as becoming "too American." At the same time, these parents seldom hesitate to spend money on whatever they consider good for their children, such as books and computer software, after-school programs, Chinese lessons, private tutors, private lessons on the violin or the piano, and other education-oriented activities.

The fourth sensitive issue is dating, particularly at an early age. Chinese parents, especially newer arrivals, consider dating in high school not only a wasteful distraction from academics, but also a sign of unhealthy, promiscuous behavior, especially for girls. They are concerned about the potential risks of unwanted pregnancy—and that this will interfere with their daughters' educational progress. Over time, parents' attitudes toward dating in high school may grow more ambivalent, and it may be interracial dating, rather than early dating in general, that "freaks them out."

These sensitive pressure points have become the sources of parent-child conflicts as the children rapidly acculturate into American ways, and as parents, in a position of authority, insist on their values and practices. These conflicts seem to be especially severe in the case of working-class Chinese immigrant parents, who are unusually demanding and unbending when it comes to their children's education and behavioral standards because they lack the time, patience, cultural sensitivity, and financial and human capital to be more compromising. Middle-class Chinese immigrant parents are also demanding and have high expectations for their children. But owing to their higher socioeconomic status and higher level of acculturation, they consciously try to be more like American parents in some ways. Some middle-class parents develop a sense of guilt for not being like American parents and become more easygoing and less strict with their children. For example, when a child refuses to do schoolwork on weekends as the father demands, and talks back by saying that "nobody works on weekends," a middle-class suburban Chinese immigrant father might simply shrug and let his child run off with his friends, because he himself doesn't have to work on weekends. A working-class Chinese immigrant father is more likely to get angry and make the child feel guilty about his own sacrifice, since he has to work on weekends to support the family.

Ethnic Networks and Institutions as Sources of Conciliation and Mediating Grounds

Tremendous parental pressures to achieve and behave in the Chinese way can lead children to rebellious behavior, withdrawal from school, and alienation from ethnic networks. Alienated children fall easy prey to street gangs. Even those children who do well in school and hope to make their parents proud are at risk for rebellious and disrespectful behavior and for flouting their parents' rules and regulations. A high school student said, "But that [doing well to make parents happy] never happens. My mother is never satisfied no matter what you do and how well you do it." This remark echoes a frustration felt by many other Chinatown youths, who are torn between wanting to please their parents and succeed educationally, but who feel overwhelmed and constrained by parental pressures, rules, and orders. Tensions in the home may seethe beneath the surface—often to a point that parents and children feel they have no room to breathe.

Yet despite these intense pressures, and the strains between the children and their parents, there is rarely an all-out war between them. And

despite severe bicultural conflicts—and the challenges that American popular culture poses to Chinese immigrant parents' values—many Chinese
immigrant children, whatever their socioeconomic background, seem to
live up to their parents' expectations. Involvement in the Chinese ethnic
community is critical in explaining why this is so.

Most remarkable is the educational success of Chinese immigrant children, who significantly outperform other Americans, including non-Hispanic whites. They score exceptionally well on standardized tests and are
overrepresented in the nation's elite universities as well as in the top lists
of many national or regional academic competitions. They have appeared
repeatedly in the top-ten award winners' list of the Westinghouse Science
Talent Search, now renamed the Intel Science Talent Search, one of the
country's most prestigious high school academic prizes. At the University of California, Los Angeles, where I teach, the proportion of Chinese
Americans in the entering class in the past few years has been 18 percent
higher than that of blacks and Latinos combined.

Is the extraordinary educational achievement of Chinese Americans a
result of the parental pressure for success and enforcement of Confucian
values? There is no simple answer. A more appropriate question is: How is
it possible for parents in the Chinese immigrant family, plagued with intergenerational strains, to exercise authority and enforce Confucian values
on education? Why do children end up doing what their parents expect
them to do? My research in the Chinese immigrant community points
to the important role of an ethnic institutional environment and multiple
ethnic involvements.

In Chinatowns or Chinese ethnoburbs, an ethnic enclave economy and
a range of ethnic social and cultural institutions have developed to support the daily needs of Chinese immigrants. As the community changed
from a bachelor society to a family community, traditional ethnic institutions also shifted their functions to serve families and children. Among
the programs they offer are weekend Chinese schools and a variety of
educational and recreational enterprises, such as daily afterschool classes
that match formal school curricula, academic tutoring and English en-
hancement classes, "exam-cram" schools, college prep schools, and music/
dance/sports studios.

Consider the Chinese language school. In New York City, the Chinese
Language School (*Zhongwen xuexiao*), run by the Chinese Consolidated
Benevolent Association (CCBA), is perhaps the largest children- and
youth-oriented organization in the nation's Chinatowns.[11] The school

enrolls about four thousand Chinese children annually (not including summer), from pre-school to twelfth grade, in its 137 Chinese language classes and other specialty classes (including band, choir, piano, cello, violin, T'ai chi, ikebana, dancing, and Chinese painting). The Chinese language classes run from 3:00 to 6:30 p.m. daily after regular school hours. Students usually spend one hour on regular school homework and two hours on Chinese language or other selected specialties. The school also has English classes for immigrant youths and adult immigrant workers.

As Chinese immigrants have become dispersed residentially, Chinese language schools have also sprung up in the suburbs. As of the mid-1990s, there were approximately 635 Chinese language schools in the United States (with 189 in California alone), enrolling nearly 83,000 students.[12] The Chinese language school provides an ethnically affirming experience for most Chinese immigrant children. In response to the question, "What makes you Chinese?" many Chinese students say that it is "going to Chinese school." In Chinese language school, Chinese immigrant children come to understand that their own problems with their parents are common in Chinese families and that their parents are simply acting like other Chinese parents. They come to terms with the fact that growing up in Chinese families is different. As Betty Lee Sung observes:

> For Chinese immigrant children who live in New York's Chinatown or in satellite Chinatowns, these [bi-cultural] conflicts are moderated to a large degree because there are other Chinese children around to mitigate the dilemmas that they encounter. When they are among their own, the Chinese ways are better known and better accepted. The Chinese customs and traditions are not denigrated to the degree that they would be if the immigrant child were the only one to face the conflict on his or her own.[13]

Ethnic institutions also allow the children to develop strategies to cope with parental constraints. For example, a girl can tell her parents that she is going out with someone at the Chinese school whom her parents know, while she actually goes to a movie with her white boyfriend. Her friends at the Chinese school will provide cover for her, confirming her story when her parents check. Chinese parents usually trust their children's friends from Chinese schools because they know the parents of the Chinese school friends.

The Chinese schools and various after-school programs not only ensure that the children spend time on homework or other constructive activities, they also help to keep children off the streets and reduce the anxieties and worries of working parents. More important, these ethnic institutions offer some space where children can share their feelings. A Chinese school teacher said, "It is very important to allow youths to express themselves in their own terms without parental pressures. Chinese parents usually have very high expectations of their children. When children find it difficult to meet these expectations and do not have an outlet for their frustration and anxiety, they tend to become alienated and lost on the streets."

Ethnic institutions also serve as a bridge between a seemingly closed immigrant community and the mainstream society. Immigrant parents and the children who live in ethnic enclaves or ethnoburbs are relatively isolated and their daily exposure to the larger American society is limited. Many parents, usually busy working, expect their children to do well in school and have successful careers in the future, but are unable to give specific directions to guide their children's educational and career plans, leaving a gap between high expectations and feasible means of meeting them. Ethnic institutions fill this gap by helping young people to become better aware of their choices and to find realistic means of moving up socioeconomically in mainstream society. After-school programs, tutor services, and test preparation programs are readily available in the ethnic community, making school after school an accepted norm. An educator said, "When you think of how much time these Chinese kids put in their studies after regular school, you won't be surprised why they succeed at such a high rate."

At the same time, ethnic institutions function as cultural centers, where Chinese traditional values and a sense of ethnic identity are nurtured. Students who participate in the after-school programs, especially those born and raised in the United States, often speak English to one another in their Chinese classes, but they learn a limited number of Chinese words each day. In the after-school programs, they are able to relate to Chinese "stuff" without being teased as they might be in school. They listen to stories and sing songs in Chinese, which reveal different aspects of Chinese history and culture. Children and youths learn to write in Chinese such phrases as "I am Chinese" and "My home country is in China" and to recite classical Chinese poems and Confucian sayings about family values, behavioral and moral guidelines, and the importance of schooling. A Chinese school principal made it clear that "these kids are here because their parents sent them. They are usually not very motivated to learn

Chinese per se, and we do not push them too hard. Language teaching is only part of our mission. An essential part of our mission is to enlighten these kids about their own cultural heritage, so that they show respect for their parents and feel proud of being Chinese."

Despite differences in origin, socioeconomic backgrounds, and geographic dispersion, Chinese immigrants have many opportunities to interact with one another as they participate in the ethnic community in multiple ways. Working, shopping, and socializing in the community tie immigrants to a closely knit system of ethnic social relations. Social networks, embedded in the broader Chinese immigrant community, reinforce norms and standards and operate as a means of control over those who are connected to them. Especially pertinent here is that involvement in different types of ethnic institutions also helps children to cope with—and indeed has the effect of alleviating—parental pressure.

"Parachute Kids": A Special Case

"Parachute kids," particularly prominent in southern California, offer a special case of intergenerational relations within the Chinese immigrant community.[14] This term refers to young people, aged eight to seventeen, who come to the United States to attend elementary or high schools, which, their parents believe, will give them advantages in getting into prestigious colleges and obtaining good jobs. The children often fly across the Pacific to live on their own, while their parents remain in Taiwan, Hong Kong, or mainland China. Although exact numbers are hard to obtain, it is estimated that about 40,000 parachute kids arrived in the United States in the 1980s and 1990s, mostly from Taiwan with smaller numbers from Hong Kong and mainland China. Most parachute kids live with relatives, friends, or unrelated caretakers in upscale neighborhoods. Out of sight does not mean out of mind. Still, absence and separation lessen the potential for conflict with parents. At the same time, parental authority—as well as the sense of obligation to parents—may lose force with distance.

Risk Factors

Unlike immigrant children who live with their parents and whose adaptational experience is influenced by the economic hardships of settlement and intergenerational clashes, most parachute kids live in a world that American teenagers can only dream of: a fully furnished house of their own in upscale neighborhoods, a fancy car, a cellular phone, plenty of cash, and no parents. For these children, going to school in America is considered not only a lifetime opportunity for a better future, but also an extraordinary adventure in searching for one's self. However, this transnational path is not without risks.

For parachute kids, the risks are associated less with physical separation from parents than with the social environment they confront in the United States. Since education takes priority in Chinese families, parents are expected to do everything possible to maximize their children's chances of educational success. Parachute kids may not like being away from their parents, but they generally accept that this is a family decision and that their parents have selected what they think is the best available option. As one said: "I didn't like being away from my parents and my family. But think about the kind of money my parents have spent on me just to get a good education. I feel they really care about me and love me." Or as another put it: "My parents do not have to send us away, but they do it because they care and because they want us to have a better future."

Neither parents nor parachute kids, however, seem to anticipate the drastic difference between separate living arrangements in the homeland and transnational living. In the homeland, when children live apart from parents, they are likely to be placed in a familiar sociocultural environment where similar values, norms, and behavioral standards are enforced. They are also likely to confront, as well as be controlled by, an adult society similar to the one in which their parents live. In a foreign country, parachute children are not only away from their families but are also cut off from social networks of support and control and from the customary patterns of social relations between children and adults.

Parents use their financial resources to ensure that their children are in the care of reliable relatives or caretakers, live in safe neighborhoods, and attend good schools. Most of them are well aware that the quality of American schools depends largely on the socioeconomic standing of the neighborhood, so they tend to choose host families or purchase homes for their children in upscale middle-class neighborhoods with reputable schools. However, they have little knowledge of the potential risks of transnational living without former social networks and support.

When looking back on their experiences, several parachute kids now in college said they had had too much free time after school and too little adult supervision. Their parents were not there to supervise the children's homework and arrange various after-school activities in the local community that are crucial to a child's educational experience. Even if parents managed to have some activities arranged (the most popular one being the Chinese school), they could not ensure that their children actually attended. In an environment where youth-oriented consumerism and anti-intellectualism are so pervasive, even the most self-disciplined parachute kids are lured by the powerful influences of popular American culture that are not necessarily conducive to educational achievement. One college student summed it up when he recalled his earlier parachuting experiences, "Three to ten is a long time to be on one's own. I didn't like it at all. I got bored, turned on the TV, played video games, ate junk food, and hung out in cafes with other parachute kids and friends. Good thing that none of my friends were in gangs."

Changing Relationships between Parachute Kids and Their Parents

In the parachute world, routine interaction between parents and children takes place through weekly phone calls. Many children miss physical closeness among family members, although they feel freer of parental controls. When asked what they disliked most, more than half of the thirty-three children interviewed said that it was being away from their parents or being unable to talk to their parents in person. The same group of respondents said that what they valued most was being independent from parental control and being able to do things without parental consent (e.g., filling out parental consent forms themselves in school).

Over time, many parachute children become used to living away from home and feel more emotionally distant from their parents. Trans-Pacific communication with parents becomes a matter of routine, and the frequency of phone calls decreases with time. One interviewee recalled, "I used to call home twice a week in the first few months, telling my parents what I did during the week and letting them know that I did well, and that I missed them. They would also give lectures like they did at home, things like to work hard, to focus, no drugs, no smoking, no dating, and no this, no that. Those kinds of phone calls got boring after a while. Now I call home only because I am expected to. I really don't have much to say on the phone with them." Another parachute kid said, "I call home regularly just so my mom doesn't get worried, but I really don't have much to say. My parents don't live here and don't know what problems and what needs we have here. I don't think they understand what I have to say."

Parents are worried and concerned about the gradually changing relationship with their children. A Taiwanese mother who was visiting her parachute children (a seventeen-year-old son and fourteen-year-old daughter) in the United States recalled, "I remember in the first few months, my children called frequently. They cried on the phone saying that they missed home. I was sad but kept saying to them that they were not babies any more, and that they should act like a big boy or a big girl. But after a while, they called less frequently. When they did, there were just those simple responses such as 'yes' or 'no' or 'OK.' Then I became very worried." When their children are in the United States, parents feel guilty and become more easygoing with them, while children feel alienated from their family and become more independent; some may even take advantage of their parents' sense of guilt to have their way. Insufficient parent-child interaction not only widens the generational gap but also puts children at risk of being further alienated from their parents and their parents' social networks in the host country.

From Direct Control to Remote Control

The changing relationship between parents and children poses a threat to parental authority in Chinese families. Traditionally, if children do not show respect for elders and maintain self-discipline or proper behavior, they are considered to be without *jiajiao* (family discipline), and parents are blamed for not raising children properly. When children live apart from parents, this central mechanism of control loses ground.

Parents of parachute kids have two main means to try to ensure that their children hold onto the *jiajiao* principles they have learned at home: parental networks with caretakers and monthly allowances. Parents usually arrange, at least initially, to settle their children in the homes of relatives, family friends, or unrelated caretakers whom their friends know well. They believe that, through these connections, they have the ears and eyes to monitor their children's behavior. If children live with grandparents, close relatives, or close family friends who make a strong commitment to help, they are likely to feel pressure to conform to parental expectations. One high school senior explained: "I am living with my aunt. My parents do not pay her for taking care of me. I guess she is doing my family a favor. She's more than my mother when it comes to rules and discipline. I don't like her much but I have to obey her because she's my mother's eye. Whatever I do that she knows, my mother knows too."

A college student who lived with her grandmother for the first two years of "parachuting" recalled, "My grandma was quite nice. She did not nag as much as my mother, except that she tried to feed me more than I needed. But one thing I used to get annoyed was that my mother seemed to know a lot of details about my life and behavior here. So I had to watch out my behavior in front of my grandma." Another college student who used to live with a family friend said, "Because they are my parents' friends, I will have to watch my behavior."

Many parachute kids agreed that the chief reason their parents chose to send them to southern California was because of the presence of relatives and family friends. Of course, things do not always go smoothly. There were some cases where parachute kids rebelled violently against relatives who were considered too "nosy" and too strict.

For children living with paid caretakers (related or unrelated), the remote control button does not always work as intended. Usually parents pay these caretakers varied amounts of money in exchange for room and board and a home-like atmosphere. Parents expect the host families to take care of their children and watch out for improper behavior. Many caretakers do live up to these expectations. One young man said: "I had few problems communicating with my caretaker. She gave me general direction and told me what to do. I basically could tell her my problems and she would give advice in return. But sometimes, I had difficulty communicating with her, especially when she overreacted to problems and yelled at me to discipline me."

But some caretakers are reluctant to deal with children's problems. They fear that any active role will cause strained relationships with the children and may lead to losing income if the parents remove the children from their homes or if the children decide to leave. In my research, I heard of no case of serious open conflict with paid caretakers, although quite a few parachute kids reported they disliked or were indifferent to their caretaker.

Generally, after a few years, parachute kids, especially those in high school, move out of their original host families—with their parents' support—to live on their own, either by renting or moving into houses owned by their parents. Independent living frees them from parents' networks of control; it puts them in a high-risk situation owing to the lack of adult supervision or even adult presence in the home.

Wherever they live, monthly allowances are a means of parental control. School performance is of great concern to parents. Parachute kids are expected to report weekly on their schoolwork, and parents double-check these reports with caretakers. They are also expected to fax copies of graded homework and report cards. When these reports do not fit parents' expectations, monthly allowances will be cut as punishment. "They can't ground us since they are so far away," a parachute kid said in an interview. "But if I don't listen to them, get good grades, they don't send money."

On average, the cost of sending a parachute kid to the United States in the mid-1990s was estimated at $40,000 annually. The cost obviously was higher when a family sent more than one parachute kid. In my sample, about a quarter of the parachute kids came with one or two siblings. Apart from caretakers' fees and tuition, parents sent each child an average of $15,000 per year. Usually parents send the monthly allowance from their home countries, although in some cases it comes from rental properties the parents own in the United States.

One student, for example, had been a parachute kid for three years and had received approximately $40,000 from her parents annually for her expenses. When she went to college, her parents bought her a house and a Mercedes and spent another $12,000 on college tuition. A high school student who had been a parachute kid since he was fourteen received a $1,200 monthly allowance from his parents; his parents promised to buy him a new car when he went to college. Parachute kids are aware that the money and material promises are rewards for educational achievement. If they do not do well in school, their ultimate punishment is usually a homebound airplane ticket and a return with shame.

While many parachute kids are willing to fax report cards to parents because they get good grades, others are not willing or only do so selectively. One young woman said, "When they [parents] are here, I watch what I do. When they're not here, there are no restraints. When they call and I'm not here, I make up an excuse, like I was in the shower or something." There is also a lot of room for what parents consider improper behavior. One parachute kid in my sample had recently married in order to help a friend get a green card. His parents had not been told.

In the parachute world, children basically control their own lives. Their parents usually fly over to visit them only once or twice a year, and the children visit home about once a year. When they are with their parents, relations have changed. Many parachute kids still respect their parents but no longer obey them as they did before. Parents gradually, though often reluctantly, accept their children's independence as the cost of this arrangement. As one parent commented, "We have always kind of bet on our belief that our children are good kids. If they decide to go the opposite way, you lose them. You really can't do much to make things work for them. They are on their own."

Conclusion

A complex and often contradictory set of forces affect parents and children in Chinese immigrant families and their relations with each other. Many Chinese immigrant parents expect the children to attain the highest levels of achievement possible and rely on them to move the family into middle-class status as a way to repay parental sacrifices and to honor the family name. Deviation from these cultural values, standards, and expectations is considered shameful or "losing face" and is strongly criticized, indeed censured, by the family and the ethnic community. Still, parents have trouble enforcing these values and behavioral standards—and guaranteeing that familial expectations are met. Both parents and children struggle constantly to negotiate cultural differences, make compromises, and resolve conflicts in order to navigate the "right" way into mainstream American society.

This undertaking is by no means limited to the family arena, nor is it simply a matter of having the right cultural values. As I have emphasized, Chinese immigrant families cannot be viewed in isolation. Many are intricately and closely connected to broader networks in the wider ethnic community. Ethnic educational institutions and children-oriented programs, as I have shown, not only provide tangible resources in the form, for example, of educational training, but also serve as effective mechanisms of social control, thereby reinforcing parental values. At the same time, they give young people a socially accepted place to develop their own coping strategies as well as social relationships with peers experiencing the same dilemmas at home. One of the many factors that set parachute kids apart is their lack of access to these kinds of support and control because they are less connected to the ethnic community than young people in immigrant families. It is also important to stress that the mobilization of educational resources in the immigrant family and community is heavily affected by immigration selectivity, in that those with education, professional skills, and money comprise a significant proportion of the Chinese migrant inflow.

The children of Chinese immigrants are motivated to learn and do well in school because they believe that education is the most effective route for them to do better than their parents—and also a way to free themselves from their parents' control. Whatever the children's motivation, parental pressure—which is supported and strengthened through participation in the ethnic community—reinforces educational goals and often leads to positive outcomes. A community youth program organizer put it this way: "Well, tremendous pressures create problems for sure. However, you've got to realize that we are not living in an ideal environment. Without these pressures, you would probably see as much adolescent rebellion in the family, but a much *larger* proportion of kids failing. Our goal is to get these kids out into college, and for that, we have been very successful."

While intense parent-child and community pressure pushes children to work hard to succeed, there are limits to its effectiveness. Beyond high school, the social capital available in the Chinese-American community is not sufficient to help children choose appropriate academic and career paths. When applying to college, many children of Chinese immigrants are forced by parents to choose institutions close to home, which can limit chances for significant social mobility. At college, the children tend to concentrate in science and engineering because their families want them to and their friends are doing it—even if this is something they are not interested or lack talent in. After graduation from college, they often lack the type of networks that facilitate job placement and occupational mobility.

A whole series of additional issues arise as the children of Chinese immigrants enter adulthood. What will their relationships with their parents be like then? Will the children be grateful to parents for pushing them to succeed? Will sources of conflict prominent in adolescence be less acute in adulthood? Will there be new sources of tension, for example, disagreements with parents over family finances, marriage, and childbearing or child-rearing methods? In the case of the parachute kids, if they stay in the United States and their parents remain in the homeland, will the children become even more emotionally distant from parents—or will some return to their homeland and reestablish close bonds with parents? These are among the many questions that deserve further research.

NOTES

1. This chapter draws on my previously published work; see Zhou 1997; 1998; 2006.

2. Foner 1999; Mahalingam 2006.

3. USDHS 2006.

4. Estimated from the Current Population Survey (CPS) data 1998–2000. See Logan et al. 2001.

5. Compared to 8 percent under age eighteen and 8 percent between ages eighteen and twenty-four in the first generation.

6. U.S. Census Bureau 2007.

7. "Ethnoburb" is a term developed by Wei Li (1997) to refer to suburban ethnic clustering of diverse groups with no single racial ethnic group dominating. Los Angeles's Monterey Park is a typical ethnoburb.

8. Gans 1992; Portes and Zhou 1993; Zhou 1997.

9. Yeh and Bedford 2003.

10. Sung 1987.

11. The Chinese Consolidated Benevolent Association (CCBA) is a quasi-government in Chinatown. It used to be an apex group representing some sixty different family and district associations, guilds, tongs, the Chamber of Commerce, and the Nationalist Party, and it has remained the most influential ethnic organization in the Chinese immigrant community.

12. Chao 1996.

13. Sung 1987: 126.

14. Data were collected during the spring and summer of 1996 by my three research assistants and myself. We conducted interviews with a snowball sample of thirty-three parachute kids, and a convenience sample of parents, caretakers, school counselors, and community social workers from southern California. The sample of parachute kids was made up of twenty-five college students and eight high school students; 55 percent were males; three were from Hong Kong, one from Singapore, two from mainland China, and the rest from Taiwan. I made a handful of prearranged home visits in Monterey Park, Alhambra, and Arcadia and conducted a number of in-home or telephone interviews with parents who were either back in their home country or were visiting their children in southern California at the time. I also talked, either in person or on the phone, to a number of school counselors and community social workers who had worked with parachute kids in Monterey Park, Alhambra, Arcadia, and Hacienda Heights, where many parachute kids were concentrated. See Zhou 1998 for a detailed discussion.

REFERENCES

Chao, Teresa Hsu. 1996. "Overview." Pp. 7–13 in Xueying Wang (ed.), *A View from Within: A Case Study of Chinese Heritage Community Language Schools in the United States*. Washington, DC: The National Foreign Language Center.

Foner, Nancy. 1999. "The Immigrant Family: Cultural Legacies and Cultural Changes." Pp. 257–74 in C. Hirschman, P. Kasinitz and J. DeWind (eds.), *The*

Handbook of International Migration: The American Experience. New York: Russell Sage Foundation.

Gans, Herbert J. 1992. "Second-Generation Decline: Scenarios for the Economic and Ethnic Futures of the Post-1965 American Immigrants." *Ethnic and Racial Studies* 15 (2): 173–92.

Li, Wei. 1997. "Spatial Transformation of an Urban Ethnic Community from Chinatown to Chinese Ethnoburb in Los Angeles." Ph.D. Dissertation, Department of Geography. University of Southern California.

Logan, John R., with Jacob Stowell and Elena Vesselinov. 2001. "From Many Shores: Asians in Census 2000." A report by the Lewis Mumford Center for Comparative Urban and Regional Research, State University of New York at Albany, accessed on October 6, 2001, at http://mumford1.dyndns.org/cen2000/report.html.

Mahalingam, Ram (ed.). 2006. *Cultural Psychology of Immigrants.* Mahwah, NJ: Lawrence Erlbaum.

Portes, Alejandro, and Min Zhou. 1993. "The New Second Generation: Segmented Assimilation and Its Variants." *Annals of the American Academy of Political and Social Science* 530 (November): 74–96.

Sung, Betty Lee. 1987. *The Adjustment Experience of Chinese Immigrant Children in New York City.* New York: Center for Migration Studies.

U.S. Census Bureau. 2007. *The American Community, Asians: 2004.* American Community Survey Reports (acs-05), accessed on September 6, 2007, at http://www.census.gov/prod/2007pubs/acs-05.pdf.

U.S. Department of Homeland Security (USDHS). 2006. *Yearbook of Immigration Statistics, 2006.* Accessed on October 9, 2007, at http://www.dhs.gov/ximgtn/statistics/publications/LPR06.shtm.

Wang, Xueying (ed.). 1996. *A View from Within: A Case Study of Chinese Heritage Community Language Schools in the United States.* Washington, DC: The National Foreign Language Center.

Yeh, Kuang-Hui, and Olwen Bedford. 2003. "Filial Piety and Parent-Child Conflict." Paper presented at the International Conference on Intergenerational Relations in Families' Life Course, co-sponsored by the Institute of Sociology, Academie Sinica, Taiwan, and the Committee on Family Research, International Sociological Association, March 12–14, Taipei.

Zhou, Min. 1992. *Chinatown: The Socioeconomic Potential of an Urban Enclave.* Philadelphia: Temple University Press.

———. 1997. "Social Capital in Chinatown: the Role of Community-Based Organizations and Families in the Adaptation of the Younger Generation." Pp. 181–206 in Lois Weis and Maxine S. Seller (eds.), *Beyond Black and White: New Faces and Voices in U.S. Schools.* Albany, NY: State University of New York Press.

———. 1998. "'Parachute Kids' in Southern California: The Educational Experience of Chinese Children in Transnational Families." *Educational Policy* 12 (6): 682–704.

————. 2006. "Negotiating Culture and Ethnicity: Intergenerational Relations in Chinese Immigrant Families in the United States." Pp. 315–36 in Ram Mahalingam, ed., *Cultural Psychology of Immigrants*. Mahwah, NJ: Lawrence Erlbaum.

Zhou, Min, and Xiyuan Li. 2003. "Ethnic Language Schools and the Development of Supplementary Education in the Immigrant Chinese Community in the United States." Pp. 57–73 in Carola Suarez-Orozco and Irina L.G. Todorova (eds.), *New Directions for Youth Development: Understanding the Social Worlds of Immigrant Youth*. San Francisco: Jossey-Bass.

2

||||||||||||||||||||||||||||||||||||||||||||||||||||||||

Emotions, Sex, and Money
The Lives of Filipino Children of Immigrants

Yen Le Espiritu

Focusing on emotions, sex and money, this chapter calls attention to the ways in which the lives of Filipino children of immigrants pivot around rigid and often contradictory expectations over the meaning of sexuality and success. This is not news: many scholars have detailed the tensions between immigrant parents and their children over perceived (im)proper sexual behaviors and (in)appropriate achievement standards.[1] However, unlike most previous works, this chapter does not approach emotions, sex, and money as mere objects of study, but rather as sources of knowledge that elucidate not only the conditions of immigrant life, but also the conditions under which the "immigrant," as a racialized and gendered subject, was produced in the first place. As such, it conceptualizes intergenerational strain not only as a private matter between immigrant parents and their children, but as a social, historical, and transnational affair that exposes multiple and interrelated forms of power relations. In the same way, it deprivatizes and denaturalizes "emotions," "sex," and "money" and emphasizes instead the ways in which they are constituted by and constitutive of gendered, sexualized, and racialized discourses and practices that circulate between the Philippines and the United States.

The data for this chapter come from in-depth interviews conducted between 1992 and 2002 with young Filipinos who lived in San Diego County.[2] It is not coincidental that Filipinos comprise the largest Asian American group in San Diego. Until 1998, San Diego was the site of the largest U.S. naval base and the Navy's primary West Coast training facility, the Naval Training Center (NTC). The Navy turned San Diego into a prominent area of resettlement for Filipino Navy personnel and their families beginning in the early 1900s. During the ninety-four years of U.S. military presence in the Philippines, U.S. bases doubled as recruiting stations for the U.S. Navy. For the majority of Filipino Navy men, San Diego was their first U.S. destination, where they received their basic training at the NTC. Filipino Navy families thus formed the cornerstone of San Diego's Filipino American community and provided the impetus for and sponsorship of subsequent chain migration.[3] As in other Filipino communities along the Pacific Coast, the San Diego community grew dramatically in the decades following passage of the 1965 Immigration Act. New immigration contributed greatly to the tripling of the county's Filipino American population from 1970 to 1980 and its doubling from 1980 to 1990. In 1990, there were close to 96,000 Filipinos in San Diego County; by 2000, the population had risen to over 120,000. According to 2004 American Community Survey Census Bureau data,[4] in San Diego County more than 135,000 people, or about one in twenty, are Filipino. Filipino Americans in the county live in relatively comfortable economic circumstances: they enjoy a median family income of $80,772; close to 70 percent own their own homes; and only about 4 percent live in poverty.[5]

"Structure of Feeling": Immigrant Lives through the Lens of Emotions

Like other immigrant groups, young Filipino American women and men identify the family (sa pamilya) as a tremendous source of cultural pride.[6] In focus groups with Filipino children of immigrants in northern California, Diane Wolf noted the "strong, spontaneous and emotional statements about family as the center of what it means to be Filipino."[7] Similarly, in my interviews with Filipino American families in San Diego County, I found that most Filipinos believed themselves to be superior to white Americans because they are more family-oriented and more willing to sacrifice for one another. However, this ideology of family cohesion contrasted sharply with many of the same subjects' experiences of pressure and conflict within their own families.[8] In the same way, the Children of Immigrants Longitudinal Study (CILS), a longitudinal quantitative study of Filipino American high school students in San Diego,[9] found that while the great majority of the respondents indicated that the ideology of family togetherness and cohesion is extremely important to them, few actually experienced this cohesion in their family. In light of the importance of family ideology for these young Filipinos, the CILS project reported that parent-child conflict was the strongest predictor of young people's self-esteem and depression: the higher the parent-child conflict, the lower the self-esteem and the higher the level of depression.[10]

When asked to describe their relationship with their parents, young Filipinos in the interviews expressed a range of intense and often conflicting emotions: from anger and resentment toward parental pressures and verbal and physical abuse; to sadness and disappointment over the lack of intimacy in their relationship; to anxiety and guilt over the inability to meet high parental expectations; to love and gratitude for their parents' many sacrifices on their behalf. Although the majority of young Filipinos have learned to live with or resolve intergenerational tensions, a small number have resorted to running away, joining gangs, or attempting suicide. But even when young Filipinos succeed in subverting their parents' wishes, parental (dis)approval remains powerful in shaping their emotional lives. And yet most scholarly research on the second generation has sidestepped the complexities, tensions, and uncertainties of their social world, focusing instead on the narrower question of their educational and economic attainment.[11] As an example, an informative edited volume on the post-1965 second generation focuses its discussion on whether today's children of immigrants will move into the middle-class mainstream or join the expanded multiethnic underclass.[12] Departing from this trend, this chapter broaches the study of second-generation Filipinos through the lens of emotions in order to illuminate the social link between the private and the public, between the biographical and the historical.[13] Grappling with the emotional lives of young Filipinos is also a way of looking for and at the gaps—those aspects of immigrant life that are not seen, as well as the forces that made them invisible.

In Western social thought, emotions are understood predominantly as the antithesis of reason and as interiorized private experience, disconnected from history and culture.[14] This elevation of reason over emotion reflects the core Western belief that being human is uniquely characterized by thought or the activity of thinking—that is, by reason. Key Western philosophers, from Plato to Descartes, and from Kant to the Logical Positivists, place reason at the center of being human and regard it as the indispensable faculty for the acquisition of human knowledge—the quest for "objectivity," "truth," and "wisdom."[15] Eighteenth- and nineteenth-century Western philosophers linked reason with human emancipation and emotions with human servitude, and they warned against emotions' alleged disruptive influence on the proper conduct of human affairs.[16] In sociology, the Americanization of Weber's Protestant work ethic, which promoted the idea of increased rationalization of the world and the rejection of the body and emotional life, led to the development of "sociologies without emotions," from at least since the 1930s to the 1970s.[17] The tendency to devalue emotions and to "disappear" them from social analysis has deflected attention from the relationship between emotions, social structure, and power.[18]

Since the 1970s, there has been a resurgence of emotion studies in virtually all of the disciplines, with philosophy, anthropology, sociology, and history taking the lead.[19] Across these disciplines, scholars have exposed and challenged the Western academic and popular association of the emotions with irrationality and biology and have insisted that the emotions are about social life rather than simply internal states.[20] In other words, emotions constitute collective ways of acting and being shaped by the historically specific social structure and culture of a particular society, group, or community. As a result of this resurgence of emotion studies, in Western academic discourse "emotions have begun to move from their culturally assigned place at the center of the dark recesses of inner life and are being depicted as cultural, social, and linguistic operators."[21]

In this chapter, I am most interested in the ways that critical perspectives on emotions open up new ways of seeing. British cultural materialist Raymond Williams coined the concept "structure of feeling" to define social experiences that are often not "recognized as social but taken to be private, idiosyncratic, and even isolating."[22] According to Williams, feelings, although "actively lived and felt," are "elusive, impalpable forms of social consciousness,"[23] and thus tend to disappear from social analysis altogether. Since the most common modes of social analysis define the *social* as the known and reduce it to fixed forms, they tend to miss the "complexities, the experienced tensions, shifts, and uncertainties, the intricate forms of unevenness and confusion" that constitute the living present.[24] Williams argues that the alternative to these analytical reductions is not the silencing or disappearance of these complexities and tensions but "a kind of feeling and thinking which is indeed social and material."[25] As Avery Gordon explains, a structure of feeling articulates "the tangled exchange of noisy silences and seething absences."[26] It is these "noisy silences" and "seething absences" in the lives of young Filipino Americans that I am most interested in documenting. Thus lies the importance of approaching migration through the lens of emotions: it enables us to see the material, cultural, and political circumstances that constrain immigrant life, the immigrant responses to and against these constraints, and the emotional tensions that result therein.

Money: A "Weapon against Social Subjugation"

In Brian Ascalon Roley's *American Son: A Novel*,[27] young protagonists Gabriel and Tomas experience anger and shame as they witness the mistreatment that their low-wage-earning, first-generation, single Filipina mother regularly endures. In the face of such indignities, the young brothers learn quickly that *money* "is the only reliable weapon against social subjugation."[28] Tomas thus turns to stealing, drug dealing, and even guard dog–training and selling to provide monetarily for his mother and to act out his anger at the many indignities she suffers. Following Roley's intense account of the layered social significance of and investment in money, this section explores the poignant and complex ways in which Filipino immigrants and their children use money to manage intimacy, to negotiate meanings of the family, and to assure their social position and dignity in the racially and economically stratified United States.

Although money is one of the most important pieces of "social technology" ever developed, many scholars have conceptualized money as an "impersonal element that exists in human life."[29] However, as a system of intricate social relations, money is "neither culturally neutral nor socially anonymous."[30] In studying money, we need to be attentive to its multiple symbolisms, its cultural and social significance beyond utility, and its attachment to and dependence on a variety of social relations.[31] For instance, anthropologist Jean Lave contends that money is employed so as to "preserve moral categories and family relations as well as to express them"; and political scientist Robert Lane concludes that Americans view money as a meaningful symbol of feelings such as personal inadequacy, loss of control, failure, security, or need for social approval.[32]

The Filipino immigrant narrative is replete with stories about and around money. For the majority of the people that I interviewed, their migration to the United States was designed to improve the lot and status of their families back home, and not only or primarily about the pursuit of personal success. A significant economic manifestation of these transnational families is the remittance flows—both in money and goods—to relatives and friends in the Philippines. Close to 90 percent of the Filipino immigrants I interviewed indicated that they or their family had sent remittances to the Philippines: to help an aging parent, to finance a sibling's college education, to alleviate an emergency, to purchase property, or to provide extra spending money for family members during the holidays. Whatever the reason, sending remittances to secure a better quality of life for one's family back home is widely perceived as a migrant's obligation. Leo Sicat, who "send[s] money home regularly," viewed sending remittances as a nonnegotiable responsibility: "We cannot get away from that. The people back home always need that support."[33] This sense of duty stems not only from traditional demands but also from a deep awareness of the income and resource differentials between the Philippines and the United States, which are the result of U.S. (neo)colonialism in the Philippines. When asked why her family continues to send money to the Philippines, Maricela Rebaya, who came to the United States in 1985 at the age of fourteen, declared, "No matter how difficult life is here, it's still better off than over there." As she saw it, their lives in the United States were intimately connected to the lives of those "back home": "For us staying here doesn't mean that's just for us. When we earn extra money, we send it home. It's a big help for them. So when we're here, we try to make better of ourselves so we can help them."

In many instances, sending remittances increases the immigrant's status back home and helps to blunt the sharpness of life—homesickness, cultural isolation, and downward social mobility—in the United States. On the other hand, remittance-based relationships entail financial sacrifices as well as personal and emotional costs. Carmina Datilles shared that for the first twenty years of their lives in the United States, her husband felt obligated to send money to his family "even though we don't have anything. We don't have telephone, anything, but he's always helping his family. Monthly. Month after month. There were seven in his family altogether. They were poor. So if someone is in need, we always provide. . . ." When Datilles's husband reduced the monthly amount sent to his family, "his Dad got mad in the Philippines because he made the allotment smaller. His brother also said, 'Why did you cut my allotment?' My husband was surprised. He said, 'I've been giving to you guys for twenty years. It's about time.'" This example suggests that decisions over who should receive remittances, how much to send, and for how long are difficult negotiations, fraught with disappointments and suspicions. Julia Cortez recounted that her mother had a "nervous breakdown" over sending money to the Philippines because "my dad's mom was jealous of my mom sending money to her mom in the Philippines. She thought that my dad was forgetting about her." Remittance-sending can also lead to marital conflicts. Ruby Cruz related that her parents fought bitterly over money sent to the Philippines:

> My dad's always proving himself to his relatives back home. So whenever they ask him for money, he just gives it to them. My mom told me that we had given our relatives over ten thousand dollars so far. That makes my mom really, really mad because she worked two jobs so that my brother and me wouldn't have to work when we are in college. But now that money is gone.

Implicit in these charges is the migrants' frustration over the perceived shift in the quality of their relationship to relatives back home from one based on love and affection to one based on the amount of goods and money remitted. These examples call attention to the *transnational* dimension of money, as family members, both here and back home, negotiate and nurse broken promises, clashing expectations, and unfulfilled dreams about and around money decisions. These transnational tensions have to be understood within the larger context of growing global inequalities— particularly between the United States and the Philippines—that forces Filipinos to live apart from their loved ones in order to better provide for them.

More compellingly, Filipino reasons for migration—and their definition of success—pivot around the projected and actual life chances for their children in the United States.[34] When asked why they chose to move from the Philippines to the United States, Filipino immigrant parents would say, "We did it for the children." In the United States, they believe, their children will have better educational and job opportunities. It is this belief in intergenerational mobility that validates their decision to migrate, even when they themselves experience downward economic and social mobility as a result. It is also what keeps them rooted in the United States. As an example, after toiling in the U.S. Navy for twenty years, Nestor Pulido gave up his dream of going back to the Philippines and living "like a king" because he "wanted to stay here to sacrifice for my kids . . . to give [them]

oetter education here." Sometimes, the transnational and intergenera-
‚ional dimensions of "success" collide, as when obligations for the family
back home conflict with those for the family here. Ruby Cruz resented
her father's generosity toward his relatives in the Philippines because it
siphoned needed resources from their nuclear family: "It's not really, really fair. I mean, because my dad has sent money to my cousin who went
to nursing school. You know, why should she have money to do whatever
she wanted, but my brother and me have to struggle and be limited and
we're here and we are his kids."

Transnational obligations, parental sacrifices, and the promise of intergenerational mobility—these are the factors that shape the money dynamics between Filipino immigrant parents and their children. In the interviews with young Filipino Americans in San Diego, clashing ideas about
"money"—expressed most often in the form of conflicts over choices of
academic majors and future careers—constitute key sources of emotion-
filled strains and conflicts between immigrant parents and their children.
Almost all respondents reported experiencing pressure from their parents
to get good grades, to attend and finish college, and to pursue "practical"
careers such as law, medicine, or engineering. Arturo Velasco, a community college student with an interest in art and graphic design, described
the toll that his parents' "high" expectations had on their relationship:

> Me and my dad . . . can't really talk to each other. My dad doesn't really
> have anything like nice to say. It's like the same thing every day, you know.
> It's like, what's your grades in school? It's like school this, school that, school
> this, school that, you know. . . . And I like arts and stuff . . . but my parents
> they want me to be an engineer or doctor. It's like the typical Pilipino fam-
> ily, you know. They want their kids to make a lot of money and stuff. . . .
> Like my parents are always getting on my case. Like, the past few years,
> there's been times that I didn't want to stay at home because they kept nag-
> ging me . . . like just about school and like what I'm doing.

When asked to explain their parents' rigid academic standards, many
respondents invoked the Philippines, claiming that it is a Filipino cultural value for parents to want a "good education for the kids." However,
when probed further, some began to describe their parents' attitudes toward education as an effort to shield children from potential racial discrimination. Romeo Morales recalled that when his immigrant mother
was passed over for a promised promotion, she dealt with her anger and

disappointment by exhorting her children to do well in school: "That's why you kids have to finish school because I want them to see that it is not just your color, you should show them that . . . this is my degree. I just want you guys to . . . have something to show so that you won't have to work like this." Many parents we interviewed confirmed that they pushed their children to succeed in part to protect them from the discrimination that they themselves had faced:

> I always tell my kids, don't let anyone ever tell you that you're not good enough, 'cause you will face a lot of racism in your field and just deal with it, you know. You don't take anything from Americans. Uh, do not let anybody demean you, degrade you, or push you around, because of color. See, you know, you have the same right as everybody around here. I told them that. I said, it's very important that you get a degree because a college education is something that nobody, nobody can take away from you.
>
> I told [my children] that they are Americans . . . because I don't want them to feel like a second-class citizen, that like the Americans, you know the people here, feel like they thought to themselves that they are the people, like, in power, you know, that you have to move out. And I don't want them to feel that they have to move out and things like that. I want them to feel like they are equal with anybody who lives here. I want them to feel that you are no better than me.

These statements constitute both a warning and an exhortation to their children: a warning to be aware and wary of racial discrimination, and an exhortation to press on toward success. Many parents grab onto education as the antidote to the effects of racism for themselves and especially for their children. On the receiving end, many second-generation Filipinos learn early on that getting good grades, attending college, and selecting a career are not personal choices, but are deeply embedded in fulfilling their parents' dream of and hope for intergenerational mobility—their reason for migrating in the first place.

The discussion above confirms that money is used to create categories of social difference, especially to mark social rank and to determine social acceptance and membership.[35] In the United States, wealth has become the basis of social esteem and a status marker. Lamont reports that for American upper-middle-class men, money means above all "freedom, control, and security"—the ability to work, play, and live by one's own rules.[36] But as the interviews above remind us, wealth accumulation

, the United States is intimately linked with racism; and as such, a study of money is necessarily a study of racial inequality. As many scholars have documented throughout U.S. economic history, from the colonial period to the industrial revolution to the present postindustrial era, the "possessive investment in whiteness" has sustained an oppressive economic system that protects the class privileges of whites and denies racialized communities opportunities for asset accumulation and upward mobility.[37]

In recent years, scholars have begun to explore how marginalized groups, and not only elites, use money and consumption to raise or secure their social standing. As Alex Kotlowitz reports, it is primarily as consumers—as "purchasers of the talisman of success"—that poor black youth claim social membership to the larger U.S. society.[38] In her insightful study of children of Asian immigrant entrepreneurs, Lisa Park likewise shows that it is through conspicuous consumption that young Asian Americans attempt to claim their, and by extension their parents', social citizenship, or belonging as Americans.[39] In other words, college and career choices are less or not only a sign of Filipino assimilation and social acceptance, and more a complex and strategic response to their and their parents' "differential inclusion" into U.S. society.[40] Cognizant of her parents' many sacrifices and their harsh lives in the United States, Alva Gonzales pressured herself to succeed in order to establish her family's worth, belonging, and acceptance into U.S. society:

> With my dad, he doesn't really acknowledge it, but he has had to, like assimilate and then some, to get where he was today. And I think that's why he really, really burned his identity, and like, he's really hard on himself, and I think that's why he's so hard on us. Um, but yeah, he achieved, um, senior chief position in the military. I think their main concern is that we have a way to sustain ourselves when we're older. And that's like, the biggest thing that I want to do, is make sure that when I'm older I have the financial means to make sure that they're okay. Yeah, like, that's like, the biggest thing. 'Cause I saw them work their asses off, ever since I was growing up, and that's the one big thing that I want to do, is just to give back to them. Yeah, I mean that's why I talk about living the American dream, and like, having a successful career and pretty good salary. . . .

As the only person in her family to have attended a U.S. university, Carmina Reyes, a college junior, faced intense pressure from her parents to do well and to graduate. She described how she has internalized her parents' pressure as her own "driving force":

> I will be the first of both my parents' sides of the family to graduate at a United States college. So I have a lot of weight on my shoulders to finish. And to, you know, make them proud. . . . It's like a driving force as like, you know, I don't wanna let them down. Because they have like supported me financially, you know, to get through this. To get this far. But also, as being a driving force. There is also that, uh, intense pressure where you wanna, where you don't wanna fail. . . .

An irony in immigrant family life is that as much as education is stressed, it is often the child's responsibility to navigate the demands of the complex U.S. educational system.[41] In many instances, this is so because immigrant parents are uninformed about the expectations and requirements of U.S. schools. In other cases, such as that of Arturo Gonzales, parents' demanding work schedules keep them from taking an active role in their children's education. For Arturo, his mother's absence has left a void that continues to affect his academic and personal life:

> My mom was working. She had two jobs, so I didn't see her all that much. Like, I had to find a way to get through my schoolwork. She doesn't even bother, actually, she never even seen, you know, schoolwork. For us it was never an issue in terms of our parents driving it home like, "do good, do good." Like, we already knew we had to do good. 'Cause my mom doesn't have the energy, like, when she comes home to sit down with us, right. . . . And so, for me, I had to take the burden of education onto myself without saying, "Oh, can you help me?" I think in these last couple of years that my mom has really seen the effect of coming to the United States, what it has done to our family, right. She blames herself for not being there. But I don't blame her because I guess that was our situation, you know. But it doesn't help, like, when you, you know, I'm twenty-one years old and I don't have the best relationship with my mother, or with the rest of my siblings. I mean, we can't blame each other, right, but you're still left with that sense of void.

Arturo's declaration that "we already knew we had to do good" encapsulates the ways in which many second-generation Filipinos have internalized parental pressure to succeed as their own. As Carmina explained, "It's

/oint . . . where even though they're not saying, 'Oh you have to get
at A's,' I already know it. I've been trained not to be average. They
ct it and so now I expect it of myself." Therein lies the source of their
ess: they feel tremendous pressure to succeed in school but receive and
xpect little assistance from their already overburdened and often uninformed parents. As a result, for many second-generation Filipinos in our
study, conflicts over grades and career choices are less about a refusal to
please their parents than about frustrations over their inability—for whatever reason—to fulfill their parents' dream of family success via intergenerational mobility.

Sexuality: The "Keepers of Culture"

As the designated "keepers of culture,"[42] immigrant women and their behavior come under intense scrutiny from both women and men of their
own groups and from U.S.-born Americans.[43] In a study of the Italian
Harlem community from 1880 to 1950, Robert Orsi reports that "all the
community's fears for the reputation and integrity of the domus came to
focus on the behavior of young women."[44] Because women's moral and
sexual loyalties were deemed central to the maintenance of group status,
perceived changes in female behavior, especially that of growing daughters, were interpreted as signs of moral decay and ethnic suicide and were
carefully monitored and sanctioned.[45]

Although details vary, young women across groups, space, and time—
for example, second-generation Chinese women in San Francisco in the
1920s, U.S.-born Italian women in East Harlem in the 1930s, young Mexican women in the Southwest during the interwar years, and daughters of
Caribbean and Asian Indian immigrants on the East Coast in the 1990s—
have all identified strict parental control on their activities and movements as the primary source of intergenerational conflict.[46] More recent
studies of immigrant families also have identified gender as a significant
determinant of parent-child conflict, with daughters more likely than sons
to be involved in such conflict and instances of parental derogation.[47]

Although immigrant parents have always been preoccupied with passing on culture, language, and traditions to both male and female children,
it is daughters who bear the unequal burden of protecting and preserv-
ing the family name. Because sons do not have to conform to the image
of "ideal" ethnic subjects as daughters do, they often receive special day-

to-day privileges denied to daughters.[48] This is not to say that immigrant parents do not have unreasonable expectations of their sons, it is rather that these expectations do not pivot around the sons' sexuality or dating choices. In contrast, parental control over the movement and action of daughters begins the moment they are perceived as young adults and sexually vulnerable, and it regularly consists of monitoring their whereabouts and forbidding dating.[49] For example, the immigrant parents I interviewed seldom allowed their daughters to date, to stay out late, to spend the night at a friend's house, or to take an out-of-town trip.

Many of the second-generation women I spoke to railed against their parents' constant surveillance, which they named as a key source of their frustrations at and even intense anger toward their parents. Below are some examples:

I couldn't get along with my family, especially my father . . . because of the experience of being the girl . . . the surveillance. I would get in so much trouble because they wouldn't let me go out, not even to the front yard even, let alone going to a dance or going out with my girlfriends, or just friends in general. And they just say, "No!" That's it. And I'm like, "Why? Why? Why? Is it because I'm a girl?" They wouldn't let me out, and I hated them for that.

As I got older, it was more about just like not being able to go anywhere or like, not being able to do certain things, like you can't take your car out or . . . go out with some friends. I couldn't go out to parties. They just wouldn't let me do stuff and it was like a big yelling competition. I just had like a lot of anger and just, would just yell back at my parents.

My childhood was so turbulent for me, very difficult. Um, just always having to fight as a female with my parents about things that I could do. You know, I played three sports in high school, was president of this, that, and I had to fight for everything and anything that I ever wanted to do. I always had to fight long, drawn-out arguments with my parents, just to move two feet from the house. And no matter what I did, I was the anti-Christ. I mean, I know that sounds like an exaggeration, but my God, "Oh my God, you're so evil! You're so bad! Da-da-da-da-da. . . ." All this. My mom, because I was dating a guy and I go see him, she calls me a slut. Because I am a girl, I should not go over there. I was twenty years old and in college. So . . . I mean they're old school, they're old-fashioned, and they're also, they're not very kind, loving parents.

Being the oldest and being the only girl in the family, my sister didn't really have a choice. . . . Mind you that my sister was like the geek of the school. . . . She was voted the most likely to succeed. . . . She was valedictorian of her class. . . . And you know, that's why it was really bad when my mom would get on her and be like, "You know you're a whore!" and stuff like that. She would call my sister a whore when guys would come to the door to ask her what the homework was in class. And so, she would be like, "You're a whore!" And blah, blah, blah, you know, and she just totally yells at her.

These young women particularly resented what they saw as gender inequity in their families—the fact that their parents placed far more restrictions on their activities than on their brothers'. Ashley Hernandez talks about this double standard:

There was definitely a double standard as far as what I could do and what [my brothers] could do. And it didn't matter that I was older. Because it mattered that I was a girl. Like I couldn't stay out late. I had to stay home. And I couldn't have a boyfriend. And if I had like a guy come over, they were strictly like, you know, we could not go in my bedroom, and I am looking at my brothers now, who, you know, they come straight in the house and they have their girls come to their room. They have the door shut and locked. I could not get away with that. . . . Even when I had dance practice, like late each night till ten, you know, they expected me home, you know, right after practice. Whereas my brothers could have basketball practice. And then hang out with the guys. And then not come home till like, one o' clock.

The restrictions on girls' movement sometimes spill over to the realms of academics. Shamita Das Dasgupta and Sayantani DasGupta recount that in the Indian American community, while young men were expected to attend faraway competitive colleges, many of their female peers were encouraged by their parents to go to the local colleges so that they could live at or close to home.[50] Similarly, Diane Wolf reports that some Filipino parents pursued contradictory tactics with their children, particularly their daughters, by pushing them to achieve academic excellence in high school, but then "pulling the emergency brake" when they contemplated college by expecting them to stay at home, even if it meant going to a less competitive college, or not going at all.[51] Gracelynn de la Cruz recounted her parents' request that she attend the local university instead of another one further away from home:

I got accepted to UCLA and UCSD. . . . And my mom voiced it for me that that they'd appreciate it if I'd stay in San Diego. So I was like, "Okay, I'll stay," but I was kind of resentful of the fact that I didn't really get to choose. I think my parents, they were really scared. And I think that really has a lot to do with me being the youngest and the girl, you know. They were really worried about me leaving. . . . So I feel like I didn't make an informed decision. It was more like my parents requested me to stay. Those two applications, those two letters in front of me and, kind of, because of my loyalty to my parents, I just said, "Okay."

I do not mean to suggest that immigrant communities are the only ones that regulate their daughters' mobility and sexuality. Feminist scholars have long documented the construction, containment, and exploitation of women's sexuality in various societies.[52] We also know that the cultural anxiety over unbounded female sexuality is most apparent with regard to adolescent girls.[53] The difference is in the ways that immigrant and non-immigrant families sanction girls' sexuality. To control sexually active girls, non-immigrant parents in the United States often rely on the gender-based good girl/bad girl dichotomy in which "good girls" are passive, threatened sexual objects while "bad girls" are active, desiring sexual agents.[54] The good girl/bad girl cultural story conflates femininity with sexuality, increased women's vulnerability to sexual coercion, and justifies women's containment in the domestic sphere.

Immigrant families, though, have an additional strategy: they can discipline their daughters as racial/national subjects as well as gendered ones. That is, as self-appointed guardians of "authentic" cultural memory, immigrant parents can attempt to regulate their daughters' independent choices by linking them to cultural ignorance or betrayal. As both parents and children recounted, young women who disobeyed parental strictures were often branded "nonethnic," "untraditional," "radical," "selfish," and not "caring about the family." To the second-generation daughters, these charges are stinging. The young women I interviewed were visibly pained—with many breaking down and crying—when they recounted their parents' charges. This deep pain, stemming in part from their desire to be validated as Filipinas, existed even among the self-defined "rebellious daughters." As Amanda Flores explained:

My mom is very traditional. She wants to follow the Filipino customs, just really adhere to them, like what is proper for a girl, what she can and can't do, and what other people are going to think of her if she doesn't follow that way. When I pushed these restrictions, when I rebelled and stayed later than allowed, my mom would always say, "That is not what a decent Filipino girl should do. You should come home at a decent hour. What are people going to think of you?" And that would get me really upset, you know, because I think that my character is very much the way it should be for a Filipina. I wear my hair long, I wear decent makeup. I dress properly, conservative. I am family-oriented. It hurts me deeply that she doesn't see that I am decent, that I am proper, and that I am not going to bring shame to the family or anything like that.

Debra Ragaza expressed a similar sentiment:

When I lived with my parents, I was going out all the time . . . just hanging out with my girlfriends. And they didn't like that because I was coming home at two in the morning. But I try to tell them [that] we're not doing anything bad . . . that was my defense growing up. "I'm not doing anything bad. Just because I'm out doesn't mean I'm bad."

These narratives suggest that even when parents are unable to control their children's behavior, their (dis)approval remains powerful in shaping the emotional lives of their daughters.[55] Even as she rebelled against her parents' restrictions, Debra Ragaza continued to seek their approval: "I was just really in a rebellious stage. . . . But I would never want my parents to find out that I was dating behind their back. I'd do anything to cover up. Any notes that I got I would hide them in a box under my bed, you know, any kind of evidence, just get rid of it so that I would have my parents believing that I was paying attention to them and not disobeying them." Therein lies the source of immigrant parents' power: they possess an emotional hold on their children because they have the authority to determine if their daughters are "authentic" members of their racial-ethnic community. Largely unacquainted with the "home" country, U.S.-born children depend on their parents' tutelage to craft and affirm their ethnic self and thus are particularly vulnerable to charges of cultural ignorance or betrayal.[56] Since U.S.-born Filipinas are often excluded from full American membership, the parental accusation "You are not Filipina enough" essentially strips the second generation of meaningful identity, rendering them doubly "homeless." Thus the emotional hold immigrant parents have on their children is their unique ability to strip them of identity in what might, in non-immigrant family quarrels, be no more than a heated exchange about curfew violations by a teenager.

When questioned about their treatment of their daughters, parents such as Ofelia Velasco explained it as an act of "cultural preservation":

> I have that Filipino mentality that boys are boys and girls are different. Girls are supposed to be protected, to be clean. . . . The girls always say that is not fair. What is the difference between their brothers and them? And my answer always is, "In the Philippines, you know, we don't do that. The girls stay home. The boys go out." It was the way that I was raised. I still want to have part of that culture instilled in my children. And I want them to have that to pass on to their children.

Pedro Gonzales also explained that he leaned "more towards the Filipino way" when it came to raising his daughter:

> I have only one daughter so I tended to be a little bit stricter. So the double standard kind of operates: it's all right for the boys to explore the field, but I tended to be overly protective of my daughter. My wife feels the same way because the boys will not lose anything, but the daughter will lose something, their virginity, and it can also be a question of losing face, that kind of thing.

Other parents, while also referencing the Philippines in discussing their daughters, took a more critical transnational perspective by calling attention to the stereotypes of Filipinas that emerged out of U.S. colonialism, especially the extensive U.S. military presence in the Philippines. As one father explained, "Filipina women, you know, when they walk on the street, the first thing people think, like, she got here from the bar in the Philippines. That's the first impression that they get." Within the context of the dominant culture's pervasive hypersexualization of Filipina women—either as the desirable but dangerous "prostitutes" and/or submissive "mail-order brides"—the construction of the "ideal" Filipina—as family-oriented and chaste—can be read as an effort to reclaim the morality of the community. However, enforced by distorting powers of memory and nostalgia, this rhetoric of moral superiority often leads to calls for cultural "authenticity" that locate family honor and national integrity in the community's female members.[57] This practice of cultural (re)construction reveals how deeply the conduct of private life can be tied to larger national and transnational structures.

Conclusion

Most popular and scholarly writings on immigrant families tend to naturalize and domesticate intergenerational tension, attributing it to the "culture clash" between "traditional" immigrant parents and their more "Americanized" children. In this chapter, I have examined intergenerational strain *not* as a private matter between Filipino immigrant parents and their children, but as a social, historical, and transnational affair that exposes, defies, contradicts, and advances multiple and overlapping forms of power relations. Whereas most scholarly research on the second generation conflates their economic and educational attainment with emotional well-being, I have shown that these "money" issues are emotionally charged—with Filipino parents and children clashing over ideas about transnational obligations, parental sacrifices, and intergenerational mobility in the racially and economically stratified United States. In the same way, I have argued that the often inflexible expectation of Filipina chastity is not only about reinforcing masculinist and patriarchal power but also about bolstering national and ethnic self-respect in light of the pervasive sexualization of Filipinas and other Asian women in the United States. These examples confirm that domestic tensions over money and sexuality express more than familial squabbles or cultural clashes, but bespeak the aftermath of gender, race, and global inequality. Therein lies the importance of studying intergenerational relations through the lens of emotions: by exposing the material, historical, and transnational circumstances that constrain immigrant life, this approach underscores the need to conceptualize intergenerational strain as a site not only for assessing the private lives of immigrants, but also for understanding the racialized and gendered economic, cultural, and political foundations of the United States and its empire.

NOTES

1. Di Leonardo 1984; Gabaccia 1994; Hickey 1996; Ruiz 1992.

2. The interview data come from two sources. The first was a set of interviews that I conducted with more than one hundred Filipinos in San Diego over the course of eight years (1992–2000). The second was from a later study conducted with Diane Wolf. With the assistance of two research assistants, one Filipina and one Vietnamese, we interviewed forty young Filipinos stratified

by sex. Our study of intergenerational tensions is distinctive in that we also interviewed immigrant parents, twenty from each group. We asked both parents and children (separately) about the nature of their relationships with each other, the points of conflict and cooperation, and how they navigate between different cultural codes and ideologies. We are particularly interested in comparing the ways in which parents and children may have different interpretations of similar dynamics. Parents were asked about their immigration, residential, and occupational histories as well. Reflecting the average socioeconomic status of the larger Filipino American population in the county, the majority of my respondents came from middle-class, college-educated, home-owning families.

3. Espiritu 2003.

4. Elena Gaona, "Thousands of Filipino-Americans Celebrate with Festival, Fiesta," *San Diego Union-Tribune*, October 2, 2005.

5. In comparison, for the total San Diego County population, the median family income was $69,099; about 57 percent owned their own homes; and 8 percent lived in poverty (U.S. Census Bureau, 2006).

6. Di Leonardo 1984; Kibria 1993.

7. Wolf 1997: 461.

8. Espiritu 2001.

9. "Children of Immigrants: The Adaptation Process of the Second Generation" (known as the Children of Immigrants Longitudinal Study, or CILS) is a comprehensive longitudinal study of the educational performance and social, cultural, and psychological adaptation of second-generation youth in San Diego. These data suggest that "certain psychosocial vulnerabilities or dynamics among Vietnamese and Filipino children of immigrants" not captured by quantitative data "may be linked to a diminished sense of self worth" (Rumbaut 1994: 785), underscoring the need for further in-depth qualitative research.

10. Espiritu and Wolf 2001: 179–81.

11. Hernandez and Glenn 2003.

12. Portes 1994: 634

13. Mills 1959.

14. Lutz 1990.

15. Barbalet 1998: 30; Bendelow and Williams 1998: xvi.

16. Barbalet 1998: 14, 30.

17. Barbalet 1998: 12–13.

18. Abu-Lughod and Lutz 1990: 3.

19. Abu-Lughod 1990; Denzin 1984; de Sousa 1987; Hochschild 1983; Kemper 1978; McLemee 2003.

20. Conceptualizing emotions as cultural constructs, anthropologists have documented the ways in which emotions are expressed, interpreted, and practiced differently across cultures and nations. See Abu-Lughod and Lutz 1990;

Barbalet 1998; Lutz 1990; Lyon 1998: 53–54. Historians have added to this discussion by showing that emotional change and difference is more than mere randomness, but results "from interaction between our emotional capacities and the unfolding of historical circumstances" (Reddy 2001: 45). And sociologists have insisted that emotions, as "social things," hold the key to our understanding of social structures and processes and provide the "missing link" between private experience and public issues (Barbalet 1998: 170; Bendelow and Williams 1998).

21. Lutz 1990: 69.

22. Williams 1977: 132.

23. Eagleton 1991: 48.

24. Williams 1977: 129.

25. Williams 1977: 131.

26. Gordon 2001: 200.

27. Roley 2001.

28. Chow 2003: 212.

29. Ingham 1996; Weber [1946] 1971: 331.

30. Zelizer 1994: 18. In a study of the changes in the public and private uses of money in the United States between 1870 and 1930, Zelizer shows that at each step in money's advance, people's values and social relations have transmuted money in ways that puzzle market theorists, investing money with varying systems of meaning and incorporating it into personalized webs of friendships, family relations, and interactions with authorities. Zelizer also reminds us that the meaning of money is gendered, in that women's money, dismissed as "purse money," is comparatively of less value than men's.

31. Ingham 1996; Veblen 1899; Zelizer 1994.

32. Lave 1988: 141; Lane 1991.

33. Except for Leo Sicat, whose life history was published in Espiritu 1995, all personal names used in this essay are pseudonyms.

34. Nauck and Settles 2001.

35. Published in 1899, Thorstein Veblen's *Theory of the Leisure Class* is one of the earliest statements of the view that consumption structures social difference. Writing in a time where the nouveaux riches used luxury consumption to elevate their social position, Veblen maintained that consumption was not apolitical but an integral part of the reproduction of inequality. Extending these ideas, Pierre Bourdieu (1984) describes how members of the French dominant class strive to uphold their social position by competing to legitimize their definition of high status markers. In a follow-up study, Michèle Lamont (1992) argues that members of the French and American upper-middle class engage in "boundary work" when they use their "distinctive" tastes and lifestyles to mark their class status and signal their ability and desirability. According to Lamont (1992), boundary work, or the process of generating distinctions, is an intrinsic part of the process of constituting the self. Since boundary work involves patrolling the borders of

one's groups, it potentially produces inequality by separating people into classes, working groups, professions, species, genders, and races, often in reference to their presumed lifestyle, habits, character, or competences (p. 10). In an articulated theory of the production of social differences through commodities, Jean Baudrillard (2000) likewise insists that it is necessary to define consumption "not only structurally as a system of exchange and of signs, but strategically as a mechanism of power" (p. 75).

36. Lamont 1992: 69.
37. Harris 1993; Lipsitz 2006; Roediger 1991.
38. Kotlowitz 2000: 257.
39. Park 2005.
40. Espiritu 2003.
41. Park 2005: 84.
42. Billson 1995.
43. Gabaccia 1994: xi.
44. Orsi 1985: 135.
45. Gabaccia 1994: 113.
46. Dasgupta and DasGupta 1996; Orsi 1985; Ruiz 1992; Waters 1996; Yung 1995.
47. Gibson 1995; Matute-Bianchi 1991; Rumbaut and Ima 1988; Woldemikael 1989.
48. Haddad and Smith 1996: 22–24; Waters 1996: 75–76.
49. See, e.g., Wolf 1997.
50. Dasgupta and DasGupta 1996: 230.
51. Wolf 1997: 467.
52. See Maglin and Perry 1996.
53. Tolman and Higgins 1996: 206.
54. Tolman and Higgins 1996.
55. See Wolf 1997.
56. Espiritu 1994.
57. Espiritu 2001.

REFERENCES

Abu-Lughod, Lila. 1990. "Shifting Politics in Bedouin Love Poetry." Pp. 23–45 in Catherine Lutz and Lila Abu-Lughod (eds.), *Language and the Politics of Emotion*. Cambridge: Cambridge University Press.

Abu-Lughod, Lila, and Catherine A. Lutz. 1990. "Introduction: Emotion, Discourse, and the Politics of Everyday Life." Pp. 1–23 in Catherine Lutz and Lila Abu-Lughod (eds.), *Language and the Politics of Emotion*. Cambridge: Cambridge University Press.

Barbalet, J. M. 1998. *Emotion, Social Theory, and Social Structure*. Cambridge: Cambridge University Press.

Baudrillard, Jean. 2000. "The Ideological Genesis of Needs." Pp. 57–80 in Juliet B. Schor and Douglas B. Holt (eds.), *The Consumer Society Reader*. New York: The New Press.

Bendelow, Gillian, and Simon J. Williams. 1998. *Emotions in Social Life: Critical Themes and Contemporary Issues*. London: Routledge.

Billson, Janet Mancini. 1995. *Keepers of the Culture: The Power of Tradition in Women's Lives*. New York: Lexington Books.

Bourdieu, Pierre. 1984. *Distinction: A Social Critique of the Judgment of Taste*. Translated by Richard Nice. Cambridge: Harvard University Press.

Chow, Karen Har-Yen. 2003. "Prose Book Prize Awardee—American Son: A Novel, by Brian Acalon Roley." *Journal of Asian American Studies* 6(2): 211–12.

Dasgupta, Shamita Das, and Sayantani DasGupta. 1996. "Public Face, Private Face: Asian Indian Women and Sexuality." Pp. 226–43 in Nan Bauer Maglin and Donna Perry (eds.), *'Bad Girls'/'Good Girls': Women, Sex, and Power in the Nineties*. New Brunswick, NJ: Rutgers University Press.

Denzin, Norman. 1984. *On Understanding Emotion*. San Francisco: Jossey-Bass.

de Sousa, Ronald. 1987. *The Rationality of Emotion*. Cambridge: MIT Press.

Di Leonardo, Micaela. 1984. *The Varieties of Ethnic Experience: Kinship, Class, and Gender among California Italian-Americans*. Ithaca, NY: Cornell University Press.

Eagleton, Terry. 1991. *Ideology: An Introduction*. New York: Verso.

Espiritu, Yen Le. 1994. "The Intersection of Race, Ethnicity, and Class: The Multiple Identities of Second Generation Filipinos." *Identities* 1 (2–3): 249–73.

———. 1995. *Filipino American Lives*. Philadelphia: Temple University Press.

———. 2001. "'We Don't Sleep Around Like White Girls Do': Family, Culture, and Gender in Filipina American Lives." *Signs: Journal of Women in Culture* 26(2): 415–40.

———. 2003. *Home Bound: Filipino American Lives across Cultures, Communities, and Countries*. Berkeley: University of California Press.

Espiritu, Yen Le, and Diane L. Wolf. 2001. "The Paradox of Assimilation: Children of Filipino Immigrants in San Diego." Pp. 157–86 in Ruben Rumbaut and Alejandro Portes (eds.), *Ethnicities: Children of Immigrants in America*. Berkeley: University of California Press; New York: Russell Sage Foundation.

Gabaccia, Donna. 1994. *From the Other Side: Women, Gender, and Immigrant Life in the U.S., 1820–1990*. Bloomington: Indiana University Press.

Gibson, Margaret A. 1995. "Additive Acculturation as a Strategy for School Improvement." Pp. 77–105 in Ruben Rumbaut and Wayne Cornelius (eds.), *California's Immigrant Children: Theory, Research, and Implications for Educational Policy*. La Jolla: Center for U.S.-Mexican Studies, University of California, San Diego.

Gordon, Avery. 2001. *Ghostly Matters: Haunting and the Sociological Imagination*. Minneapolis: University of Minnesota Press.

Haddad, Yvonne Y., and Jane I. Smith. 1996. "Islamic Values among American Muslims." Pp. 19–40 in Barbara C. Aswad and Barbara Bilge (eds.), *Family and Gender Among American Muslims: Issues Facing Middle Eastern Immigrants and Their Descendants*. Philadelphia: Temple University Press.

Harris, Cheryl. 1993. "Whiteness as Property." *Harvard Law Review* 106(8): 1709–95.

Hernandez, David Manuel, and Evelyn Nakano Glenn. 2003. "Ethnic Prophesies: A Review Essay." *Contemporary Sociology* 32(4): 418–26.

Hickey, M. Gail. 1996. "'Go to College, Get a Job, and Don't Leave Home without Your Brother': Oral Histories with Immigrant Women and Their Daughters." *Oral History Review* 23(2): 63–92.

Hochschild, Arlie. 1983. *The Managed Heart: Commercialization of Human Feeling*. Berkeley: University of California Press.

hooks, bell. 2000. "Eating the Other: Desire and Resistance." Pp. 343–59 in Juliet B. Schor and Douglas B. Holt (eds.), *The Consumer Society Reader*. New York: The New Press.

Ingham, Geoffrey. 1996. "Money Is a Social Relation." *Review of Social Economy* 54(4): 507–30.

Kemper, Theodore. 1978. *A Social Interactional Theory of Emotions*. New York: John Wiley and Sons.

Kibria, Nazli. 1993. *Family Tightrope: The Changing Lives of Vietnamese Immigrant Communities*. Princeton, NJ: Princeton University Press.

Kotlowitz, Alex. 2000. "False Connections." Pp. 253–58 in Juliet B. Schor and Douglas B. Holt (eds.), *The Consumer Society Reader*. New York: The New Press.

Lamont, Michèle. 1992. *Money, Morals, Manners: The Culture of the French and the American Upper-Middle Class*. Chicago: University of Chicago Press.

Lane, Robert. 1991. *The Market Experience*. Cambridge: Cambridge University Press.

Lave, Jean. 1988. *Cognition in Practice: Mind, Mathematics and Culture in Everyday Life*. Cambridge: Cambridge University Press.

Lipsitz, George. 2006. *The Possessive Investment in Whiteness: How White People Profit from Identity Politics*. Philadelphia: Temple University Press.

Lutz, Catherine. 1990. "Engendered Emotion: Gender, Power, and the Rhetoric of Emotional Control in American Discourse." Pp. 69–91 in Catherine Lutz and Lila Abu-Lughod (eds.), *Language and the Politics of Emotion*. Cambridge: Cambridge University Press.

Lyon, Margot L. 1998. "Limitations of Cultural Constructionism." Pp. 39–59 in Gillian Bendelow and Simon J. Williams (eds.), *Emotions in Social Life: Critical Themes and Contemporary Issues*. London: Routledge.

Maglin, Nan Bauer, and Donna Perry. 1996. "Introduction." in Nan Bauer Maglin and Donna Perry (eds.), *'Bad Girls'/ 'Good Girls': Women, Sex, and Power in the Nineties*. New Brunswick, NJ: Rutgers University Press.

Matute-Bianchi, M. E. 1991. "Situational Ethnicity and Patterns of School Per-
    formance among Immigrant and Nonimmigrant Mexican-Descent Students."
    Pp. 205–47 in M. Gibson and J. U. Ogbu (eds.), *Minority Status and School-
    ing: A Comparative Study of Immigrant and Involuntary Minorities*. New York:
    Garland.

McLemee, Scott. 2003. "Getting Emotional: The Study of Feelings, Once the
    Province of Psychology, Is Now Spreading to History, Literature, and Other
    Fields." *Chronicle of Higher Education*, February 21, p. 14.

Mills, C. Wright. 1959. *The Sociological Imagination*. London: Oxford University
    Press.

Nauck, Bernard, and Barbara Settles. 2001. "Immigrant and Ethnic Minor-
    ity Families: An Introduction." *Journal of Comparative Family Studies* 32(4):
    461–66.

Orsi, Robert Anthony. 1985. *The Madonna of 115th Street: Faith and Community
    in Italian Harlem, 1880–1950*. New Haven, CT: Yale University Press.

Park, Lisa. 2005. *Consuming Citizenship: Children of Asian Immigrant Entrepre-
    neurs*. Stanford: Stanford University Press.

Portes, Alejandro. 1994. "Introduction: Immigration and Its Aftermath." *Interna-
    tional Migration Review* 28(4): 632–39.

Reddy, William M. 2001. *The Navigation of Feeling: A Framework for the History
    of Emotions*. Cambridge: Cambridge University Press.

Roediger, David. 1991. *The Wages of Whiteness: Race and the Making of the Amer-
    ican Working Class*. New York: Routledge.

Roley, Brian Acalon. 2001. *American Son: A Novel*. New York: W. W. Norton.

Ruiz, Vicki L. 1992. "The Flapper and the Chaperone: Historical Memory
    among Mexican-American Women." Pp. 141–58 in Donna Gabaccia
    (ed.), *Seeking Common Ground: Multidisciplinary Studies*. Westport, CT:
    Greenwood.

Rumbaut, Ruben. 1994. "The Crucible Within: Ethnic Identity, Self-Esteem, and
    Segmented Assimilation among Children of Immigrants." *International Migra-
    tion Review* 28(4): 748–94.

Rumbaut, Ruben, and Kenji Ima. 1988. *The Adaptation of Southeast Asian Youth:
    A Comparative Study*. Washington, DC: U.S. Office of Refugee Resettlement.

Tolman, Deborah L., and Tracy E. Higgins. 1996. "How Being a Good Girl Can
    Be Bad For Girls." Pp. 205–25 in Nan Bauer Maglin and Donna Perry (eds.),
    'Bad Girls' / 'Good Girls': Women, Sex, and Power in the Nineties. New Bruns-
    wick, NJ: Rutgers University Press.

U.S. Census Bureau. 2006. "American Community Survey: S0201, Selected Popu-
    lation Profile in the United States; Filipinos Alone." Accessed online June 6,
    2008: http://factfinder.census.gov.

Veblen, Thorstein. 1899. *The Theory of the Leisure Class: An Economic Study in
    the Evolution of Institutions*. New York: Macmillan.

Waters, Mary C. 1996. "The Intersection of Gender, Race, and Ethnicity in Identity Development of Caribbean American Teens." Pp. 65–84 in Bonnie J. Ross Leadbeater and Niobe Way (eds.), *Urban Girls: Resisting Stereotypes, Creating Identities.* New York: New York University Press.

Weber, Max. [1946] 1971. "Religious Rejections of the World and Their Directions." Pp. 323–62 in H. H. Gerth and C. Wright Mills (eds.), *From Max Weber: Essays in Sociology.* New York: Oxford University Press.

Williams, Raymond. 1977. *Marxism and Literature.* Oxford: Oxford University Press.

Woldemikael, T. M. 1989. *Becoming Black American: Haitians and American Institutions in Evanston, Illinois.* New York: AMS Press.

Wolf, Diane L. 1997. "Family Secrets: Transnational Struggles among Children of Filipino Immigrants." *Sociological Perspectives* 40(3): 457–82.

Yung, Judy. 1995. *Unbound Feet: A Social History of Chinese Women in San Francisco.* Berkeley: University of California Press.

Zelizer, Viviana. 1994. *The Social Meaning of Money.* New York: Basic Books.

3

|||||||||||||||||||||||||||||||||||||||||||||||||||||||

Spare the Rod, Ruin the Child?
First- and Second-Generation West Indian Child-Rearing Practices

Mary C. Waters and Jennifer E. Sykes

In the early 1990s, when one of us interviewed West Indian immigrants to New York City, she asked them if there was anything about the United States that surprised or shocked them when they first arrived.[1] She expected many to mention the extent of racial discrimination in the United States, the huge size and impersonal relations of New York City, and even the cold weather that is a terrible shock to people who have lived all of their lives in the tropics. And some people did mention these issues. But she was very surprised at the number of parents who answered this open question with a discussion about methods of disciplining their children. For many parents, the most shocking aspect of American society was the difference they perceive in the social norms about the correct way to discipline children.

This difference was usually described as one between "strict" Caribbean parenting and "lax" American parenting. By this they mean the use of corporal punishment to deal with children who do something wrong, and stricter rules about child behavior and freedom among West Indian families than among American families. In this chapter we explore the attitudes of first-generation immigrants about these issues, as well as the experiences of second-generation West Indians as they grow up and reflect on the methods their parents used in raising them. We draw on 30 in-depth interviews conducted for the New York Second Generation

Study in 1999–2000 in New York City, as well as 124 in-depth interviews conducted by Waters in the early 1990s in New York City.[2] We explore the ways in which this issue of discipline is seen differently by parents and children, and the changing of West Indian cultural norms over time.

We find that "strict" parenting and the use of corporal punishment (described as "beatings" by immigrants and the second generation) are widespread and do not vary much by social class. Middle-class and working-class West Indian families seem to adopt these "authoritarian" parenting techniques in equal numbers. This is at odds with the patterns among American families, where parenting techniques vary a great deal by social class. We find some evidence of change in parenting practices among the second generation—a slight move away from corporal punishment on the part of some respondents. But we also find that the second generation wants to preserve many of the practices of their parents' generation. We discuss the implications of these findings for the literature on parenting practices. Specifically, we argue that beliefs about how to discipline children and parenting behaviors are culturally determined, rather than a reflection of class position, and as such, they offer a way to measure cultural change over time.

The Parents' View

The parents in the New York study in the early 1990s believed that physical punishment was the way to deal with a child who had misbehaved. They were shocked that this is unacceptable in the United States, and consistently said that it was one of the most disturbing aspects of living in this country. Over and again, among both middle-class and working-class immigrants, the issue of corporal punishment and its apparent unacceptability in the United States was described as a very serious problem. That the state can dictate that a parent cannot beat a child is seen by these parents as a real threat to their ability to raise their children correctly. Parental discipline of children was most often mentioned in responses to the very general questions, "How is the United States different from your country?" or "What do you miss the most about your country?" Discipline clearly was an issue very much on people's minds:

Q: How was New York different from Guyana?
A: New York is very different from our country. For instance, the training. Back home, we beat our kids. Over here, you can't beat your kids. It's child abuse.

That's the first thing they want to say. Right? You know, well whenever our kids do wrong, something wrong, we beat them. We punish them too. You know and even in the schools, right, our schools, they beat the kids. But over here, the schooling, they don't beat the kids. . . . I think it's very bad. I think they should beat the kids. To me, they learn better that way. (Guyanese female worker, age thirty-seven, in the United States eight years)

Q: Is there anything you miss about your country?
A: Well yes, I'm not accustomed to the cold. The other thing is you come up here, it's different in bringing up your kids. Number one, you know, you have no control of them than when you were back home. This is different when they are here. The people used to say, don't spare the rod and spoil the child. You know, teachers would scold them, and would be able to handle them. But I wouldn't advise anyone to bring their kids up in this town. Always live in the country until they reach an age, then you bring them in; if they choose to work and go to college, then they take it from there. But it's very hard for you to have control of your kids in this city. They adopt the American styles real fast. Back home they were more restricted. And here you find if you try to put pressure on them they become rebellious.
Q: But back there, they wouldn't?
A: No, you know, you would slap them. And you could be more stern with them. Even the teachers and so on at the school, they were able to slap them. They were afraid of that. But here it's different. It's not the American way. Because the first thing, when you beat them, you hear child brutality and things like that. I am kind of afraid of that. (Guyanese female worker, age thirty-eight, in the United States nine years)

A teacher gave his opinion:

As they say, don't spare the rod and spoil the child. But in this system, if you do that, the child can call the police and you will be in trouble. So that's why some of the parents are finding it hard and the kids know it. They know what they can get away with and they play it into trouble and then what are you gonna do? You're gonna beat them and they'll call the police. 'Cause I, at open school night, I was speaking to parents and he told me one of the kids did call the police. But I guess after talking to the police, the police, I think, give them a warning. Said the next time they would have to press charges. And he's telling me you know because he's from Trinidad and the kid was born there and the kid stays out late, coming in at eleven, twelve in the night. On the telephone all the time and he's talking and not listening. I mean, you could talk, talk, talk so far, and then, when time come to punishment what are you going to do? Can't lock him in the house. You gonna open the door and go out. Now if you lock him out, and if they're under age, the police gonna bring them back. You have to take them? With my kids I am on them very hard. (Trinidadian male teacher, age forty-one, in the United States eighteen years)

The issue of corporal punishment came up in two contexts: whether parents should be allowed to hit or beat their children; and whether teachers and other school personnel should be allowed to hit children. The issue of corporal punishment in the home and the schools and the wider philosophical differences about child-rearing that this issue touches on represent the key behavioral cultural change that assimilation to America calls for among West Indian people. It is a widely discussed, contentious issue in the public schools in the West Indian community. It brings many West Indian immigrants into direct conflict with the American state, in the form of the Department of Social Services. And, like the contentious issues of Muslim girls wearing scarves in French schools or male African immigrants who have more than one wife, the issue of corporal punishment brings up very hard questions for multiculturalists. West Indians see corporal punishment as an integral part of their culture and of child-rearing. They feel that the American state is making them abandon a practice they believe to be the best way to raise their children.

While the immigrants and their children believe that it is illegal in New York for parents to hit their children at all, the law does not outlaw spanking. It does prohibit excessive force, and teachers are required to report parents if they leave any mark or welt on their children. Strictness in dealings between parents and children does seem to be a key component of West Indian culture. It has been commented on by a number of scholars who have studied West Indians both at home and in the United States.[3] In fact, the former prime minister of Jamaica, Edward Seaga, in his earlier life as an anthropologist wrote an article on the use of corporal punishment in the schools of a rural Jamaican village.[4] David Lowenthal noted that corporal punishment was an accepted, even taken-for-granted, aspect of West Indian child-rearing:

Upbringing is felt to require physical chastisement; parents regularly resort to the rod. Outsiders may interpret frequent beatings as symptoms of parental insecurity, but West Indians consider them normal and appropriate. Flogging is considered essential not only for effective punishment but for education; teachers vie with parents as disciplinarians. Beatings are no evidence of cruelty, opines a local authority; people of nearly all classes in Jamaica who are very violent with children at any other given moment are often at other times loving and warmhearted.[5]

In a review of child-rearing practices in Jamaica, Delores Smith and Gail Mosby argue that in the Caribbean more widely but specifically in Jamaica, "child rearing and disciplinary practices that would warrant child abuse charges in other Western societies are rampant."[6] Although Smith and Mosby conclude that severe beatings, emotional distance, and lack of communication between parents and children are destructive behaviors and should be changed, many West Indian professionals would profoundly disagree and argue that condemnation of these practices is a result of cultural misunderstanding. Many of the teachers and social workers Waters interviewed argued that true child abuse does exist in the West Indian community as it does in every community, and that it is very apparent to professionals when it does occur. These professionals argue that corporal punishment is not a harmful experience unless it is extreme, and that when it is extreme the West Indian community can recognize it and deal with it.

West Indians are not the first or the only immigrant group to experience challenges to their methods of child-rearing. Historian Selma Berrol describes the same friction between parents and children and the same concerns of social service agencies about Italian and other southern and central European families in the beginning of the twentieth century.[7]

> When a son criticized the decor at home for being too Italian, his father beat him. This was also the fate of a daughter in another family who came home later than the hour her father had specified. One young girl attempted to wear lipstick at age 13, which brought out a harsh scrubbing from her mother. Resentment at such treatment sometimes escalated into crisis; even if their youth and poverty forced them to stay at home, immigrant children left their parents in terms of culture, behavior, and affection.[8]

The West Indians' perception that Americans do not hit their children is actually mistaken, yet it does pick up on recent changes in norms about corporal punishment in the United States. According to sociologists

Murray Straus and Denise Donnelly,[9] the laws in all fifty states give parents the right to hit a child with an object provided no serious injury results. Figures on the prevalence of corporal punishment show that 90 percent of toddlers experience some form of corporal punishment, and 52 percent of the adult population of the United States recall having experienced corporal punishment as a teenager.[10] Yet Straus and Donnelly show that norms about corporal punishment have been changing rapidly for some segments of the American population in the last few decades. They note that while no state outlaws corporal punishment by parents completely, in the way Sweden and nineteen other countries now do, the laws in the United States have been changing:

> Other categories for adults with responsibility for children (such as foster parents and craftsmen supervising apprentices) previously also had the right to use corporal punishment. Today essentially the only type of person besides a parent who can legally hit children is a teacher or other school official. Moreover, despite opposition from most teachers' organizations, this is changing rapidly, and by 1990, 27 states had banned the use of corporal punishment in schools.[11]

This change has been uneven across U.S. regions, racial groups, and social classes. In 1968 "there was almost complete consensus concerning the cultural norm which permitted and expected parents to use corporal punishment. At that time 94 percent of the U.S. adult population approved of spanking a child."[12] By 1994 that number had decreased to 68 percent. But the decline in approval of corporal punishment was greater among whites, among the highly educated, and among people who did not live in the South. Thus in 1994 there was less normative consensus on the issue.[13]

Indeed, African Americans voice greater support of corporal punishment than whites. (Eighty-four percent of African Americans approve of corporal punishment compared to 66 percent of European Americans.) Some recent research about this issue shows some southern black Americans experiencing the same frustrations as the West Indians in this study because of the disparity between their method of discipline for their children and the parenting methods approved by child welfare agencies. Lynne Vernon-Feagans studied low-income African American children in rural North Carolina and compared them to a group of middle-class or white families in the same area. She noted that in African American families, "physical punishment was the norm and other relatives and respected adults were obliged to physically punish children for transgressions, even if they were not their own children." While the middle-class whites lectured or talked to their children, the low-income African Americans used physical punishment.[14]

Low-income African American parents in rural North Carolina had the same fear as the New York West Indians that the government could interfere with their chosen method of child-raising. Vernon-Feagans reports:

> One mother told us that after she had recently spanked her 5-year-old daughter for disobedience, the child threatened to tell the social worker she was being abused. The mother was somewhat surprised that such a young child could already play one adult's value against another's for her own benefit. The mother told us that this conflict between her strong-held views about the value of physical punishment and the more mainstream view had caused many of her friends and family difficulty with the social service system and the schools.[15]

Since the law does allow parents to hit their children, the real dispute between immigrant parents and state child protection agencies is about the line between allowable physical punishment and actual child abuse. Some scholars argue that any amount of corporal punishment by parents can have serious negative consequences for children. Straus, the foremost sociological expert on family violence in the United States, believes this to be the case. He and Donnelly conclude: "Corporal punishment of adolescents is particularly likely to be harmful because as existing evidence shows, it is associated with an increased probability of violence and other crime, depression, and alienation and lowered achievement. Although not tested in this article, we suspect that corporal punishment is also likely to interfere with the development of independence and to humiliate, antagonize and infantilize adolescents."[16] Yet other scholars argue that to deny ethnic minority parents their preferences in something as private as how to raise one's children is wrong. George Hong and Lawrence Hong conclude that adequate definitions of child abuse and neglect should include ethnic minority perspectives and that "[o]ne has to find a balance between honoring society's obligation to protect children and providing safeguards for minority groups from unwarranted interference in their preferences and practices."[17]

Despite a decline in the general opinion-poll support for corporal punishment in the United States since the late 1960s, actual practice has been far slower to change. In 1957, Sears, Maccoby, and Levin reported in *Patterns of Child Rearing* that 99 percent of the parents they studied hit their children. Today, the vast majority of American parents—approximately 90 percent—still admit to using corporal punishment on young children, with about half of all parents reporting that they slap or spank their children into early adolescence.[18]

Although such widespread use suggests that the practice is deeply embedded in American cultural norms of child-rearing, its prevalence and frequency/intensity of use is unevenly distributed along class lines. There is convincing evidence of an association between lower income and lower educational attainment and the use and approval of corporal punishment. One attitudinal study found that those least likely to support corporal punishment are highly educated (graduate degree–holding), non-southern women.[19]

Several studies indicate that parents with lower incomes and lower educational attainment are more likely to say they use corporal punishment, more likely to use it frequently, and more likely to continue to use corporal punishment on teenage children.[20] Tracy Dietz finds that severe poverty is associated with the use of frequent corporal punishment. She argues that stress associated with poverty, rather than income per se, is directly related to the use and support of corporal punishment.[21] Work by Glenn Wolfner and Richard Gelles provides evidence of a "structural social stress of family violence" wherein the youngest, poorest, most economically frustrated caretakers are the ones most likely to act violently toward children. Parents who experience financial stress, parenting stress (such as parenting a younger child), and those with fewer resources (such as less education) are more likely to use both corporal punishment and *severe* corporal punishment.[22]

Finally, there are some reasons to believe that racial and religious differences deeply influence the ways that parents discipline and punish their children.[23] Vonnie McLoyd's qualitative work on poor black families, for example, suggests that corporal punishment might be a reaction to living in certain types of neighborhoods or a deep-seated part of black cultural tradition.[24] Additionally, C. G. Ellison and D. E. Sherkat examined results from the General Social Survey and argued that the "spare-the-rod" ideology in America remains an especially salient narrative of parenting for southern males and fundamentalist Protestants.[25]

As for the effects of highly controlling disciplinary styles or harsh punishment styles, recent research has indicated harmful outcomes for children.

Analyzing National Longitudinal Survey of Youth (NLSY) 2000 data, Andrew Grogan-Kaylor found that parental use of corporal punishment was associated with a substantial increase in children's externalizing behavior problems, even when several parenting behaviors and neighborhood quality were taken into account.[26] This link between antisocial behavior and corporal punishment held across racial groups.[27] A large body of research has found strong associations between corporal punishment and the following negative child outcomes: increased aggression, antisocial behavior, criminal activity, depression, suicide, and lower academic performance.[28]

However, a few studies question the strength of the association between corporal punishment and negative child outcomes; some even suggest benefits of corporal punishment as an effective parenting tool.[29] Vernon-Feagans concludes that the research literature has a strong middle-class bias and that it is a myth that all physical punishment is the same as child abuse:

> Much has been written in the middle-class research literature about the "evils" of physical punishment of children and the myth has been created that physical punishment borders on child abuse. No doubt there are families in which physical punishment can lead to abuse, and coupled with poverty and the stress of family life, this form of punishment may indeed be dysfunctional, but the judicious use of physical punishment should not be dismissed as merely a "bad" parenting practice without understanding its roots and its effect on the children.[30]

The overwhelming majority of West Indians interviewed in New York believed that parents had a moral obligation to discipline their children, and that if parents did not beat them children would turn out badly. In fact, the absence of physical punishment was often cited by respondents as the cause of America's juvenile delinquency problem:

Q: Have there been any times you feel you have benefited from being a person from the Caribbean?
A: Yes. And this is more personal than anything else. I was explaining to this guy the other day, to me being from the Caribbean, you have a little bit more sense of respect. And that, you know, you are brought up learning to respect, to obey. You know over here they won't scold the kid with a lash or anything because the cops are going to be on you. Back in the Caribbean we had the wild cane. This is like a very slim thing. When you

misbehave that cane is on you. Over here you can't do that. Over here they can't discipline children and that is why I think they have a lot of problems, a lot of delinquents. It stems from the home. (Trinidadian male teacher, age forty-one, in the United States fourteen years)

Because West Indian immigrants believe that it is the good parents who physically punish their children and the bad ones who do not, the parents were very forthright about "beating" their children:

A: Because home, a twelve-year-old at home and a twelve-year-old here is two different things. A twelve-year-old at home is a twelve-year-old child. A twelve-year-old child here is a twelve-year-old man. You know—he out on the street by himself because if he was twelve at home and six o'clock come and it getting a little dark and he not home, prepare yourself you are gonna get licks when you cross that door because why you let outside getting dark and you not. . . . But here you just see twelve-year-olds on the train by themselves and going places by themselves and if the parents scold them, that is child abuse. I didn't know about child abuse until I come here.

Q: And how will you raise your son?

A: Well, my son is raised as a West Indian child because he is only five. But if he do something that he not supposed to do, I give it to him good. And I tell him, you never do that again and he would say, yes mommy. . . . But he is strange, because sometimes my mother be so strict with him and if he want to say something, he will say it anyway. I say, boy, you have this American thing in you that I'm gonna beat, you know? (Trinidadian female worker, age thirty, in the United States ten years)

One of the first things children learn when they arrive is that parental beatings are considered child abuse in the United States, and that they can report their parents to child welfare:

If my mother hit me, all I gotta do is go to the child welfare agency and say, look at what my mother did to me, and they come and they arrest her. My mother says you can't even touch a kid nowadays without getting into trouble for it. (Jamaican male, age eighteen, in the United States fifteen years)

Many teens do report their parents. Two West Indian teachers and three food-service workers in the New York study had encounters with the police over beating their children. The parents were outraged that the state can come between a parent and a child. Indeed, many parents spoke defiantly of how they would beat their children regardless of the consequences:

> When I came here my father was telling me, oh you cannot hit a child as long as it's here. 'Cause they will call the cops on you. But I'll be telling my father, there's no way I'm gonna bring a child in this world, and if I want to hit him, and he's done something wrong, and they decide to call the cops, then he gonna have to live with the cops, not with me anymore. 'Cause when I was coming up, my mother would hit me, with a belt. She did this thing called a tambering rod. She picks it off a tree like a branch, she splice it together, and she would beat us with that. And that's to discipline us. So when I bring a child into this world, I prefer to discipline my child, and then let him call the police, 'cause the cops going to take him or her if they call them. (Barbadian female, age nineteen, in the United States four years)

One teacher told the following story about a father who defied anyone preventing him from disciplining his children the way that he wanted to:

> Haitian kid decided to get one of the new kinds of haircuts—one of those flattops. And he got home and his father beat him. Matter of fact, when he came to school he pulled up his shirt, and I saw the fist mark right there. And we called Social Services and they sent a representative to the house. And the father was about, maybe six-foot-ten, ten zillion pounds. And he let the worker know that yes, I did it. He cuts his hair like that again, I'll do it again. The father said he comes in here looking like these Yankee kids. And if he comes in here doing it again, he would do it again. At that point the worker left and that was it. End of story. (Barbadian male teacher, age forty-three, born in the United States)

We heard of one case where a teenager was misbehaving very badly. The parents tried to discipline him and threatened him with a beating, but in turn he threatened to call Social Services to report his parents. The parents bought the child a one-way ticket back to Jamaica and forced him to go home. When he got off the airplane, many members of his extended family met him in the airport and beat him very badly right then and there.

Some West Indian parents, however, are trying to learn new ways to discipline their children. Some learn new techniques from their children, who explain how their American or Americanized friends are disciplined.

Some parents are forced to consider change because of encounters with the Department of Social Services or because of referrals to family therapists due to a child's problems in school. But changing parenting behavior when parents think they are doing the right thing—particularly when it is such an ingrained part of their upbringing and often acted out in private settings—is difficult. A guidance counselor at a New York City public school described how he tries to convince the parents to use other techniques to deal with their children:

> We have to deal with a child coming into school and he has a bruise or you can see he has been verbally abused. You have to report that. In this society here, we don't allow that. That is the law. I try to talk to the parent about how we try to talk to the child as opposed to beating the child. And that stuff they learned from their parents, to their parents, on down the generations. That is part of their culture now. However, in parent training programs when they come to talk to me, I try to make it another way to deal with, a way to talk with a child. But a lot of that will probably continue, and it means that when we report it to the system of child abuse, the social worker might go to the house and investigate. And I have to call the parent after that and let them know, this is what you have to do in America. And I will let them know that when you move from Haiti, or wherever, any part of the West Indies, that's something you have to be faced with here. And personally, I understand what they are saying. They say, "It's the only way I can keep my daughter in line." I say, "But in America you don't do it. And you have to see your daughter get out of line." I don't know what's worse really. (African American guidance counselor, age fifty)

Parents who have sought help from community mental health centers for dealing with their troubled teenagers are referred to group sessions for West Indian parents to discuss their difficulties and to share coping mechanisms. One worker's sixteen-year-old daughter had run away and was living in a group home run by Child Protective Services; the parent said with true astonishment that she had learned in the group sessions that she should give her teenage daughter "privacy." She said the word with the utmost disdain—as if people who would recommend privacy for a sixteen-year-old were completely out of their minds. She planned to continue searching her daughter's possessions for anything illicit.

But the main thing West Indian parents are introduced to in these sessions is the idea that they should talk to their children, that they should share emotions and feelings with their children and be open to the children's emotions and feelings, and that instead of physical punishment they should use techniques like denying them privileges. It is difficult for these parents to change. One teacher who was told never to hit a child when she was angry exclaimed, "But when you are calm, who wants to hit?" It still seemed to her that physical punishment was the only way to control an unruly child.

A few parents did say they were trying the new technique of talking rather than hitting:

> Where I'm from you don't talk to parents that way, you don't say what's on your mind. You don't get a chance to express yourself. And here, it's more free speech. I'm even practicing. Although I couldn't tell my parents anything, I try to open up to my children so that they can talk to me about anything. (Jamaican female teacher, age thirty-seven, in the United States seven years)

A second-generation teacher described the frustrations he felt about raising his children so differently than the way he was raised:

> Q: What is the best way to raise kids, the American way or the West Indian way?
>
> A: I try to talk to mine, which is frustrating, you know. So, you know, I have teenage daughters and I have the two little ones, the two foster ones, sometimes it's difficult 'cause I like talking, 'cause I like to hear what the kids have to say. But I have created lazy children. You know, I want your chores on Saturday, well, you know, there's not going to be any real punitive kind of, we're not gonna do them. And that's a frustration. You know, my day, we had an old belt. Well, actually, she used to give it to me with the cuckoo stick. That's the stick that is used to turn the cornmeal. And you have to take it. You'd go sulk and you would learn. But because you try to do things in this modern way, I don't know if it works. I don't have bad kids, but they're lazy as hell. And, you know, that's the bottom line. So I tend to think the old-fashioned way is better, but you just can't do it here. (Barbadian male teacher, age forty-three, born in the United States)

Not one of the teenagers interviewed in New York in the early 1990s was completely opposed to the use of physical punishment. Many defended their parents' practices and argued forcefully that they would raise their children the same way:[31]

Q: Do you think Jamaicans have a different way of raising their children than Americans do?

A: I think a Jamaican parent is more stern with their kid than an American parent. Then again, in Jamaica a parent could like spank her kid, give her kid a good spanking and so he will listen. But in America, if you do that, this system is against it. They say, well you know, you can't beat up your kid or you'll go to jail.

Q: Which way do you think is best?

A: Well, a beating is good. A good beating is good sometime, you know. I don't think you should murder the kid, you know. Just, if he deserves a good beating, give it to him. In the right places. You know, on his butt, on his foot. But I think the Jamaican is good because there's a lot of kids turn out to be good kids when they finally grow.

Q: If you had kids, which way would you raise them?

A: Oh, the Jamaican way, definitely. Actually I don't really like the American way of raising kids 'cause as you can see, I mean most of the violence and crime that's going on right now it's done by the young kids, youth, all ranging from age fourteen to twenty-one. (Jamaican male, age twenty-two, in the United States six years)

The teens did not think that Social Services was protecting them or looking out for them. Rather, they echoed the parents' concerns that Social Services came between parents and children and was responsible for high rates of delinquency among youngsters in the United States:

In Jamaica the families try hard to raise their kids properly, you know. When you do something wrong, they beat you or something. But up here, do something wrong and they beat you, some neighbor going to call Social Service that you're beating your kids and you're doing all this and so you have more guidelines to follow. But in Jamaica, you raise your kids better 'cause there's no Social Service come knocking on your door saying why you doing this to your kid, you know. . . . [With Jamaican parents] if you don't follow guidelines then you're in trouble, a lot of trouble, you know. (Jamaican male, age eighteen, in the United States eight years)

But the majority of the students interviewed said when they grew up and had children, they would try to combine West Indian strictness with American freedoms and openness. The students identified "talking" and "withdrawing privileges" as American ways of punishment, and even if their parents were not using these methods, the teens anticipated using them with their own children:

A: Over there, if a child misbehaves, they give them a spanking or a whipping. Over here, they talk to them and they punish them.

Q: Which way do you think is best?

A: I believe a little bit of both because a child needs discipline, but they also need space. You know, a little bit of both.

Q: If you had kids, which way would you raise them?

A: Little bit of both. I would be strict up to a certain point, but I'll be flexible. They could talk to me, you know, I would say OK, but I'm not gonna be like, oh well, this is what I think, and what I think is gonna go. You know, I am going to be flexible. (Jamaican female, age seventeen, in the United States three years)

The Second Generation in Young Adulthood

The New York Second Generation study interviewed West Indian young adults age eighteen to thirty-two about how they were raised, how they were raising their own children, and, for those who did not yet have children, how they planned to raise their children. Strict parenting appeared throughout the interviews as a central tenet of West Indian parenting. When asked whether West Indian parenting differs from American parenting, respondents overwhelmingly described the fundamental difference as one of disciplinary rigor, with West Indian parents being far more restrictive than their peers' American parents. Specifically, respondents said their parents were more restrictive when it came to dating (in one case, until a female was twenty-two), not being allowed to leave the house overnight (such as for an overnight school trip), not being given as much freedom on their own block, and so forth.

Overall, the parenting style described by respondents fits Diane Baumrind's typology of authoritarian parenting: high control (high demanding and high directive) and low warmth/responsiveness.[32]

Q: Would you say you were raised in the West Indian way or the American way?

A: It was structured. I think my mother was the hardest on me. This is to be done when I say it's to be done, no questions asked, don't touch anything, walk in a straight line, don't get off—you know, it was just "Do as I say, and do not ask anything about it." (West Indian female, twenty-three years old)

A twenty-eight-year-old man described a typical West Indian upbringing and the image he had of how white Americans are raised—indulgent, permissive parents who make few demands:

Q: Do you think West Indian families here in the U.S. have a different way of raising children than other Americans do?

A: I'll set out what I think is the West Indian way. It's all about responsibility for the kids. Kids have work to do as soon as they can walk. As long as you can push a broom one of your jobs can be sweeping up the floor or the yards. If you're old enough to run the vacuum cleaner, if you're tall enough to reach the shelves, you can dust the shelves. Once you can negotiate the sink and all that, you can wash the dishes, you can clean the tub, you can always make your own bed. So that's one thing. You start working very early. I don't know anybody, any West Indian who did not have chores as a child. So I think that's a very . . . teaching responsibility through work is very important. Respect for elders is very important. You can be right and they can be wrong but their elder status trumps everything. And you have to show them respect in certain ways regardless. They are very respectful of the title somebody has. Father, mother, grandmother, forget it. So all that is very important. That kind of age hierarchy is very important. Discipline. You do wrong, you get punished and they are not afraid. They do not spare the rod. They do not spare the rod. You will be punished in a way that you will remember the next time you think about doing that thing that you did.

Q: When you were growing up did you ever disagree with your parents about the way they raised you?

A: As I was growing up, yeah. As a kid you want to be raised the way the white kids are being raised. (Laughter) You want to be able to just play Atari all day and have your parents buy you a bike because you got a good grade on a test and all that kind of stuff and not have to deal with all the responsibility and the discipline. So as a kid I definitely wished that I was being raised more like some of my white friends were.

Respondents often described corporal punishment and frequent "beatings" that kept them in line as children. They contrasted this with what they see as softer American methods of punishment, such as time-outs, standing in the corner, and being grounded from television:

> Jamaican parents, they are usually into the discipline, and the parents over here they really are into punish them, put them in a corner kind of thing. Do a different kind of punishing. My family is different. You just know you're going to get beaten for it. And the parents over here, "Oh I can't watch TV for a week." Or something. No. (West Indian female, twenty years old)

An eighteen-year-old West Indian man put it this way: "We get beat. In West Indian countries there is no time-outs and stuff like that." A few second-generation respondents quoted the aphorism that it is important to "bend the tree while it is young." Interestingly, many respondents described resenting this harsher parenting style as children, but appreciating it (understanding the motivation for it) as adults.

> Q: When you were growing up, did you ever disagree with your parents about the way they raised you?
> A: At the time maybe. Maybe I fought for more freedom or maybe I felt it was a little unfair of me to be in a certain situation, but when I grew up and I see how things turned out, then I thanked them. (West Indian man, twenty years old)

A twenty-eight-year-old lawyer attributed his success to his parents' strict control and discipline when he was a child:

> Q: Do you think West Indian families here in the U.S. have a different way of raising children than other Americans do?
> A: Yeah. Most of my friends are from an American descent and they had a lot more freedom at a young age but they didn't become as responsible.
> Q: What do you mean?
> A: Let's put it this way, I was doing my sacrifice thing when they were having fun. They were always able to walk the streets and go out to parties and stuff like that much more than I could. I had to beg to go to a party. It was a big deal for me to go to a party. Yet they could go all the time. So they had their fun at a young age but they didn't do as well in school. They didn't go to college. And the ones that did, didn't finish. So I guess all the time I was sacrificing I was gaining more responsibility. There

were things that I had to do that it wasn't put upon them to do as much as it was in my family.

It was not just strictness, but specifically corporal punishment that most respondents saw as distinctively West Indian and, for the most part, beneficial for child outcomes—although they admitted that sometimes strictness could be taken too far:

> You can't do anything without your mother and father knowing. I know a woman, till the time she was twenty-five, she still had to ask her mother if she could go out on a date. And her mother even beat her when she was in her twenties. (Guyanese male, thirty-one years old)

Respondents described the authoritarian parenting style West Indian parents use as being directed at developing two things in children: (1) educational achievement (homework, school attendance, and college); and (2) respect (often mentioned was not talking back to parents or other authority figures, such as teachers). Respondents noted that their childhood experience was filled with more responsibility than that of their American peers:

> Q: Do you think West Indians have different ways of raising their children than white Americans do?
>
> A: Definitely. It's totally different. I mean, nowadays, it's startin' to get more on the same wavelength, but when I was growing up, in Jamaica or even up here, there was a strict rule that you couldn't do certain things, but now the culture's sort of blending and mixing and getting more watered down 'cause now you can't spank your children, you can't do certain things, but when I was growing up, it wasn't like that, and I was raised in a way that I don't believe any white person, child or grown-up, has ever been raised in. The same things that I had to go through and do that they never had to do. I have friends that are white and I see that they've been doing that from when they were little. They talk back to their parents. I could never talk back to my mother—no matter how old I get, or how grown I think I am, I could never talk back to my mother. . . . Americans, at a certain age, they tell their mother, well, I'm eighteen, nineteen, now I can do what I want. West Indians, it doesn't matter how old you are, your mother will still say, "You're my son, and I'm telling you what to do."
>
> Q: Is that the same way you plan to raise your children, with that West Indian discipline?

A : Well, it's gonna be a mixture, because I feel that it's certain things I didn't gain because of how I was brought up, the discipline, and I believe that, you know, it affected me in some ways so in those ways. I'll kind of ease back on my children, but it will be discipline, so it'll be a mixture. (Jamaican male, twenty-one years old)

When they face decisions about their own children, or think about their potential children, many second-generation respondents say they will replicate the harsher parenting style because they think it explains why they turned out well:

Q : How do you plan to raise your children?
A : The same way.
Q : When you were growing up, did you ever disagree with your parents about the way they raised you?
A : Of course I did because sometimes you think what you did . . . nobody likes beating, so you try to justify, saying, "You don't love me." Or something like that. But later on you'll realize that what they did was pretty much for your own good. Because when you know that you have that consequence coming for you, you tend to not want to do it again. If you're going to miss TV, no big deal. You remember the consequence and decide not to do it. (Jamaican female, twenty-one years old)

Even a man who said that his father beat him excessively when he was a child saw no problem with being quick to hit his own children when they get out of line:

My dad was very abusive so he didn't have to do any of the things that he did. Throwing a kid across the room. Kicking him with the army boot, 'cause he was in the Army. Thick boots. All those things wasn't necessary. A smack on the head or a belt with it is good enough. Not beat you with anything that you catch. Stuff like that. I wasn't really caring too much for that.

White families, though, they give their children a whole lot more leniency. The kid really have to drive them to the point of where they'll smack them. And even me, I'm not like that. The instant you do something, you mess up, I'm smacking you. I'm putting you back in line right away. Let you know that's not something acceptable. And I don't like to speak twice. I tell you once. I will tell you once without smacking you but if I see you do it a second time, I don't even give you a third time thing. I don't do that. So I think we are more strict with our children, keeping them in line, than I would say Americans and white folks and Jews and all these other types of people. (Jamaican male, twenty-nine years old, in the United States for eighteen years)

Only those respondents who felt that corporal punishment was a positive child-rearing method complained of the state's intervention through Child Welfare to stop it. Like first-generation immigrants, they believed that the state was intervening incorrectly by trying to prevent a proven parenting technique. One twenty-four-year-old Grenadian man described how Child Protection Services makes things worse:

You can't scold your kids any how any way up here. Cops will come and DCW [Department of Child Welfare] will be down on your back. You whip your child ass and nobody will ask you a question back home. The child would know not to do that again or know the right thing. I seen kids up here cursing their moms. "F you mom." You can't do that. You can't do that. If the law protects you sometimes too much protection makes it worse. It makes it worse.

Or, as a twenty-eight-year-old man of Trinidadian ancestry put it, "In Trinidad . . . the children are just more disciplined because you can hit them and you don't have to worry about the cops taking away the kids from you. Like up here they would take your child away from you if you hit them."

At the same time, some respondents consciously decided to raise their children very differently than the way they were raised: to incorporate more American methods of discipline and to communicate more with their children. In describing how she planned to raise her children, a twenty-five-year-old Jamaican woman explained:

I know how it was to grow up with my father and I'm going to try my damnedest to be the opposite of what he was to me. 'Cause he felt that you can't be a parent and have a relationship with your child. So that was where he went wrong and he still believes that to this day, and that's not what I want. 'Cause if you can't talk to your parents, then who can you talk with?

The comments of a thirty-two-year-old Guyanese man indicate similar intentions:

A: Now I can see why my father got violent. I mean, if you're a parent and you love your children, male or female, and you see what's going on, how this is going to screw your children up, if physical violence is the only thing you have standing between your children being crazy and healthy, I would use it too. I think any parent in their right mind would.

Q: Were you beaten as a child?

A: Constantly.

Q: How do you plan on raising your children?

A: Not the way I was raised. I plan to speak to my children to tell them that I love them. And that they can be anything that they want to be and I will support them.

Q: When you were growing up, did you disagree with your mother about the way she raised you?

A: Every single day that I thought that something was being done wrong. Of course I either got a very rude awakening with a belt or a slap or some very belittling statement, like, "You're just like your father."

Conclusion

Unlike the literature on parenting practices in the United States, which emphasizes class differences in parenting styles,[33] we did not find class differences in parenting practices in the West Indian first or second generation. Competing explanations for the class differences are found in the literature. Some point to the stressors that economically and socially disadvantaged parents experience in contrast to middle-class parents, some to structural differences in the jobs and social-class positions of parents that lead them to prepare children for different types of lives. What our analysis points to is another factor in understanding parenting practices that has received little attention: the role of culture.

The research on New York West Indians indicates that in the first and second generation, whatever their social class, the use of corporal punishment was ubiquitous, and the modal parenting style was authoritarian—with a strong notion that children should be obedient and never question authority, and that respect and deference to elders was the way in which children should behave.

This suggests that West Indian parenting practices are cultural in nature and not directly tied to occupational characteristics of jobs requiring little education, or to the economic and social stresses accompanying poverty. The American-based research on parenting practices would do well to consider the variation among immigrant groups on these measures. The West Indian case, we believe, suggests that cultural models of the transmission of parenting practices should be given more serious attention.

Of course, this does not mean that parenting practices are static. As Julia Wrigley and others have argued, American middle-class norms and practices have changed dramatically over time.[34] We also see some change among the second-generation West Indian respondents. Although most second-generation young adults did not reject their parents' methods of child-rearing or say they were adopting a middle-class American model, they were eager to combine the best of the American and West Indian methods. Many said that while they would use corporal punishment with their own children, those who had experienced severe beatings said they would "tone it down" with their kids. Many respondents said they would try to communicate more with their children than their parents had with them, telling their children that they loved them and that they wanted an emotional closeness that they had not experienced with their own parents.

In this way one can see the creative potential of being a member of the second generation. Rather than being torn between two worlds, the second generation has the advantage of being able to selectively combine those aspects of their parents' culture and American culture that they see most positively.[35] This selective combination means that cultural innovation will occur over time in the West Indian community, but also that norms and behaviors around child-rearing will still be distinctive in this community for some time to come. The interviews suggest that corporal punishment will be part of the upbringing of a large number, most likely the majority of the West Indian third generation. But over time there will also be an adoption of some middle-class American ideas of what constitutes good parenting. Researchers interested in assessing the degree of assimilation of immigrant groups over time and over generations would do well to measure attitudes and behaviors around child-rearing as these can be a very good indicator of how rapidly or not cultural change might occur.

NOTES

1. The material in the section on parents' views in this chapter draws heavily on Waters 1999: chap. 6.

2. The respondents in Waters 1999 included 59 adult West Indian immigrants. There were 25 middle-class teachers and 40 working-class food service workers from the English-speaking islands of the West Indies. In addition this study included 83 first- and second-generation youth age 14–27; the vast majority were age 16–18. Among the young people, 13 (16 percent) were from very poor families on public assistance, 40 (48 percent) from families with at least one parent working at a low-wage job, and 30 (36 percent) from middle-class families with at least one parent in a job requiring a college degree. The individuals interviewed for the New York Second Generation Study were age 18–32 in 1999–2000. They were born in the United States or had arrived by age 7, with one or both parents from the English-speaking islands of the Caribbean (including Guyana). Among the in-depth respondents in the New York Study, 55 percent were female, 45 percent male. Their parents came from Jamaica, Trinidad, Guyana, Barbados, and five other small island nations. Thirteen percent of the respondents had dropped out of high school, 8 percent had a high school degree, 50 percent had some college but no degree, and 29 percent had a B.A. or more. This was a marked improvement over their parents' educational backgrounds. Among those who reported their mother's education, 60 percent had mothers with a high school degree or less, while 40 percent had mothers with some college or above. For more information on these respondents see Kasinitz et al. 2008.

3. Brice-Baker 1994; Gopaul-McNichol 1993.

4. Seaga 1955.

5. John Figueroa quoted in Lowenthal 1972.

6. Smith and Mosby 2003: 370.

7. Berrol 1995: 81.

8. Berrol 1995: 94.

9. Straus and Donnelly 1993: 421.

10. For those who experienced it, it was not a rare event; the mean was eight times and the median was five times (Straus and Donnelly 1993).

11. Straus and Donnelly 1993: 439.

12. Straus and Mathur 1995.

13. Also see Hong and Hong 1991 on differences among Chinese, Hispanics, and whites.

14. Vernon-Feagons 1996: 56.

15. Vernon-Feagons 1996: 56–57.

16. Straus and Donnelly 1993: 439.

17. Hong and Hong 1991.

18. Straus and Stewart 1999.
19. Flynn 1994.
20. Flynn 1994; Wolfner and Gelles 1993.
21. Dietz 2000.
22. Wolfner and Gelles 1993.
23. Flynn 1994; Giles-Sims et al. 1995; Wiehle 1990.
24. McLoyd 1990.
25. Ellison and Sherkat 1993.
26. Grogan-Kaylor 2005a.
27. Grogan-Kaylor 2005b.
28. Donnelly and Straus 2005; Fontes 2002; Giles-Sims et al. 1995.
29. Gershoff 2002; Larzelere 2000.
30. Vernon-Feagans 1996: 212.
31. Straus and Donnelly (1993) also argue that many children who have experienced corporal punishment defend the practice: "Almost all children defend the use of corporal punishment. However, neither the normality of corporal punishment nor its advocacy by its victims is evidence that it does no harm" (p. 439).
32. Baumrind 1991.
33. Darling and Steinberg 1993; McLoyd 1990.
34. Wrigley (1989) describes how American parents' notions of good parenting have changed over the last century due to changes in "expert advice." Other work (Giovanonni and Becerra 1979; Gordon 1989; Zuravin 1991) highlights how even child protection agencies' definitions of maltreatment have evolved.
35. Kasinitz et al. 2008.

REFERENCES

Baumrind, Diane. 1991. "Parenting Styles and Adolescent Development." Pp. 746–58 in J. Brooks-Gunn, R. Lerner, and A. C. Peterson (eds.), *The Encyclopedia of Adolescence*. New York: Garland.

Berrol, Selma. 1995. *Growing Up American: Immigrant Children in America Then and Now*. New York: Twayne Publishers.

Brice-Baker, J. R. 1994. "Domestic Violence in African-American and African-Caribbean Families." *Journal of Social Distress and the Homeless* 3 (1): 23–38.

Darling, N., and L. Steinberg. 1993. "Parenting Styles Context: An Integrative Model." *Psychological Bulletin* 113(3): 487–96.

Dietz, Tracy. 2000. "Disciplining Children: Characteristics Associated with the Use of Corporal Punishment." *Child Abuse and Neglect* 24(12): 1529–42.

Donnelly, Michael, and Murray A. Straus (eds.). 2005. *Corporal Punishment of Children in Theoretical Perspective*. New Haven, CT: Yale University Press.

Ellison, C. G., and D. E. Sherkat. 1993. "Conservative Protestantism and Support for Corporal Punishment." *American Sociological Review* 58: 131–44.

Flynn, Clifton P. 1994. "Regional Differences in Attitudes toward Corporal Punishment." *Journal of Marriage and the Family* 56(2): 314–24.

Fontes, L. A. 2002. "Child Discipline and Physical Abuse of Children in Immigrant Latino Families: Reducing Violence and Misunderstandings." *Journal of Counseling and Development* 80: 31–40.

Gershoff, E. T. 2002. "Corporal Punishment by Parents and Associated Child Behaviors and Experiences: A Meta-analytic and Theoretical Review." *Psychological Bulletin* 128: 539–79.

Giles-Sims, J., M. A. Straus, and D. B. Sugarman. 1995. "Child, Maternal and Family Characteristics Associated with Spanking." *Family Relations* 44: 170–76.

Giovannoni, J., and R. Becerra. 1979. *Defining Child Abuse*. New York: Free Press, 1979.

Gopaul-McNichol, Sharon-Ann. 1993. *Working with West Indian Families*. New York: Guilford Press.

Gordon, L. 1989. *Heroes of Their Own Lives: The Politics and History of Family Violence*. London: Virago Press.

Grogan-Kaylor, Andrew. 2005a. "Relationship of Corporal Punishment and Antisocial Behavior by Neighborhood." *Archives of Pediatric Adolescent Medicine* 159(10): 938–42.

———. 2005b. "Corporal Punishment and the Growth Trajectory of Children's Antisocial Behavior." *Child Maltreatment* 10 (3): 283–92.

Hong, George K., and Lawrence K. Hong. 1991. "Comparative Perspectives on Child Abuse and Neglect: Chinese versus Hispanics and Whites." *Child Welfare* 70(4): 463–75.

Kasinitz, Philip, John H. Mollenkopf, Mary C. Waters, and Jennifer Holdaway. 2008. *Inheriting the City: The Children of Immigrants Come of Age*. Cambridge: Harvard University Press.

Larzelere, R. E. 2000. "Child Outcomes of Non-abusive and Customary Physical Punishment by Parents: An Updated Literature Review." *Clinical Child and Family Psychology Review* 3(4): 199–221.

Lowenthal, David. 1972. *West Indian Societies*. Oxford: Oxford University Press.

Maccoby, E. E., and J. A. Martin. 1983. "Socialization in the Context of the Family: Parent-child Interaction." Pp. 1–101 in E. M. Hetherington (ed.), *Handbook of Child Psychology*. New York: Wiley.

McLoyd, Vonnie C. 1990. "The Impact of Economic Hardship on Black Families and Children: Psychological Distress, Parenting, and Socioemotional Development." *Child Development* 61: 311–46.

Seaga, Edward. 1955. "Parent-Teacher Relationships in a Jamaican Village." *Social and Economic Studies* 4(3): 289–302.

Sears, R., E. E. Maccoby, and H. Levin. 1957. *Patterns of Child Rearing.* Stanford: Stanford University Press.

Smith, Delores E., and Gail Mosby. 2003. "Jamaican Child-Rearing Practices: The Role of Corporal Punishment." *Adolescence* 38(150): 370–81.

Straus, M. A., and J. H. Stewart. 1999. "Corporal Punishment by American Parents: National Data on Prevalence, Chronicity, Severity, and Duration, in Relation to Child and Family Characteristics." *Child and Family Psychology Review* 2: 55–70.

Straus, Murray, and Denise Donnelly. 1993. "Corporal Punishment of Adolescents by American Parents." *Youth and Society* 24(4): 419–42.

Straus, Murray, and Anita K. Mathur. 1996. " Social Change and Change in Approval of Corporal Punishment by Parents from 1968 to 1994." Pp. 91–105 in D. Frehsee, W. Horn, and K. D. Bussmann (eds.), *Family Violence against Children: A Challenge for Society.* New York: Walter de Gruyter.

Vernon-Feagons, Lynne. 1996. *Children's Talk in Communities and Classrooms.* Cambridge, MA: Blackwell.

Waters, Mary C. 1999. *Black Identities: West Indian Dreams and American Realities.* Cambridge: Harvard University Press.

Wiehe, Vernon R. 1990. "Religious Influence on Parental Attitudes toward the Use of Corporal Punishment." *Journal of Family Violence* 5(2): 173–86.

Wolfner, Glenn, and Richard J. Gelles. 1993. "A Profile of Violence toward Children: A National Study." *Child Abuse and Neglect* 17: 197–212.

Wrigley, Julia. 1989. "Do Young Children Need Intellectual Stimulation? Experts' Advice to Parents, 1900–1985." *History of Education Quarterly* 29(1): 41–75.

Zuravin, S. 1991. "Research Definitions of Child Physical Abuse and Neglect: Current Problems." Pp. 100–128 in R. J. Starr and D. A. Wolfe (eds.), *The Effects of Child Abuse and Neglect: Issues and Research.* New York: Guilford.

"Marry into a Good Family"

Transnational Reproduction and Intergenerational Relations in Bangladeshi American Families

Nazli Kibria

The work of families includes that of intergenerational cultural reproduction—the passing on of traditions and affiliations from one generation to another. Among immigrant families, such work may be especially significant, constituting a critical element of their strategies of survival and adaptation to the receiving society. In this chapter I draw on a qualitative study of Bangladeshi immigrant families in the United States to explore some of the dynamics of cultural reproduction that mark the relations of Bangladeshi immigrant parents and their U.S.-born and/or raised young adult children. I focus in particular on strategies of *transnational reproduction*, that is, those aspects of family socialization that are concerned with ensuring the continued meaning and significance of transnational social ties for the next generation. As we will see, for Bangladeshi immigrant families in the United States, these strategies can be a source of intergenerational tension, making visible the divergent understandings across the generations of the meaning and significance of transnational ties between the United States and Bangladesh.

Transnational Reproduction

The community ties of immigrant groups, based on a sense of shared origins and culture, are widely seen as an important resource for their members. These ties are increasingly viewed by scholars in transnational terms, in explicit contrast to a conception of the immigrant community as territorially bounded by the destination nation. From the perspective of transnationalism, the community of support for immigrants is one that crosses national borders to stretch from the receiving to the sending society. Indeed, an extensive body of literature shows transnational ties to be an important source of social capital or trust networks which immigrants can draw on for social support. For example, in her study of West Indian immigrants in London and New York, Vilna Bashi[1] describes how transnational social networks can successfully organize the migration process, providing access to employment and housing as well as legalized immigration status.

In addition to such critical material resources as jobs and visas, transnational ties may offer other types of benefits, such as emotional support. Active engagement in transnational networks and institutions can sustain the meaning and significance of the society of origin—the "homeland"— as a point of social reference for immigrants. As scholars of immigration have often noted, a dual frame of social reference is what helps many immigrants to cope with the challenges that they face as racialized, low-wage workers in the receiving society.[2] That is, they are able to resist the dehumanizing effects of race and class stigma in the receiving society by turning to another social context—the "homeland"—to understand themselves. Under these conditions, considerable energy and resources may be directed toward maintaining transnational ties, especially in ways that strengthen one's sense of self-worth. Hung Cam Thai's study of remittances by Vietnamese immigrant men vividly illustrates this point.[3] Toiling in low-wage jobs in the United States, these men remit money to kin in Vietnam, often at considerable material hardship to themselves. The remittances, however, are what enable them to cope with the degradations of their life in the United States, offering a means for claiming and valorizing social worth in the community of origin.

Given its general significance, the transnational sphere is likely to be an important focus of cultural reproduction in immigrant families. That is, integration into the transnational sphere of members is a vital aspect of immigrant family life. However, transnational reproduction is also a highly variable process, shaped in its character and significance by the diverse conditions of immigrant life, including that of the transnational sphere that is part of it. As Peggy Levitt has noted, transnational ties differ greatly in their organization and significance across immigrant groups.[4] While in some cases these ties are sparse and informal, in others they are dense, multifaceted, and institutionalized, encompassing not just economic but also religious, political, and other dimensions of life. If intergenerational transnational reproduction is challenged by conditions of sparse transnationalism, it may be supported by dense transnationalism, which can facilitate the efforts of immigrant parents to socialize the second generation into the cultures of the transnational sphere.

A portrait of intergenerational transnational reproduction under conditions of dense transnationalism is offered by Robert Smith in an ethnographic study of Mexican migrants and their children in New York.[5] The cultural socialization strategies of the immigrant parents included the widespread practice of sending adolescent children to the home community of Ticuani for extended visits. During these trips, the second-generation Mexican Americans participated in the community life there, attending festivals and dances, in many cases experiencing a richer and less restricted social life than in New York. Smith argues that for these second-generation persons, Ticuani remains an important point of reference they use to affirm self-esteem and forge an identity that is distinct from that of the stigmatized ethnic minorities with whom they are often equated in New York, such as African Americans and Puerto Ricans.

Bangladeshis in the United States and the Emerging Transnational Social Field

According to the 2000 U.S. census, there are more than 200,000 persons of Bangladesh origin in the United States. Informal estimates are much higher; one study puts the number at about 350,000.[6] Much of this immigration has occurred since the 1980s through family reunification channels as well as the Diversity Program.[7] According to census figures in the United States, in 1980 there were 5,880 foreign-born Bangladeshis; in 2000 there were 92,235.[8] Because of the relatively brief history of settlement in the United States, the Bangladeshi community is largely an immigrant one, and U.S.-born and/or raised persons tend to be of relatively young age.

As far as socioeconomic status, almost half of all foreign-born Bangladeshis report that they are college-educated,[9] suggesting that many are from middle-class backgrounds in Bangladesh. In the United States, however, only about 24 percent of foreign-born Bangladeshis are in managerial and professional jobs; 30 percent are in service and manufacturing jobs, and 8 percent are self-employed.[10] Reflecting these conditions, the accounts that I gathered from immigrant Bangladeshis were often marked by a sharp sense of downward class mobility after migrating from Bangladesh.[11]

Since the 1990s a number of notable Bangladeshi geographic concentrations have developed, in such states as New Jersey, California, and Texas. The New York area, in particular the borough of Queens, is especially prominent, with an estimated 40 percent of foreign-born Bangladeshis having settled there. It is not surprising, then, that New York is widely viewed by Bangladeshis as the center of a nascent transnational public sphere between the United States and Bangladesh. For example, many media companies in Bangladesh, including television channels and newspapers, have begun to open offices in New York, as have various political parties and religious groups. A growing transnational business sector provides services in both locations, including real estate, travel, food, and clothing. Throughout the United States, there has also been a mushrooming of local "hometown" associations, as well as larger community organizations that maintain branches in Bangladesh and are often focused on specific charitable projects.

Among the notable characteristics of this emerging Bangladeshi American transnational social field is the prominence of immigrants and the relative invisibility of second-generation Bangladeshi Americans within it. Besides the recent history of Bangladeshi settlement in the United States, this pattern may also be related to a larger trend of second-generation disengagement from the transnational sphere. In the course of my research, I found a widespread stance of ambivalence toward Bangladeshi affiliation among second-generation Bangladeshi Americans.[12] Many informants identified themselves either as "Muslim" or "South Asian," seeing these as more powerful and meaningful bases of identification than "Bangladeshi." In fact, Bangladeshi identity could even be a point of disidentification—an affiliation from which young people tried to dissociate themselves due to its negative connotation, stemming in part from the images of poverty and corruption that surround the country. Thus, transnational reproduction in Bangladeshi immigrant families unfolds within a larger context in which second-generation Bangladeshis may be quite uncertain about the meaning and significance of the transnational sphere for themselves and their futures.

In what follows I explore some of the strategies of transnational reproduction evident in Bangladeshi immigrant families and the divergent perceptions and experiences for parents and young adult children that were part of them. I draw on research from a larger project on the contemporary diaspora from Bangladesh that is concerned with developments of national and religious identity among the settled communities of Britain and the United States, as well as the labor migration streams to the Persian Gulf states and to Malaysia.[13] I focus in this chapter on my findings for the United States From 2001 to 2007, I conducted 72 in-depth interviews with Bangladeshi Muslims[14] in the Boston, Detroit, and New York metropolitan areas; 40 involved first-generation immigrants, and 32 were carried out with second-generation persons whom I defined to include persons either born or raised in the United States from the age of twelve or earlier. Almost all of the interviews were tape-recorded and transcribed; they were conducted in Bangla and/or English, depending on the wishes of the informant. To supplement the interviews, I also conducted participant observation at community and family gatherings.

"Marry into a Good Family": Children's Marriage Decisions

I interviewed Mahbub[15] and Shaheen over tea and snacks at their comfortable Long Island, New York home. The couple had been living in the New York area for about fifteen years and were raising three children, ages eight, thirteen, and nineteen. Both Mahbub and Shaheen were college-educated and from urban, middle-class backgrounds in Bangladesh. After some difficult initial years in the United States, Mahbub had successfully entered into a real estate business with the assistance of relatives.

Mahbub and Shaheen spoke at length about their preferences for whom their children should marry in the future. Like most Bangladeshis of middle-class background, they did not expect to formally arrange the marriages of their children. They did, however, hope to be matchmakers in what may be described as a semi-arranged marriage. That is, they hoped to introduce children to a list of potential partners whom they had scrutinized for suitability. If the children did not allow them to play this role, they hoped at the very least to weigh in on the choices that the children made. In terms of specific criteria, they were especially adamant about the importance of marrying into "a good family":

> SHAHEEN: With my oldest son in college, he is getting to the age when we think about marriage. I tell him, the best thing would be a nice, well-educated girl from a good family in Bangladesh. There are many girls now in Bangladesh who are smart, speak English, and could adjust quite well here. If he wants to marry a Bangali[16] girl who is already here in America, who was brought up here, that is OK, but I would worry more about the family.

> NK: What about the family do you look for?
> MAHBUB: A good name.
> SHAHEEN: Devout Muslims, honest, smart. . . .
> MAHBUB: A good family is one in which the girl is well brought up. It's also one in which the family has a good name in the sense that they are well-known and well-established. They have a good position in society as a family. If you marry into a family like that, you can count on them to help you if you ever need something or you are in trouble.

The frequently mentioned notion of a "good family" appeared in the accounts of Bangladeshi immigrants as a reference to such desirable traits as religiosity, education, and honesty. These traits were furthermore signaled by the social reputation and status of the family and its extended kin networks. That is, the "good family" was one that had a "good name," reflecting both the perceived moral conduct of family members and their social standing, as indicated by occupation, wealth, education, and political connections. Here it is relevant to note the central role of political connections and state protection in the historical development of the middle-class in modern Bangladesh.[17] For middle-class Bangladeshis, marriage into a "good family" is often viewed as a potentially important route to enhanced social capital. In the specific case of Mahbub and Shaheen, the experience of needing and receiving assistance from kin during the trying initial years in the United States gave them a particular consciousness of the measure of security that could be provided by kin, especially those with resources, during difficult times.

As we have seen, Mahbub and Shaheen, like many other Bangladeshi immigrant parents, expressed a preference for their children to marry Bangalis from Bangladesh, rather than Bangalis from the diaspora. Those from Bangladesh, I was told, would be more familiar with Bangali culture and thus more able and likely to approach their family relations in a manner that was in keeping with Bangali traditions. For those in the United States, Bangladesh also tends to offer better opportunities for contracting marriages that represent gains in family-based social capital. This is because in Bangladesh, marriage to a U.S. citizen may carry positive value, offering the possibility of legal migration through family sponsorship and, more generally, the prestige of having family members in the United States. Under these conditions, those in the United States may be able to effectively exchange their legal presence there for family-based capital, through marrying into families of higher social standing than their own.

Jamal, a Bangladeshi immigrant in his early fifties, favored a strategy of marriage to a Bangladeshi citizen for his U.S. citizen children, seeing it as a way to garner family-based social capital. Jamal spoke to me with some satisfaction of the successful negotiation of the marriage of his daughter Jhumpa to a young man from Bangladesh. Jamal came from a rural family of modest means in Moulvibazaar, Sylhet, a district in northeastern Bangladesh. Over the course of his twenty-seven years in the United States he had worked as a waiter, a security guard, and a newspaper vendor. In 2005 he had arranged the marriage of Jhumpa, the youngest of his four children, to a man from a prominent and well-educated family in Moulvibazaar. He spoke of the reciprocal benefits derived from the marriage. On his daughter's side, there was the formation of ties to a well-connected family of good social standing in Bangladesh. The son-in-law had gained the opportunity to live and work in the United States, and to provide resources from abroad to his family in Bangladesh:

> Our new son-in-law is from a good family. You know the MP [Member of Parliament] ____; that man is their close relative. One of the brothers in the family is a manager at Sonali Bank [a major government bank], and another brother has a successful business as a building contractor. My son-in-law is a good person, of good character (*bhalo chele, bhalo choritro*). He has a BCom (Bachelor's of Commerce) degree. Here I hope that he will study further and then find a good job. His family knew that there were more opportunities for him here.

At a later point in our conversation, I asked Jamal about his other children, in particular the two others who had been raised in the United States. In a tone of sadness and resignation, he told me that his older son had married a Puerto Rican woman and one daughter was studying in college, determined to be a doctor and refusing to get married. We see then that the parents' ideas about how children should marry are not necessarily accepted by the children themselves. Indeed, the issue of marriage was a frequent point of tension and argument, if not overt conflict, between Bangladeshi immigrant parents and their teenage and young adult children.

As one might expect, the U.S.-born and/or -raised Bangladeshis framed their talk of marriage decisions around popular notions of romantic love: you married the person with whom you were in love. With some exceptions, most were quite opposed to the idea of arranged marriage and, to a lesser degree, to that of semi-arranged marriage as described earlier. However, there was also widespread appreciation among the young Bangladeshi Americans for the parental desire to see children marry endogamously, that is, to others who were also Muslim and Bangali in origin. Endogamous marriage made sense to the second generation on the basis of the common background, and thus the enhanced "cultural compatibility," of spouses. In contrast, there was much frustration and indeed disgust over what one second-generation informant described to me as "the older folks' obsession with 'good family.'" Take for example the comments of Khoka, the nineteen-year-old son of Shaheen and Mahbub, the immigrant parents whose comments appeared earlier. When I spoke to Khoka alone, he strongly rejected his mother's concerns with "good family":

KHOKA: My mom is starting to talk about marriage. It's always like [making a face] 'a nice Bangali girl, from a good family.' I say to her, 'What should I do with a good family, I'm not marrying the family.' I don't even know what 'a good family' actually means.

NK: Really, what do you think it means?

KHOKA: It's all about this status stuff which is not all that important to me. It's the person inside that matters.

NK: So you're not concerned about marrying Bangali?

KHOKA: It's not a priority, although I do think it would be nice because there are the similar cultural values.

As suggested by Khoka's comments, the children of Bangladeshi immigrants chafed at their parents' urgings to "marry into a good family." This was an idea that ran counter to the egalitarian ethos of intimate relationships that is part of the dominant U.S. culture and to which they subscribed. The resistance of the young adults here may also be attributed to the idealism of youth, which sees true love as having no social bars. But what was also at play was the second-generation's generally weak appreciation for the value of ties to Bangladesh and, more generally, for the significance of the transnational social networks in which their immigrant parents were embedded.

Many of the second-generation Bangladeshi Americans I spoke to felt "Muslim" to be a more meaningful basis of self-identification than "Bangladeshi." Marriage to a fellow Muslim was thus a higher priority than marriage to a fellow Bangali. Tanya, a twenty-three-year-old who had graduated from a state college in New Jersey, was deeply aware of how her ideas on this matter were different from older family members. Tanya had grown up in the New York–New Jersey area, surrounded by a large extended family. The "whole clan," as Tanya put it, had been enthusiastically engaged in trying to find her a suitable partner since she graduated. Honoring Tanya's sharp concerns about the supposed chauvinism of men from Bangladesh, they had agreed to limit their search to Bangladeshi men in the United States. Just a few weeks before I interviewed her, Tanya had been introduced at a party orchestrated by her aunt to a young Bangladeshi man from Texas who was studying in Connecticut. Much to the dismay of her aunt and other family members, she rejected him:

I tried to explain to my aunt (*khala-moni*) that we just had nothing in common. He seemed to be into Texas culture and I'm a real New Yorker. . . . I don't know, there was something about him, I just didn't like him. My family was going on and on about him, "Oh, he comes from such a good family." His father is a doctor in Texas, and I guess the family in Bangladesh is very high-status. My aunt kept on going on and on about how they were such a good family (*bhalo family*). I told them I didn't care about that. So then we had this big discussion, like a family meeting, and they asked me, what did I care about? I told them that there had to be some compatibility there. And the most important thing to me was marrying a Muslim; I didn't really care about whether they were Bangladeshi. I would be happy to marry someone who was white or black or whatever, so long as they are Muslim. My family is quite religious but they didn't seem to like that idea. My father said, you are Muslim and Bangali, you cannot separate those things. I was thinking to myself, maybe you can't separate them, but I can separate them.

Tanya's account suggests how family discussions about the characteristics of acceptable marriage partners could make visible the generational divide about the importance of Bangladeshi identity. The challenges of transnational reproduction under these conditions were also made apparent by the divergent perspectives of the generations on another immigrant socialization strategy—family trips to Bangladesh—a topic to which I turn next.

"We Come from a Good Family": Family Trips to Bangladesh

Immigrant Bangladeshis described visits to Bangladesh as times of great excitement and joy at reuniting with family and friends. Nayla, a forty-year-old immigrant who had lived in the New York area for about fifteen years, described the intense feelings of belonging that flooded her senses when she visited *desh*—the homeland:

> Last summer we went back for two months. I am very excited about going back. Before I went I did shopping of ten thousand dollars, filling twelve suitcases. Everyone expects a gift; it is something special, to get an item from America.
>
> We enjoyed ourselves very much. My son and daughter [ages ten and twelve] spent some time with our family and they came to understand our culture a little more. There was a lot of visiting and chatting [*adda*], shopping. We lived like royalty . . . no cooking, no cleaning, no laundry, no grocery shopping. I would like to go back, I dream about that day. *Desh* is *desh*.[18] There are so many people, transportation is very bad, no one respects the law. The government is corrupt, the politicians do nothing but call strikes. In spite of all the problems, I miss *desh*. We are respected [*maan-shomman*] there. When I go there I forget about the hard life here, where you are nobody, just another dark-skinned person.

For Nayla, as for many other Bangladeshi immigrants, trips to *desh* were a respite from the drudgery and indignities of life in the United States. There was relief from the daily, often harried routines of jobs and housework. Perhaps most importantly, they were a time of self-affirmation, an opportunity to renew one's sense of social worth. As suggested by Nayla's remarks about feeling like "not just another dark-skinned person" when she was in Bangladesh, there was escape, albeit temporary, from the racial marginality she experienced in the United States. There was also an affirmation of class privilege. Immigrants from middle-class backgrounds in Bangladesh could feel the burdens of working-class status in the United States lift from their shoulders, at least for a while, when they were in Bangladesh.

Immigrants spoke of the trips to Bangladesh as opportunities for their children being raised in the United States to become acquainted with the extended family and with the country in general. These desires were accompanied, however, by an awareness that many children were somewhat uncomfortable if not ambivalent about being in Bangladesh. The validity of these perceptions was largely confirmed by my conversations with second-generation Bangladeshi Americans, who were in general far less cheerful about their trips to Bangladesh than their parents. To be sure, there were positive aspects to being in Bangladesh for them as well. Many spoke of the pleasures of getting to know cousins and other family members and of the novel comforts of being in an environment where one could "blend in" with respect to skin color. And there were certainly appreciative accounts of being pampered, of being taken care of in unaccustomed ways, such as being chauffeured around and eating lavishly prepared and served meals. At the same time, the visits were typically a time of deep unease.

When I spoke to Abedin, an immigrant who had been in the United States for about eighteen years, he and his family had just returned from a six-week trip to Bangladesh. Abedin came from a middle-class family with roots in the district of Kushtia. After studying English for a few years at a college of modest academic reputation in Dhaka (the capital city), he had come to the United States, seeing little economic future for himself in Bangladesh. Only after several years of intense economic hardship had he managed to bring his wife and young child to join him. He and his wife were now operating a twenty-four-hour convenience store in which they also held partial ownership. As the children (ages thirteen and twenty) had started to grow older, Abedin and his wife had resolved to visit Bangladesh as frequently as possible, at least every two to three years. Abedin was well aware of his children's ambivalence about these visits. He hoped nonetheless that the trips would give them a sense of connection, especially an awareness of their family lineage. It was, in fact, with this particular consideration in mind that he had made it a point while in Bangladesh to take his children out of the urban comforts of Dhaka for a visit to their ancestral village home (*gramer bari*) in Kushtia. For the urban middle class in Bangladesh today, the ancestral village home continues to hold considerable symbolic significance as a place of heritage and belonging. Ties with the village are usually maintained through land holdings and the upkeep of often uninhabited family homesteads. The ancestral village is also a focus of charity for urban residents. Among the diaspora, for example, *zakat*[19] payments as well as other charitable donations are often directed to the ancestral village, to institutions such as schools, medical clinics, and orphanages, as well as mosques and madrasahs (Islamic schools). As we see in Abedin's account, these contributions may serve to affirm ties and status within village society:

> My children, Kamal and Samia, are like others who are raised here [in America]. They find the environment in Bangladesh to be difficult, you know, the heat, the crowds. I made it a point this time to take them for five days to our ancestral village home. Usually I send my *zakat* money to the mosque and madrasah there. When we were there, I gave a feast for all the people of the village, almost twenty-five hundred people. Everyone has great respect for our family. At the mosque there they say prayers for our family. I wanted the children to know our ancestry [*bongsho*], that we are a respected family. My hope is that they will come to understand the importance of these things, even after I am gone.

When I later spoke to Kamal, Abedin's son, he affirmed much of what his father had to say about their recent trip to Bangladesh. He and his sister had been reluctant to go and had done so only under considerable parental pressure. He rushed to assure me that this was not because he disliked the country or that he wanted to deny his connection with it. He just found it difficult to adjust to the climate, food, and especially the daily, unrelenting sights of poverty that one confronts there. When I asked Kamal about the best part of his recent trip, he described the visit to the ancestral home village in Kushtia, the one that had been purposefully arranged for him by his father:

> KAMAL: My parents like to go to Bangladesh every two years or so but I don't like to go as often as them. The climate is really harsh for me. Every time I go there I get sick, it gets very difficult for me to adjust. I think it's the mentality, too, because you walk through the streets and see all the poverty, that's very difficult. And I'm not used to the food.
> NK: What would you say is the best part about being there?
> KAMAL: It's the feeling that you get from helping people. That's why I liked going to the village, even though the living conditions there are tough. My dad does a lot to try and help relatives and people he knows in our village. When we were there we were treated like celebrities, there were

people coming and touching my father's feet [a gesture of respect]. One day, if I'm financially successful, I may want to do some things to help there, like set up some scholarships and a foundation to give medicine and food to people. I want to help Bangladesh. It's hard to think about it because the country is so messed up. The corruption, the bureaucracy, it's all so bad. The country is always high on the most-corrupt list.[20] How can you make a difference under those conditions?

Abedin's plan to give his children a sense of connection to the ancestral village had clearly been successful, although perhaps not exactly in the manner that he had intended. For Abedin, giving to the village was certainly a project of charity, of moral obligation. But it was also one of identity, of family status and self-worth. For Kamal, however, it was largely if not exclusively a way to channel the desire and effort to help the poor of Bangladesh. Of note, too, is Kamal's stance of frustrated resignation about the efficacy of charitable efforts in Bangladesh, given the nation's political and other problems. All in all, he seemed uncertain about the prospects of maintaining ties with Bangladesh in the future.

If, as in the case of Kamal, many second-generation Bangladeshi Americans emerged from their trips to Bangladesh with a sense of uncertainty about the significance for themselves of ties with Bangladesh, I did encounter some notable exceptions to this pattern. Arun, who had grown up in Boston, was in the midst of a graduate program in architecture when I spoke to him. After graduating from college he had, at the urging of his parents, spent a summer in Bangladesh, visiting relatives and touring the country. He had enjoyed himself immensely, so much so that he now planned to move there after completing his degree:

When I went to Bangladesh, people there were complaining about how hot it was and I was telling them, stop complaining, it's not really that hot [laughing]. I'm like, turn off that AC. I liked the experience of blending in, not being different. I feel like life here is kind of one-dimensional, whereas in Bangladesh it feels multidimensional, it's all in living color and it's so rich in terms of relationships.

There are also a lot of opportunities there. Just when I was there, even before I had enrolled in the master's program, I was being offered jobs. My uncle was saying, you come here and you can do some work for that person, we'll hook you up with that company. Here it's more difficult. First of all, it's pretty hard to get established as an architect. And then I do feel that it's easier for white people to get professional breaks. In Bangladesh I would be the one getting the breaks.

Arun had felt a great sense of affinity with the country, but he had also been attracted by the possibility of greater professional opportunities there. His well-connected relatives in Bangladesh had indicated to him that they would be able to open professional doors for him there. In contrast, he saw the professional opportunities in the United States to be more limited. This was because of the generally challenging nature of the architecture field in the United States, as well as his status as a racial minority. In Bangladesh, he would be able to harness his family background of class privilege to his advantage. Second-generation transnational engagements may be enhanced by such conditions, when these ties are seen as an economic resource, even a path of upward class mobility.

Conclusions

In this chapter I have explored some of the strategies of transnational reproduction that are part of Bangladeshi American family life. As we have seen, Bangladeshi immigrant parents urged their children to marry in a manner that would integrate them into transnational social networks, especially those that were rich in social capital. And in an effort to expand their children's understanding of the meaning and significance of transnational social and family ties, they took them on trips to Bangladesh, at times going to great lengths to ensure that these trips were enjoyable and memorable. The course of these strategies could make visible the profound differences between the generations in their relationship to the transnational sphere and, more generally, to identification with Bangladesh. For the most part, second-generation Bangladeshi Americans, unlike their immigrant elders, were uncertain about the meaning and significance of ties with Bangladesh.

As I have argued, the ability of immigrant elders to successfully integrate the next generation into the transnational sphere is shaped by the richness of the transnational ties and institutions that are a part of their lives. Although the Bangladesh–U.S. transnational sphere is a growing one, it is also recent, developing since the expansion in the 1990s of the size of the Bangladeshi population in the United States. Thus the second-generation Bangladeshi Americans in my study grew up, for the most part, in the context of a sparse transnational sphere. Furthermore, as noted by scholars of transnationalism,[21] second-generation immigrants often turn to transnational ties in response to conditions of racialized exclusion in the receiving society. Second-generation Bangladeshi Americans have turned not to transnational ties with Bangladesh but rather to involvement with Muslim and South Asian American communities in order to cope with their sense of marginality in the United States, much of which is informed by the post-9/11 growth of anti-Muslim sentiment. This does not necessarily mean that transnational engagements will be absent from the lives of second-generation Bangladeshi Americans in the future. My findings do, however, emphasize that their transnational engagements are likely to be quite different from those of their immigrant parents, and also mediated by their identification as Muslim Americans and/or South Asian Americans.

NOTES

1. Bashi 2007.
2. See Waldinger and Lichter 2003; Waters 1999.
3. Thai 2006.
4. Levitt 2001: 9.
5. Smith 2006.
6. See BAFI (Bangladesh-American Foundation Inc.), "Community Profile: Bangladesh-Americans at-a-Glance," available online at http://www.bafi.org/community/community_profiles.asp.
7. The Diversity Program, popularly known as the Green Card Lottery, accounted for 30.5 percent of Bangladeshi admissions during the 1996–2002 period. Reflecting its purpose of achieving diversity from countries with low levels of immigration to the United States, the lottery, established in 1990, has been open only to those from countries that have sent fewer than 50,000 people to the United States in the past five years.
8. Kibria 2007: 618.
9. Kibria 2007: 618.
10. Kibria 2007: 618.
11. According to the 2000 U.S. census, median household income for the general U.S. population was $42,148; for foreign-born Bangladeshis, it was $40,000. As far as poverty levels, 16.3 percent of foreign-born Bangladeshis were reported to be below the poverty line, in comparison to 9.4 percent for the general U.S. population.
12. Kibria 2008.
13. Kibria forthcoming.

14. While Muslims constitute the majority, the Bangladeshi immigrant population includes Hindus, Christians, and Buddhists. Reflecting my concern with negotiations of Muslim identity, my study focused on Bangladeshi Muslims.

15. All names have been changed to protect the identity of study participants.

16. The term "Bangali" is the one that is most often used by persons from Bangladesh to describe themselves and others from the region of Bengal, which encompasses part of present-day India and Bangladesh.

17. Islam 2004.

18. This expression is meant to underscore the point that Bangladesh is *the* homeland.

19. *Zakat* is one of the core requirements for Muslims, involving the donation of a proportion of one's money to the poor and needy.

20. A reference to the widely reported international rankings of country corruption by Transparency International.

21. Smith 2006.

REFERENCES

Bashi, Vilna F. 2007. *Survival of the Knitted: Immigrant Social Networks in a Stratified World*. Stanford: Stanford University Press.

Islam, Aminul S. 2004. "Is the Candle Still Burning? Weber and the Crisis of Democratic Transition in Bangladesh." *Bangladesh e-Journal of Sociology* 1: 1–13.

Kibria, Nazli. 2007. "South Asia: Pakistan, Bangladesh, Sri Lanka, Nepal." Pp. 612–23 in M. C. Waters and R. Ueda (eds.), *The New Americans: A Guide to Immigration since 1965*. Cambridge: Harvard University Press.

———. 2008. "The New Islam and Bangladeshi Youth in Britain and the U.S." *Ethnic and Racial Studies* 31: 243–66.

———. Forthcoming. *At Home and the World: Bangladeshi Muslims in Diaspora*. New Brunswick, NJ: Rutgers University Press.

Levitt, Peggy. 2001. *The Transnational Villagers*. Berkeley: University of California Press.

Smith, Robert C. 2006. *Mexican New York: Transnational Lives of New Immigrants*. Berkeley: University of California Press.

Thai, Hung Cam. 2006. "Money and Masculinity among Low Wage Vietnamese Immigrants in Transnational Families." *International Journal of Sociology of the Family* 32: 247–92.

Waldinger, Roger, and Michael Lichter. 2003. *How the Other Half Works: Immigration and the Social Organization of Labor*. Berkeley: University of California Press.

Waters, Mary. 1999. *Black Identities: West Indian Immigrant Dreams and Immigrant Realities*. New York: Russell Sage Foundation.

||||||||||||||||||||||||||||||||||||||||||||||||||||

Images of a Wounded Homeland
Sierra Leonean Children and the New Heart of Darkness

JoAnn D'Alisera

There is a woman whose features, in expression, are sad and noble, but which have been degraded, distorted, and rendered repulsive by disease; whose breath is perfumed by rich spices and by fragrant gums, yet through all steals the stench of the black mud of the mangroves and the miasma of the swamps; whose lap is filled with gold, but beneath lies a black snake, watchful and concealed; from whose breasts stream milk and honey, mingled with poison and with blood; whose head lies dead and cold, and yet is alive; in her horrible womb heave strange and monstrous embryos. Swarming round her are thousands of her children, whose hideousness inspires disgust, their misery compassion. She kisses them upon the lips, and with her own breath she strikes them corpses by her side. She feeds them her breasts, and from her own breasts they are poisoned and they die. She offers them the treasures of her lap, and as each hand is put forth the black snake bites it with his fatal fangs. . . . Look at the map of Africa. Does it not resemble a woman with a huge burden on the back. . . . ?
—Winwood W. Reade, *Savage Africa* (1864)[1]

True, by this time it was not a blank space any more. It
had got filled since my boyhood with rivers and lakes
and names. It had ceased to be a blank space of delight-
ful mystery—a white patch for a boy to dream gloriously
over. It had become a place of darkness.
—Joseph Conrad, *Heart of Darkness* (1902)[2]

There's death a dozen times over down the river!
—Humphrey Bogart,
The African Queen (dir. John Huston, 1951)

This essay explores the way in which problematic representations define
"Africa" for Sierra Leonean children living in Washington, D.C., and the
crisis of identity that ensues for both parents and children.[3] In particular,
the static image of Africa as a timeless continent teeming with disease and
other "horrors" frames it as a new "Heart of Darkness." While these images at times seem to be defined by contemporary realities (such as AIDS,
Ebola, famine, and civil conflict), they nevertheless are deeply connected
to constructed images of the past. As Philip Curtin has pointed out, "There
is a 'black legend' . . . that lives in spite of the knowledge geographers,
meteorologists, and specialists in tropical medicine have gained," that is,
that "most people in the Western world carry a half-conscious image of
'the White Man's Grave' . . . elaborated with such elements as 'primitive
tribes,' burning heat, fever-laden swamps, swarming insects, and miles of
trackless jungle." These images, while embedded in the fixed past, nevertheless persist in the contemporary construction of Africa.[4]

For Sierra Leonean children living in the diaspora, images of Africa,
and more recently a war-torn Sierra Leone, often challenge a parental
narrative that constructs Africa in general, and Sierra Leone in particular, in profoundly romantic terms. Children become the sites upon which
collective cultural memories, informed by competing master narratives
about the past, are produced, reproduced, and made manifest. Through
children the *remembered* and *forgotten* past becomes an "active *practice*"
in which parents struggle to re-enact an imagined homeland while at
the same time resisting the essentializing and popular discourses prevalent in American society, in which Africa is constructed as the Heart
of Darkness. How do Sierra Leonean children and their parents experience these popular media images? For parents, the images challenge and

disrupt idealized depictions of their homeland. How do their reactions to such media images affect their North American–born and –raised children? And, ultimately, how do views of the homeland influence family as well as community dynamics? Images encode worldview, and for Sierra Leonean children these images are often at odds with how their parents imagine Africa/home. As such, the way in which the Sierra Leonean community constitutes itself in a transnational context is often a struggle between what these images proclaim and what the adults of the community envision. The children sit in the middle, a border on which much of the conflict is played out.

My analysis is based on extensive ethnographic fieldwork with the Sierra Leonean community in the Washington, D.C., metropolitan area conducted from 1991 to 1993 and 2001 to 2003. According to estimates, the Sierra Leonean community in the metropolitan area numbers about five thousand, although my own research focused on Muslims within the community.[5] It mainly consisted of participant observation at Sierra Leonean and wider Muslim community gatherings: communal prayer, national and religious holiday celebrations, lifecycle rituals and rites of passage, religious instruction, and U.S. holiday events. Most of my key informants were highly educated and came to the United States in the late 1960s and early 1970s to attend American universities. As members of the first post-independence generation (Sierra Leone gained independence in 1961), the majority intended to return home to accept positions in government agencies and bureaucracies. However, political instability—a succession of coups and a bitter and bloody civil war that lasted from 1991 to 2002[6]—left many disillusioned and, understandably, loath to go back. They stayed in the United States and raised families, although many continued to hope that conditions would improve in Sierra Leone and allow them to return.[7]

"What Kind of People are These?"

Amie arrived in the United States in the mid-1980s. Her ten-year-old daughter, Mawa, joined her five years later. In the early 1990s, Amie worked as a nanny, taking care of a two-year-old whose parents were both lawyers in the District. Like many other Sierra Leoneans in Washington, Amie, who had attended college in Sierra Leone, experienced marked downward mobility in the United States. She held this particular job for two years. She would arrive at her employers' home at 7 a.m., before their child woke up; her day ended at 7 p.m., after she had fed the child dinner and prepared her for bed. For twelve hours of work five days a week, she was paid, by my calculations, less than minimum wage. As with many women in similar circumstances, her employers had promised to sponsor her for a green card. Amie was all too aware of the risks involved and of her own vulnerability. At any time her employers could yank the rug out from under her, leaving her no recourse other than to seek new employers and start the process again.

I moved in with Amie and Mawa early in my fieldwork in 1991. One day Amie returned home despondent. She had been let go. The frustrations of two years of abusive working conditions erupted.

These people [her employers] are too much for me to deal with anymore! They have told me that they don't want me to work for them any more! What will I do now? They are my sponsors and I must be employed by them to keep the green card processing going. They are evil people! These evil Americans! They take my blood for two years and pretend to care for me! Now they tell me they can not employ me anymore because I am too concerned with my own child! Sister, when Mawa arrived I was so happy. I had not seen her in four years. My firstborn was coming to be with me, and I could give her things that she could not have back home. They [her employers] seemed happy for me and told me I could bring her to work with me until the school year started. So I did.

She recounted how her relationship with her employers had changed after Mawa had arrived. Mawa had come from Sierra Leone during the summer school vacation, and Amie's employers had agreed that she could bring Mawa to work with her. For Amie this was a relief from worry. Not only could she keep an eye on her daughter, but Mawa could help her care for the child while she did the numerous chores required of her.

I thought while I did the laundry Mawa could play with the child. This is normal back home. Children should play with children. Mawa is good with babies. But these two thought differently. After one week of this they told me on Friday not to bring Mawa anymore. I asked why. They said, "She just came from Africa and we are concerned that she may give our daughter a disease." What do these fucking people mean! A disease! What kind of disease! My daughter is healthier than they are!

Mawa, underweight but healthy when she arrived, was sitting with her mom when this concern was expressed. Fearful of losing her job—and her prospective green card—Amie demurred. Her Sierra Leonean friends all had jobs, so her only option until school started in the fall was to leave Mawa home alone. Amie became increasingly depressed, worried about her daughter and angry at her employers.

Amie called home every hour to check on her daughter, but her relationship with her employers soon soured. "I could not stop thinking that these people knew my daughter was at home locked up in a hot apartment and didn't care," she told me. She wondered aloud, "What kind of people are these?"

Genealogy of a Myth

The answer to her question, I believe, is to be found, at least in part, in the deeply embedded constructs that Curtin speaks to—the prevailing image of Africa as a continent teeming with deadly contagion and darkness.[8] Contrary to modern scientific knowledge, medical topographies and fantastic myths of the past remain embodied in the way in which African bodies are envisioned and inscribed in the West at the start of the twenty-first century. As Curtin relates,[9] the image of "Darkest" Africa "emerged out of the haze of the unknown with the first voyages down the West African coast in the fifteenth century," growing increasingly dark "as explorers, missionaries, and scientists flooded it with light . . . [a light] refracted through an imperialist ideology that urged the abolition of 'savage customs' in the name of civilization."[10] This historical encounter set the stage for a complex set of tropes that constructed Africa as "dangerous" and "grotesque," forming the template for a "basic grammar and vocabulary" by which the Western sense of self and other was and continues to be constructed.[11]

For example, the myth of a "Dark Continent" gained currency in Britain in the early nineteenth century in the wake of the abolitionist campaign against the slave trade.[12] Abolitionist literature, with its detailed accounts of inhuman violence, lay the foundations for a continent seen largely in terms of atrocities committed against its inhabitants.[13] Such images persisted after the slave trade ceased. However the focus on the "horrors" of the human condition in Africa took a different, less altruistic cast. As the British began to re-envision themselves no longer as perpetrators of horrors, but now as the potential saviors of the continent, blame was increasingly displaced onto the Africans themselves, who were seen as desperately in need of civilizing. A new literature, promulgated largely by traders and missionaries, presented Africans as "bound in the chains of the grossest ignorance [and] prey to the most savage superstitions"— human sacrifice and cannibalism.[14] As Europeans pressed inland into the "kingdom of darkness,"[15] disease became a powerful and dominant trope in writings about Africa.

Since the late eighteenth century West Africa had been recognized as an area of hyperendemic malaria, with yellow fever epidemics spaced about five to ten years apart.[16] By the 1830s, appalling death rates for Europeans, coupled with the publication of medical topographies, contributed to the popular image of Africa as the "White Man's Grave."[17] The phrase had become the dominant idiom through which statements about Africa were conveyed. It appeared in popular literature such as Charles Dickens's *Bleak House* (1852–53), in book titles such as R. H. Rankin's influential 1836 travelogue *The White Man's Grave: A Visit to Sierra Leone in 1834*, and in the press.[18] Even as medical science began to gain a greater understanding of fevers and how to treat them—regular quinine prophylaxis was introduced to combat malaria in the 1840s—the specter of the White Man's Grave continued to haunt European popular imaginings of Africa. Despite a sudden drop in mortality rates that sparked optimism, encouraging new commercial and missionary ventures, relations between Europeans and indigenous peoples inland continued to be informed by past perceptions of the coast. By the 1850s, Curtin writes, "the image had hardened. It was found in children's books, in Sunday school tracts, in the popular press. Its major affirmations were 'common knowledge' of the educated classes."[19] Rooted in a merger of racial and evolutionary doctrines, these texts shaped the views of those traveling to Africa and provided the social and spiritual justification for imperialism.[20]

In addition, prevailing understandings of contagion, along with medical evidence that diseases were less prevalent on higher ground, led to recommendations that places of European habitation be established "away from the noxious odors of 'native' habitation, preferably windward."[21] New medical advances in the latter decades of the nineteenth century, particularly the discovery that mosquitoes transmit yellow fever and malaria, gave impetus to sanitary segregation. It was also discovered that Africans, once believed to be immune, also contracted malaria. The solution devised by colonial officials was to isolate Europeans, as best as possible, from the source areas and carriers of malaria. Based on research carried out by doctors from the Liverpool School of Tropical Medicine, who argued that mosquitoes were race-specific in their taste for human blood, preferring the African, areas to be inhabited by the Europeans were ordered cleared of all native inhabitants and their houses, and clear, uninhabited sanitary lines between European and native areas of habitation were established. The doctors expressed particular caution with regard to children. Because they were thought to be the prime source of infection, it was imperative to protect Europeans from them, particularly children under the age of five. Servants were allowed to work in hill stations, but they were not allowed to spend the night, and children were rigorously excluded.[22]

In excavating the "career" of a set of tropes, it is thus possible to see how those discourses become fused into a consistent ideology that still resonates today. Responses to late-twentieth-century epidemic diseases, such as AIDS, form the platform upon which the intersection of historical discourse about the African other and, in particular, the mobile African other are played out. The power of these tropes to sustain themselves in the present was revealed to me through a personal experience around the same time as Amie's falling out with her employers. Facing minor surgery and the prospect of a potential blood transfusion, I decided to donate my own blood. At the hospital blood bank I completed the required forms: name, address, travels abroad, and so on. When I had finished, the nurse approached me, smiling and wearing a pair of latex gloves. As she read my card I noticed her smile change to a worried expression.

> NURSE: You've been to Africa?
> ME: Yes. Why?
> NURSE: Yes, well I will be right back. I need to consult with my supervisor.

She returned, seemingly dismayed, even rather angry, and proceeded to place four more pairs of latex gloves over the one pair she was already wearing. I asked her if she always wore multiple layers of gloves to take blood. Ignoring my question, she responded in a hurried, annoyed way:

> Well, my supervisor says I have to take your blood. But you should know that it will be disposed if you don't use it. I noticed that you indicated on the form that if you do not need a transfusion you will donate your blood

to the bank. You were in Africa and there is no way we can keep your blood here. We have to be careful.

As I watched my blood trickle into the bag, I imagined it hanging in a segregated part of storage with those of others whose blood had been deemed tainted—by national origin, sexual orientation, travel, and what else?

My body, like Mawa's, had been inscribed with disease purely because of our common association with Africa. We were both, each in our own way, products of the "Heart of Darkness," a construct that runs deep in the collective memory of the West and that continues to define the way in which we view the continent and its people. Both Mawa and I were seen as sites of contagion, tainted by contact with a diseased continent and its people. While it is clear that a multitude of sociocultural factors have invested human bodies with a wide range of shifting and at times conflicting meanings over time, the idea that the *polluted body* is a *socially disruptive body* to be contained has been a thread that has run and continues to run through community discourses.

These popular paradigms of a diseased continent, so entrenched in the Western mind at the turn of the twentieth century, persist at the start of the twenty-first century and continue to have a negative impact on the lives of Africans, particularly when they move to the West, where images of jungles, disease, fantastic customs, and savage minds are so dominant. For example, how do the photographs we all know too well of malnourished children, disembodied, disconnected from mother and father, a mere fact of the horror of Africa, affect views of African immigrants and their children? As Catherine Lutz and Jane Collins argue, images are central to contemporary society and have played an important role in the construction of ethnic and racial difference.[23]

For many Westerners the most familiar image of Africa in the late twentieth century is that of the starving/diseased African child. The wounded bodies of these children have pathologized renditions of the African body. These renditions are "not only perceived, received, [but are] *read*, connected more or less consciously by the public that consumes [them] to a traditional stock of signs."[24] Whatever the image maker may have intended, the reader can imagine something else. In this case, that something else is structured by cultural elements or models that we have learned in order to interpret these images. Hence the gaze of the onlooker is constructed not only by the immediate image, but by the deeply embedded tropes attached to that image.[25]

"What Jungle?"

For Sierra Leonean migrants, the sting of these images is most apparent in the cultural and spiritual lives of their children. Parents often express dismay at the ideas that their children have about the family's homeland, a homeland that is often generalized to an entire continent, a monolithic "Africa." Children, for their part, often express dismay at their parents' need to regularly convey to them what they perceive to be a romantic, idealized sense of homeland. This dismay challenges many of the constructs that the children see as "real" and "natural." A recent phone conversation with an informant highlighted this conflict:

> Can you believe what my son said to me? He came home from school today and told me that I should clean the house. Eiii! He said to me: "Where do you think you are, in the jungles of Africa!" I asked him, What kind of jungles? I grew up in the city, I never saw a jungle or a wild animal!

Many parents have responded to this kind of exchange by attempting to construct positive images of Sierra Leone and to imbue in their children a sense of national/transnational belonging.[26] The images that parents evoke are often images from their own childhood. Many of these parents came of age at the time of independence. For them, the images of Sierra Leone, of Africa in general, were positive: hope, freedom, and above all the call to rid the continent of underdevelopment, endemic disease, illiteracy, and corruption.

For the children, their parents' attempts to construct a homeland that challenges the popularly constructed Western images of a continent often fall on deaf ears. As parents evoke positive images, children are bombarded outside the home and community with more powerful negative images that construct their lives in terms of disease, war, and corruption, endemic and spreading. If yesterday's images of Africa come from Sierra Leone and Rwanda, today's come primarily from Darfur and Congo. The conflict between the positive images of their parents' nostalgic longing and the negative images of the nightly news plays itself out in children's lives in profound ways. The children often experience a profound sense of displacement that is conveyed in the way in which they present themselves to the world. Often that presentation is a mixture of pride and shame. On the one hand, they are proud that they can point to place on a map of Africa that evokes feelings of family, community, deep-rooted culture, and religion. On the other, they feel shame that their homeland has increasingly grown distant as they and their parents find themselves cut off from country and continent, bombarded by a steady flow of general bad news and terrifying images out of Africa. For my Sierra Leonean informants, this includes too many horror stories—in the news and via informal networks (the Internet especially)—emanating from their own war-torn country.

For many Sierra Leonean parents the solution is to bring "home" to the United States, that is, to map Sierra Leone onto their community, to instill a sense of cultural, ethnic, national, and religious pride in their American-born children. But, as Arjun Appadurai has pointed out, "the work of cultural reproduction in new settings is profoundly complicated by the politics of representing a family as normal (particularly for the young) to neighbors and peers in the new locale."[27] For Sierra Leonean parents the search for powerful identity markers (ethnicity, kinship, ritual, etc.) for their children in an atmosphere affected not only by the fluidities of the transnational experience, but by a complex history of representations, "becomes both politicized and exposed to the traumas of deterritorialization as family members pool and negotiate their mutual understandings and aspirations."[28] Some children will embrace the message their parents impart, but others do not. Some even hold their parents up to ridicule, as did the young man above. Frustration and even shame often enter the picture, albeit in different ways for parents and children. For example, while discussing marriage and childbirth rituals that included animal sacrifice with one informant, her twelve-year-old daughter, who was quietly listening to our conversation, visibly cringed and interrupted her mother as she described her daughter's naming ceremony:

KHADI: When Fatmata was about three weeks old, we had her naming ceremony, we slaughtered a goat and a sheep . . .

FATMATA: Mommy, don't tell that story to JoAnn. She is American and will think we are uncivilized Africans!

Khadi, deeply disturbed, glared at the child until she fell silent. She turned to me and said:

You see what we have to put up with! Not only are they losing their culture, but they are ashamed of it! They think we are uncivilized, savage! When I tell my children that my mother and father were first cousins they tell me that this is incest! They put their hands over their ears when I tell them their grandfather had four wives and that my mother was the first wife. They are ashamed. But we are ashamed that they are losing their culture! My daughter is always asking me, "How can you tell people here that your parents were cousins? They will think we are mentally slow." I asked her, "Am I slow?!" She doesn't like me to tell these stories, but these stories are a way to keep our children connected to home.

For most U.S.-born Sierra Leonean children, monogamy and non-kin marriage partners are the norm. For these children, Sierra Leonean cultural practices, particularly the marriage practices of their parents and grandparents, including polygamy and cross- and parallel-cousin marriage, contradict North American notions of incest and views of cousin marriage as medically suspect. For these children, Sierra Leonean bodies, particularly bodies tainted in their estimation by North American notions of incest, become stigmatizing symbols of inferiority, primitiveness, and questionable health. For their parents, who grew up in a society where polygamy and cousin marriage were widely accepted, indeed ideal practices, the customs and the stories about them emphasize core cultural practices that transcend locality and are meant to instill a sense of pride and in many instances superiority. Parents want their children to listen to their stories about Sierra Leonean cultural practices with pride and not shame, and to feel connected to a homeland that many of these children have never been to. As one parent told me, "Sharing our stories, our traditions, is the only way we can show our children that they are Sierra Leonean and not American." For many children, the stories are a consistent reminder that they are expected to conform—in many instances, to their horror—to the ways of their parents. The result is many conflicts between children, especially teens, and their parents. While visiting a Sierra Leonean friend whose son is in his late teens, I was drawn into an intense argument between mother and son. Isatu wanted Ali to escort his sixteen-year-old cousin to her prom.

ALI: You want me to take my cousin to her junior prom?! First, I am nineteen years old and would not be caught dead at a prom! Second, she is my cousin. I know this is an African thing to date and marry cousins, but no way!

ISATU: What do mean, no way?! She is a good girl, she is Sierra Leonean, and she is the daughter of my cousin and friend!

ALI: Ahh, so you and Auntie are plotting marriage! It isn't good to marry a cousin! We are not in the jungle!

ISATU: What jungle?! I grew up in Freetown!

Both mother and son turned to me, exasperated. Isatu expected me to give Ali an anthropological lecture on the importance of maintaining tradition, and Ali expected me to side with him. I was between a rock and a hard place, but I admit I was sympathetic to Ali's cause. Quietly, I said, "I think Ali should make his own decisions about who he dates." Isatu stared at the two of us, and with disgust in her voice she said, "You are both so American!" and left the room. Ali looked at me and said, "Africans!" and also left the room. Isatu returned and let me know that she was disappointed in me for not defending her position.

ISATU: How am I going to teach him that he is Sierra Leonean? Our children are lost to this country. Everywhere we turn there are challenges. Why do they want to be so American? Americans look at us as if we are infectious.

ME: What do you mean "infectious"?

ISATU: My friend Rayne told me her [ten-year-old] daughter fell during recess and scraped her knee. She was bleeding and her friends came over to help her. Can you believe this, the teacher screamed out, "Don't touch her, she is from Africa, you might get AIDS!" This is what they think of us. We are all infected with AIDS, we are incestuous. What is going to become of our children. It makes me so angry.

Through the stories they tell, parents want and expect their children to "feel Sierra Leonean" and to experience pride in this identity. For many parents it is a frustrating, uphill battle, particularly in the face of profoundly destabilizing popular representations that have a long and powerful history. These representations not only challenge parental cultural values and disrupt parental narratives of difference and belonging, they also convey a powerful set of tropes that inscribe a complex range of historical, social, and cultural discourses onto the lives of their children that construct them and their children as socially and medically inappropriate. Children are consistently confronted with a wide range of shifting and conflicting meanings about who they are in relation to their parents, the Sierra Leonean community, and the world of their everyday lives.[29] And parents fight back.

Fighting Back

As Sierra Leonean migrants confront negative images of Africa in the U.S. media and elsewhere, they increasingly devise strategies to challenge these images, especially for their children, who they see as their link to Africa. "We will not allow our children to think of Africa as a jungle, wild and untamed mostly populated by elephants," an informant told me. For Sierra Leonean parents these expressive representations are the means by which their sentiments are conveyed to their children. As another informant said, "Sierra Leonean children need links that are beyond what we as parents tell them about Sierra Leone. It is a way of making the abstract concrete."

Through communal representations of community such as naming ceremonies, weddings, graduation parties, and fundraising events for the community and those back home, parents endeavor to offset the power of negative outside images and affirm for their children a place in the community both here and abroad.[30] These events give parents a place to authenticate and validate the positive aspects of Sierra Leonean cultural practices for their children.

I have written elsewhere about some of the events listed above,[31] particularly life-cycle rituals. Here, I would like to focus on community action, and especially community aid organizations and the way in which they directly challenge the essentialist images of Africa that I have described. Moreover, they challenge images of a wave of terror that washed over Sierra Leone from 1991 to 2002. Images of chaos, mass amputation, piles of dead bodies, and child combatants as young as eight years old, easily available via the Internet, home videos, Hollywood movies, and documentaries, have come to embody for many of my informants the dismemberment of a nation. In this context, they seek to create, for themselves and their children, a way to view their homeland positively and to feel an allegiance with it, despite the awful events of recent years. By instilling a sense of national and cultural belonging in their children, community aid organizations in particular provide a vehicle through which parents can counter the prevailing images of war from afar.

Sierra Leonean community aid organizations, most of which formed just after the 2002 ceasefire, are involved in a variety of activities. Several are committed to an educational mission, paying school fees for children orphaned by the war, rebuilding schools, and purchasing badly needed books and supplies. Others are focused on medical care, such as purchasing prosthetics for amputees and providing needed medicine. Still others have a more generalized mission, raising money to help support the economic activities of Sierra Leonean citizens as they rebuild their lives and providing money for housing and food for those in grave need. The majority of these organizations are committed to the idea of self-help and shun offers from outsiders to contribute. Most have formed across ethnic and class lines and are generally non-denominational, although several groups have a distinctly Muslim-inspired mission. Group membership varies, with the average being anywhere from twenty to fifty people. Most importantly, attendance at meetings increases access to information from home and creates a sense of inclusiveness for those touched by the Sierra Leonean civil war.

For my informants, these organizations have created a social space in which the constant struggle to negotiate feelings of extreme displacement, reinforced by the horrific images of a war-torn Sierra Leone, is actively played out in public meetings. Although children usually do not attend organizational meetings, they were uppermost in my informants' thoughts as they worked together to counter a displacement inflected by grief and despair. For many it has become hard to talk about home. As one informant related:

My younger brother was killed by ECOMOG [Economic Community of West African States Monitoring Group] and my father died of a broken heart. I am the oldest, and my father expected me to carry on after he was gone. I have no money, so how can I go back when I can't even build a single house? So I continue to work here. To do what I can. But talking about home makes me sad: Sad because what it was when I was a child isn't there anymore; sad that my children can know only this nightmare.

Nevertheless, adults feel, as one informant told me, that "to give up on the idea of home is to give up on making Sierra Leone live again." For many migrants it is imperative that Sierra Leoneans living in the diaspora work together to solve the problems of their home country so that people, according to the president-elect of one organization, "understand that there is still hope in the face of loss." Thus narratives of homeland, peaceful or not, continue to construct a sense of belonging that creates cultural citizenship, which resonates with a profound desire for home. Emotionally wounded and overcome at times by the pain and suffering of family and friends left behind, the organizations create a social space in which migrants can negotiate those extreme feelings of loss and displacement. In this way, they recast, for themselves and their children, a Sierra Leone that links past perceptions (nostalgic longing) with present realities (war-torn devastation). For parents, whose children may look to a decade of horror in their parents' homeland as proof that the timeless images of jungles, disease, and savagery resonate with reality, community aid work serves as a way to remind themselves and their children that the post-independence euphoria that brought them to the United States still strikes a powerful chord in many. As one informant said after a particularly emotional meeting:

> I know there are Sierra Leoneans here who say we need to forget home because it is destroyed, it isn't what it was before, the home we remember. But I know that Sierra Leone is still there. I don't think it is right to give up on Sierra Leone. I can't do that. I still believe we can make a good country. We need to work for our country, so that our children will know the real Sierra Leone. So that they can feel pride and not shame. There is a lot of work to be done. We all have to work to help build the nation. We have to remember why we came here in the first place. Many of us came to live and participate in a democracy, to get educated and bring that back home. It is time to complete our mission so that our children don't get lost here in America. If we don't rebuild our country how will they ever go home?

Narratives of home, inflected with tales of marriage, ritual, kinship, and now the horrors of war, that are shared in community settings and at home with children not only are continually reinvented and transformed but also provide a vehicle in which Sierra Leoneans living in the diaspora seek to negotiate the experience of exile for themselves and provide an identification with the homeland for their children. The success of their attempts has been mixed. For many Sierra Leonean children born and raised in the United States, Sierra Leone has become the cultural periphery, the "old country" of the classic American immigrant experience. Caught between two worlds, they often challenge their parents' need to bring "home" to the United States, to instill a sense of cultural, ethnic, national, and religious pride in their American-born children. At the same time, they seek to build bridges between their experiences and parental longing for Sierra Leone, trying their best to accommodate their parents' desire for them to stay connected to a place they have never seen. Betwixt and between, these children, like the children of other immigrants, migrants, and transnationals before them, inevitably find themselves seeking solutions to their dilemma. Some will retreat behind community boundaries, drawing thicker boundaries between themselves and all outsiders. Others will redraw community boundaries to allow greater accommodation of the larger society in which they live. In either case, the foundation has been laid for the emergence of a creative and unique way of being an American-born Sierra Leonean.

Conclusion

More than a hundred years ago, at the turn of the twentieth century, Africans were seen by Europeans and Americans as the ultimate carriers of disease. At the turn of the twenty-first century, they are still a focus of a horrified gaze from abroad, although one which is often more sympathetic as horrific representations are designed to underscore the tragedy of civil war, famine, pandemic disease, and ethnic cleansing. For Sierra Leoneans living in the diaspora, these representations erect boundaries and create conflicts between parents and children. While parents try to instill a sense of pride in, and a link to, Sierra Leone, their children grow increasingly alienated from their parents' homeland. This conflict between the first and second generation is, of course, common to many groups in the United States. Yet in the Sierra Leonean case, there is an additional element involved: a popular discourse inflected with the myth of the "Dark Continent."

Sierra Leonean parents feel increasingly displaced and caught between the powerful dreams of their youth and nostalgia for a Sierra Leone that used to be, which they struggle to convey to their children. The children struggle to live between two worlds, as their parents' dreams often collide with their own visions of self, origins, and futures. Parents seek to develop strategies to maintain an intense involvement in the cultural and political life of home to counter prevailing negative images of Africa and Sierra Leone, and set new frameworks of national and cultural belonging for their children. Through community aid organizations, a powerful post–civil war national sentiment helps parents to construct multiple frames of reference and meaning in which nation and cultural practice are produced and transmitted. Tales of homeland connected to social activism transform the experience of displacement into an exercise in empowerment in which notions of nation and culture are fixed and framed. Within this framework, despair and grief are made sense of and children's perceptions of home can be challenged. Whether the parents' efforts will, in the end, be successful, and the American-born children will ultimately feel connected in a positive way to their parents' homeland is a question that future studies will need to investigate.

ACKNOWLEDGMENTS

I would like to thank Nancy Foner for inviting me to participate in this volume and for her keen editorial eye; and Lynda Coon for her critical reading of this essay.

NOTES

1. Reade 1967 [1864]: 383.
2. Conrad 1989 [1902]: 33.
3. Curtin 1961: 94.
4. Curtin 1961: 94.
5. No official demographic figures, governmental or nongovernmental, exist for this or most sub-Saharan African communities in the United States. Community leaders in the Washington, D.C., area gave me an estimate of five thousand Sierra Leoneans throughout the district and nearby Maryland and Virginia. This population is composed of members of most, if not all, of the many ethnic groups found in Sierra Leone. My fieldwork has to date focused on Sierra Leonean Muslims, their interaction in a cosmopolitan American city with a diverse Muslim population, and ways in which they have come to define and express themselves as Muslims, Sierra Leoneans, and Sierra Leonean Muslims in a transnational context.
6. The Sierra Leonean civil war, the product of local political and regional instability, and fueled by the country's rich diamond deposits, erupted in full force in 1991 when Foday Sankoh, a cashiered army officer, seized control of key diamond fields along the border with Liberia. With the support of Liberian warlord (and later president) Charles Taylor, Burkina Faso's Blaise Compaore, and Libyan leader Muammar Qaddafi, Sankoh's Revolutionary United Front (RUF)—composed primarily of teenagers from provincial cities and towns—was able by 1994 to extend its control throughout much of the north and east of the country, areas rich in diamonds as well as titanium and bauxite. In response, the government turned first to a coalition of West African nations known as the Economic Community of West African States Monitoring Group (ECOMOG), then, with

the RUF on the verge of overrunning Freetown, to Executive Outcomes, a mercenary organization founded by white former officers in the South African army. Facing an enemy that "consisted largely of teenagers on drugs" (Traub 2000: 62), two hundred mercenaries fighting alongside West African troops drove the rebels away from Freetown and, reluctantly, to the bargaining table. Despite a wave of terror in the countryside—including mass amputations—60 percent of registered voters elected a civilian, Ahmad Tejan Kabbah, president. In what has been called a "Faustian bargain," Kabbah signed a peace accord with Sankoh and dismissed Executive Outcomes. In the spring of 1997, another rebel army, led by Lieutenant Colonel Johnny Paul Koroma, joined forces with the RUF and drove Kabbah out of the country. A year later, ECOMOG forces restored Kabbah to power, but throughout the following year both they and the RUF ravaged the countryside. The chaos culminated in the January 6, 1999, rebel onslaught on Freetown, during which "whatever happened in 1996 and 1997 pales by comparison" (ibid.).

The period that ensued brought only further chaos. In July 1999, after negotiations held under the auspices of the Reverend Jesse Jackson, who acted as special envoy for the Clinton administration, President Kabbah signed another ceasefire with the RUF, granted amnesty to RUF fighters, and brought Foday Sankoh into the government (ironically, as Minister of Mines). In October 1999, the United Nations authorized a peacekeeping force; troops, drawn primarily from ECOMOG, soon found themselves the targets of Sankoh's supposedly disarmed rebels. In May 2000, following the abduction of fifty U.N. peacekeepers by rebel forces, and with the rebels outside Freetown, British troops intervened. Eight hundred paratroopers secured Freetown's airport and oversaw the evacuation of British citizens. Shortly thereafter, Sankoh was captured. In September 2000, British forces mounted an operation to rescue comrades taken hostage by the West Side Boys, a breakaway rebel faction. In early 2001, with presidential elections postponed, U.N. troops, followed by British-trained Sierra Leonean forces, moved into former rebel-held territory and began disarming the rebels. In January 2002, the U.N. mission declared the disarmament of 45,000 rebels complete and the war over. Plans to create a war crimes tribunal were announced. In May 2002, Kabbah and his Sierra Leonean People's Party won a landslide electoral victory—the headline of one foreign correspondent's report called it a "humiliating defeat" for the rebels (Farah 2002).

7. D'Alisera 1998, 1999, 2001, 2002, 2004.

8. Equally relevant, most employers of child-care workers do not want or allow workers to bring their children to work. Amie's feeling that she was entitled to bring her daughter to work not only stems from her assumption that her employers would hold to their word, but from different cultural patterns that clash with employer expectations of child-care workers in the United States.

9. Curtin 1964: v.

10. Brantlinger 1985: 166.

11. Comaroff and Comaroff 1991, 1992; Torgovnick 1990:8.

12. Brantlinger 1985; Comaroff and Comaroff 1991, 1992; Curtin 1964; Jablow and Hammond 1977.

13. Brantlinger 1985: 170.

14. Buxton quoted in Brantlinger 1985: 173.

15. Buxton quoted in Brantlinger 1985: 173.

16. Curtin 1961, 1985, 1989.

17. According to Philip Curtin (1961:95), the death rate for any group of newcomers from Europe to the west coast of Africa was between 300 and 700 hundred per thousand per annum.

18. Jablow and Hammond 1977: 38.

19. Curtin 1964: vi.

20. Brantlinger 1985.

21. Curtin 1985: 595.

22. For more detailed description of these practices, see Curtin 1985, 1989.

23. Lutz and Collins 1993.

24. Barthes 1977: 19.

25. Lutz and Collins 1993: 196.

26. For a further and more detailed discussion, see D'Alisera 1998, 1999, 2004.

27. Appadurai 1996: 44.

28. Appadurai 1996: 44.

29. For example, children, much to their parents' dismay, may see themselves as Sierra Leonean, perhaps as African, but they also see themselves as African American. How African American identity is coded is dependent upon the circumstances in which it is or is not used. For Sierra Leonean children racial and ethnic identity is not an either-or proposition. This reflects, as Sherri-Ann Butterfield (2004; see also Waters 1999) has argued for second-generation West Indians living in New York City, the complex and unique way that ethnic and racial identities are formed in context. Sierra Leonean children, like second-generation West Indians, make racial and ethnic identity choices that are dependent on circumstances and audience. While their parents may assume that one negates the other, and in fact go to great lengths to differentiate themselves from African Americans, it is clear that ethnic and racial identities for many of the children I spoke to are fluid identities embraced without contradiction. This ultimately complicates further parental concerns about the "Americanization" of their children.

30. For a more detailed description of these representations, see D'Alisera 1997, 2004.

31. See D'Alisera 1998, 1999, 2001, 2002, 2004.

REFERENCES

Appadurai, Arjun. 1996. *Modernity at Large: Cultural Dimensions of Globalization.* Minneapolis: University of Minnesota Press.

Barthes, Roland. 1977. "The Photographic Message." Pp. 15–31 in idem., *Image-Music-Text.* Glasgow: Fontana.

Brantlinger, Patrick. 1985. "Victorians and Africans: The Genealogy of the Myth of the Dark Continent." *Critical Inquiry* 12: 166–203.

Butterfield, Sherri-Ann P. 2004. "'We're Just Black': The Racial and Ethnic Identities of Second Generation West Indians in New York." Pp. 288–312 in Philip Kasinitz, John Mollenkopf and Mary C. Waters (eds.), *Becoming New Yorkers: Ethnographies of the New Second Generation.* New York: Russell Sage Foundation.

Buxton, Thomas Fowell. 1967. *The African Slave Trade and Its Remedy.* London: J. Murray. (Reprint of *The Slave Trade [1839]* and *The Remedy: Being a Sequel to the African Slave Trade* [1840]).

Comaroff, Jean, and John Comaroff. 1991. *Of Revelation and Revolution: Christianity, Colonialism, and Consciousness in South Africa,* vol. 1. Chicago: University of Chicago Press.

——— . 1992. *Ethnography and the Historical Imagination.* Boulder, CO: Westview Press.

Conrad, Joseph. 1989 [1902]. *Heart of Darkness.* London: Penguin Books.

Curtin, Philip. 1961. "'The White Man's Grave': Image and Reality, 1780–1850." *Journal of British Studies* 1: 94–110.

———. 1964. *The Image of Africa: British Ideas and Action, 1780–1850.* Madison: University of Wisconsin Press.

———. 1985. "Medical Knowledge and Urban Planning in Tropical Africa." *American Historical Review* 90: 594–613.

———. 1989. *Death by Migration: Europe's Encounter with the Tropical World in the Nineteenth Century.* Cambridge: Cambridge University Press.

D'Alisera, JoAnn. 1998. "Born in the USA: Naming Ceremonies of Infants among Sierra Leoneans Living in the American Capital." *Anthropology Today* 14(1): 16–18.

———. 1999. "Field of Dreams: The Anthropologist Far Away at Home." *Anthropology and Humanism* 24: 5–19.

———. 2001. "I ♥ Islam: Popular Religious Commodities, Sites of Inscription, and Transnational Sierra Leonean Identity." *Journal of Material Culture* 6(1): 89–108.

———. 2002. "Icons of Longing: Homeland and Memory in the Sierra Leonean Diaspora." *PoLar: The Political and Legal Anthropology Review* 25 (2): 73–89.

———. 2004. *An Imagined Geography: Sierra Leonean Muslims in America.* Philadelphia: University of Pennsylvania Press.

Farah, Douglas. 2002. "Sierra Leone's Voters Inflict Humiliating Defeat on Rebels." *Guardian Weekly*, May 23–29, p. 36.

Jablow, Alta, and Dorothy Hammond. 1977. *The Myth of Africa*. New York: Library of Social Science.

Lutz, Catherine, and Jane L. Collins. 1993. *Reading National Geographic*. Chicago: University of Chicago Press.

Rankin, F. H. 2002 [1836]. *The White Man's Grave: A Visit to Sierra Leone in 1834*, 2 vols. Boston: Adamant Media Corporation.

Reade, Winwood W. 1967 [1864] .*Savage Africa*, 2 vols. New York: Johnson Reprint Corporation.

Torgovnick, Marianna. 1990. *Gone Primitive: Savage Intellects, Modern Lives*. Chicago: University of Chicago Press.

Traub, James. 2000. "The Worst Place on Earth." *New York Review of Books* 47(11): 61–65.

Waters, Mary. 1999. *Black Identities: West Indian Immigrant Dreams and American Realities*. Cambridge: Harvard University Press.

6

||||||||||||||||||||||||||||||||||||||||||||||||||||

Caregiving across Generations

*Aging, State Assistance, and Multigenerational Ties
among Immigrants from the Dominican Republic*

Greta Gilbertson

In this chapter I explore the nature of multigenerational relations among a group of Dominican immigrants in New York City. I examine some of the ways that multigenerational relationships are manifested in transnational contexts and how they change over the life course. In the analysis, I focus on "young old"[1] grandparents' relations with their foreign-born and U.S.-born children and grandchildren over a period of more than ten years.

A focus on aging immigrants is important because multigenerational bonds form a vital part of the immigrant's social world. Most extant literature highlights the relationship between parents and children but ignores the important role played by grandparents, particularly grandmothers, in immigrant families. Some studies do address this issue: Wei Wei Da,[2] for example, describes grandparents' role in providing child care—in both home and host societies—among contemporary Chinese immigrants in Australia. Robert Smith[3] argues that grandparents continue to play an important role in the transnational socialization of first and second generation Mexican children. Loretta Baldassar[4] finds that the elderly are active members in transnational family networks.

Even if grandparents are no longer key figures in the lives of their grandchildren—Dwaine Plaza,[5] for example, argues that grandparents in Caribbean-origin families (from Trinidad, Jamaica, Barbados) no longer play a central role in the lives of their British-born and -raised grand-children due to the "enculturation to certain 'British' norms and values for the third generation of Caribbeans"—they often serve as a "latent net-work." Latent networks provide support and well-being for younger family members.[6]

Dominican families are an ideal source for the study of intergenera-tional relations. Family and kinship ties are the most important basis of support and organization among Dominicans, both abroad and in the Dominican Republic. Grandparents are significant socializing agents in Dominican families. Moreover, grandparents may be an especially criti-cal resource for the large and growing number of Dominicans in single-parent families in the United States.[7]

The study of the family life of low-skilled Dominican immigrants brings out how it has been structured by state policies, including those related to immigration and to social provisioning. A focus on aging im-migrants is important because the elderly are more likely than those in other age groups to depend on the state and its institutions for services and sustenance.[8] At the same time, aging immigrants may return to their origin societies, creating shifts in family and household arrange-ments and the authority structures and social practices of family life. Increasingly expensive housing and a rising cost of living may encour-age return migration. Moreover, because many immigrants see their mi-gration as centered on work, the transition away from or out of paid employment heightens questions of belonging and membership. Indeed, return migration resonates with dominant constructions of aging, that is, as a process characterized by economic, social, and physical decline[9] and informed by discourses of "home" and the dangers of urban life linked to old age.[10]

The analysis of multigenerational relations in this chapter is framed by a transnational perspective. Dominican immigration is highly transna-tional, and the transnational nature of migration is reflected in accounts[11] that document how families "operate across borders, through the regu-lar circulation of goods, resources, individuals and information."[12] Indeed, as Baldassar points out, "family identities and kin relations can be main-tained across time and distance and are not necessarily or completely de-termined by particular localities or by state borders."[13]

This chapter also approaches multigenerational relations with attention to unpaid, informal caregiving. Caregiving is an important component of multigenerational relations; it often entails the care of a spouse, child, parent, or grandchild and refers to different forms of support, including emotional, companionship, and instrumental. In transnational families, relations are spread across space and caregiving takes place in multiple contexts. Caregiving is relevant when exploring the realm of grandparents, particularly grandmothers, because social and familial expectations construct it as women's work.[14] However, the nature and construction of caregiving is contested; multigenerational relations in a transnational context provide a fertile context to explore this dynamic.

In the pages that follow, I draw upon long-term observation and interviews with more than sixty Dominican immigrant residents who are part of an extended family. Members of the Castillo (pseudonym) family reside in and outside of New York City and in Mao, a rural community in the northwest region of the Dominican Republic. My observations of Castillo family members have been ongoing over a period of twelve years (1995–2007). This long-term observation allows me to describe and assess how the complex family trajectories shift over time. Most studies of immigrant families rely on cross-sectional data or short-term observations that may misrepresent the nature of dynamic family relationships[15] and give short shrift to the many complexities of immigrant family life. A longitudinal, ethnographic approach can better explore and contextualize the changing nature of multi- and intergenerational relationships. The richness that results from this research strategy outweighs its disadvantages, in particular, its limited scope and generalizability.

The Castillo family was chosen because of its large size, both in terms of generations and number of family members, its concentration in New York City, and its cohesiveness, all of which facilitated observation and interaction with all family members. The Castillo family migration chain is both different from and similar to other family migration chains from the Caribbean. Like the Domínguez family described by Vivian Garrison and Carol Weiss,[16] the initial Castillo migrants had relatively low levels of education compared to the overall U.S. population[17] and, like most Dominican immigrants in the United States, were incorporated into low-wage jobs. However, the Domínguez family relied much more extensively on clandestine migration and unlawful strategies for obtaining legal status, such as various kinds of marriage arrangements, overstaying tourist visas, and using false passports. Unlike the middle-class family group from Dominica described by Karen Fog Olwig,[18] the Castillos migrated primarily to work, rather than to pursue educational goals and professional employment.

The Castillo Family Diaspora

Not long after the fall of the dictator Rafael Trujillo in 1961, the Castillos' world in the Dominican Republic was beginning to be shaped by the expansion of commerce, the development of industry, and the massive outmigration to the United States, as well as the growth of towns and cities that characterized the post-Trujillo era.[19] Large numbers of Dominican immigrants arrived in the United States in the 1960s, 1970s, and 1980s, mostly through family reunification policies.[20] In 2000, according to census figures, there were almost 800,000 persons of Dominican ancestry living in the U.S. mainland, just under 70 percent of them foreign-born and about two-thirds living in the New York / northern New Jersey metropolitan areas.

The first member of the Castillo family to migrate to the United States, Zena, left the sending community of Mao in 1969 when she was twenty-eight years old. Female social networks facilitated Zena's migration, a pattern characteristic of Caribbean immigration flows.[21] After a short stay in Puerto Rico, where Zena worked as a nanny, she went to New York City. Her brother followed; in turn, he petitioned for Julia, their mother, who subsequently filed a petition for her remaining six children. (Filing an immigration petition is the first step in applying for an immigration visa for a family member.) Five of these six children subsequently migrated to the United States.[22] As of 2007, the family spanned five generations[23] and included ninety-two members, eight of whom resided in the Dominican Republic. The family consisted of four groups: eight children of Julia, twenty-seven grandchildren, fifty-two great-grandchildren, and four great-great grandchildren (see Fig. 1).

The Castillos, like other Dominican immigrants in the 1970s and 1980s, converged on New York City, relying on family networks to secure housing and employment. They integrated into low-wage, segregated labor markets, mostly in manufacturing. As industrialized employment declined in New York, later arrivals shifted into low-end jobs in the service sector. The Castillo family members settled in Manhattan communities inhabited by earlier waves of immigrants, including Puerto Ricans and Cubans, and later Dominicans, facilitating the development of ethnic and transnational identities.[24] Later arrivals bypassed traditional settlement areas in Manhattan, moving to more affordable, but poorer, multiracial neighborhoods outside of Manhattan, mostly in the Bronx.[25]

FIGURE 1. *The Castillo Family, 2007*

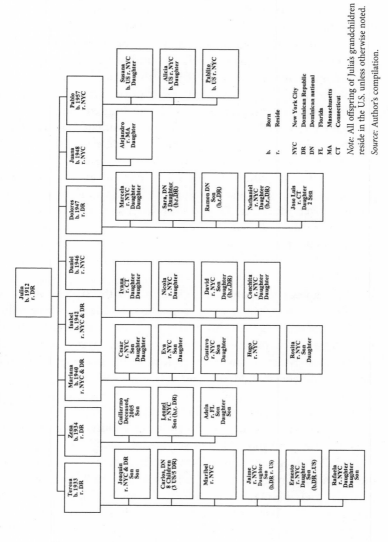

Note: All offspring of Julia's grandchildren reside in the U.S. unless otherwise noted.

Source: Author's compilation.

b.   Born
r.   Reside

NYC   New York City
DR   Dominican Republic
DN   Dominican national
FL   Florida
MA   Massachusetts
CT   Connecticut

Generations of Intergenerational Ties: Julia and her Daughters

Julia, born in 1912, is the head of the Castillo family, and at the time of this writing, lives in the Dominican Republic. A brief look at her family situation provides a context for analyzing the intergenerational ties that characterize the subsequent generations of the Castillo family.

Julia's five daughters came of age in the 1930s, 1940s, and 1950s. During these decades, which were the heart of the Trujillo era, the Dominican Republic was an agrarian society with limited industrial capacity, a low literacy rate, and a small gross national product.[26] Julia's relationships with her children were shaped by the economic difficulties of the time as well as the insecurities that women faced in a society where men were often absent from family life. Although Julia's husband, Lilo, contributed part of his wages to household support, this income was not household property over which Julia could exercise direct control, and his contribution was often affected by such factors as his involvement with other women. In a pattern not unusual among Dominican families, Julia's husband had two families; he had six children with Julia and five with his second "wife."[27]

Julia's difficult economic situation shaped the nature of intergenerational relationships; she worked long hours outside the home, selling food at a local marketplace, and had little energy to focus on providing a warm and nurturing environment for her children.[28] Many of Julia's children describe her as harsh, and they remember the beatings they endured as children. Moreover, children, especially girls, were expected to contribute to the household by helping to cook, clean, and care for younger siblings. Given the small size of her house, Julia, like many other poor Dominican women, was hard pressed to raise her children in domestic privacy; dwellings were not thought of as private retreats.[29]

As Julia's daughters formed their own families, many stayed close to their mother, relying on her to help raise their children, especially when they left their hometown in search of opportunities elsewhere. Indeed, Julia provided a base from which her children could, as Plaza[30] has put it in another context, "take on whatever new challenge came" their way. Several moved out of Mao, to Puerto Rico and Santo Domingo, in search of better economic opportunities. Eventually, four of Julia's five daughters, with and without husbands, built houses near hers, two of which are located on either side of her house.[31]

Julia's daughters—Teresa, Isabel, Mariana, Zena, and Juana—had strong ties with their own children, re-creating the strong, mother-centered households characteristic of their upbringing. Their relationships with their children reflect the continued importance of children for women's economic and social status and the prevalence of men's extramarital liaisons. Although Julia's daughters were better off than their mother—none worked in domestic service or in vending as their mother did for so many years—they also struggled with husbands who were *machista* (macho) or *mujeriegos* (womanizers). By the 1960s, migration to the United States held out possibilities to women, including the hope for a better life and more liberal ideals about marriage.[32]

Transnational Family Networks

Over time, Julia's daughters established themselves and their families in the United States. The daughters returned frequently to Mao, usually staying in their own home or with a relative. They could be called, in today's language, "transnationals," retaining a foot in two worlds, a story told in much of the recent literature on transnational migration.[33]

Family reunification immigration policies, which allowed Julia's daughters to petition for their spouses and minor children, played a key role in structuring outmigration from the Dominican Republic and settlement in the United States. Unlike other migration streams, where parents could not or did not bring children with them, Julia's daughters filed petitions for their children as soon as they could, and their children arrived in the United States no more than five years after their mothers had received their own visas. Julia's grandchildren did not experience a "care drain"[34] in the Dominican Republic; many of Julia's children were cared for by extended family members, and many report, albeit a good many years later, that they scarcely noticed when their parents were away. Most of Julia's grandchildren came to the United States in their late teens or early twenties. (The youngest arrived at the age of eleven and the oldest was thirty-six; Julia's youngest son's children are the exception in that three are U.S.-born.) Apart from Teresa's children, who were older when they migrated, and Pablo's (the youngest son's) children, who were born in the United States, Julia's grandchildren had their childhood socialization in Mao and their adult socialization, including entry into waged work, in New York City. This is significant because these children had multiple reference groups, both in the United States and in the Dominican Republic. Moreover, they all spoke Spanish fluently, further consolidating their identities as Dominicans and interchange with the Dominican Republic. Transnational and panethnic identities were also bolstered by residence in Spanish-speaking neighborhoods and by Spanish language media in the United States.

In New York City, Dominican immigrants reside in communities marked by substandard housing, poor social and educational opportunities, and racism.[35] Strong ties among family members helped the daughters to cope with the difficulties they faced in New York. Interdependence was not only a response to their incorporation in low-wage, segregated labor markets and expensive housing markets, but also a way to create a safe space. The daughters encouraged their children to look within the family to meet their physical and emotional needs;[36] Julia's grandchildren thus often secured independent housing at a relatively late age and sometimes only after they had their own children.[37] In many cases, they found a place to live close to their parents, sometimes in the same neighborhood or even the same apartment building.

In the case of smaller families, such as those of Juana and Zena, intensive patterns of nuclear family co-residence and interdependence have been less feasible because of small family size, divorce and separation of family members due to return migration, and settlement outside of New York. In 2007, Juana's only child lived in Massachusetts; of Zena's two surviving children only one lived in New York City.

Aging, the State, and Caring Relations

By the mid-1990s, Julia's daughters were in their fifties and sixties. Their families had been living in or visiting the United States for an average of fifteen years. By this time, their residences had stabilized, their children had begun to work and form their own families, and they were considering returning to the Dominican Republic. Between 1995 and 2005, Julia's daughters struggled to maintain a sense of belonging in the United States as they faced numerous challenges: economic vulnerability as aging women, increasing health problems, concerns about access to state resources, changing needs of their children and grandchildren, a desire for leisure, and a need to feel valued and valuable.

One important factor that has shaped the nature of multigenerational relations in the daughters' families is state assistance. Because Julia's daughters and their husbands had worked in the United States they were eligible for various kinds of benefits. For example, Teresa's husband, Pedro, began receiving Supplemental Security Income (SSI) in 1990. Isabel's and Mariana's husbands received disability benefits after about a decade in the United States. Several other unmarried sisters (Zena, Juana) received SSI after working in the United States for various periods of time, due to injury or health problems. Several of the sisters have also qualified for and received subsidized housing for the elderly.

State aid has both solidified and disrupted relationships with children and grandchildren. For example, several of Julia's daughters have obtained subsidized apartments in a complex for the elderly in New York City. Teresa has used the apartment she rents with her husband Pedro as a gathering place for her family in New York City. Accustomed to a busy social life—Teresa and Pedro's home in Mao was once a well-known gathering place that also housed Pedro's thriving business—and strongly invested in a caring identity, Teresa does her best to forge connections to her children and grandchildren in the United States. She is a good cook; she prepares "authentic" Dominican food as a way to draw her family to her and to feel valuable.

On the other hand, public housing can be disruptive to family. City-owned housing for the elderly imposes restrictions on occupancy that contradict how immigrants see their ideal living arrangements. Consider the case of Teresa and Pedro, who live in a subsidized apartment when they are in the United States. According to city regulations, only the elderly may live in the apartment with a spouse or partner. However, Teresa and Pedro do not like being alone when they are in the United States, that is, without regular contact with family members and, to a lesser degree, close family friends. Sharing an apartment with their children is a way to minimize social isolation, draw their children closer, and build social capital. Over a period of several years, Teresa and Pedro's subsidized apartment, despite its small size, housed several of their children and grandchildren and has been the center of many family social gatherings. On one occasion, neighbors complained that the apartment was being occupied illegally. At that time, one of Pedro and Teresa's children lived there for a year with his recently arrived wife and two children. Pedro and Teresa were investigated by the N.Y.C. Housing Authority and Teresa's son and his family left, although the agency did not evict Teresa and Pedro.

Aging has added other dimensions to intergenerational relations. Although Teresa and her sisters are strongly tied to their children and grandchildren, caring for grandchildren has become more difficult as they have aged. For example, Isabel and Mariana entered the United States in the early 1980s, after which they petitioned for their husbands and children, who arrived between the ages of twelve and nineteen. Isabel and Mariana worked sporadically in various manufacturing jobs, combining paid employment with domestic labor. Their children also found work in low-wage manufacturing and service jobs, and several began their own small businesses. Over the years, Isabel and Mariana have taken on much of the responsibility for the domestic labor of the household and played a major role in raising several of their grandchildren.

Caring for grandchildren, cleaning, and cooking often fall disproportionately on the shoulders of aging immigrant women; domestic and caring labor is not only difficult for women, but it can isolate them. For example, in 1996, fifteen years after Isabel first came to New York, three of her four adult children, then in their late twenties, continued to reside in the family's household in Washington Heights. Isabel felt unfairly burdened with the work of the household. She reported that neither her husband nor her children helped with the household labor, with childcare, or with regular contributions to household expenses. Isabel also has had ongoing conflicts with her youngest daughter, Conchita. In 1998, Conchita's two children were five and two years old. Isabel temporarily assumed custody of the children because her daughter was continually absent from the household and her children were about to be taken by the city welfare agency.

Julia's daughters and their husbands envision "retirement" in the Dominican Republic. Both Isabel's and Mariana's husbands prefer being there because it is more restful and they find the slower pace more conducive to their health. When their grandchildren were young, Isabel and Mariana would sometimes bring them back with them when they visited the Dominican Republic. By 2007, when both Isabel and Mariana were spending much of the year in the Dominican Republic, their "partial return" had resolved some of the tensions of their family situation in New York.

However, reliance on state resources, particularly in the form of subsidized health care and housing, complicates permanent return owing to the requirement to spend time in the United States. In the case of Isabel, ties to medical and welfare institutions in the United States pulled her and her husband back to New York, illustrating how state resources can help to organize family relations. The chronic health problems of Isabel's husband, which had become increasingly severe with age, have structured their mobility; he has had several serious heart attacks and is diabetic.

Although they use some medical services in the Dominican Republic, the cost of health care there has increased, making the purchase of health care services on a regular basis prohibitively expensive. Isabel's medical needs have also increased over time and she has developed relationships with various medical personnel and institutions in New York City.

Mariana and her husband returned to New York in 2000, in part to help several of her children and grandchildren. Her eldest son's wife had left him and their two children, ages three and eight. The son and his children moved back to the family's apartment, relying on Mariana for child care. Mariana also helped her daughter Evelyn with her two children when Evelyn moved back to the family's apartment after her husband died. Mariana's other son relocated to an apartment downstairs; when she is in New York, Mariana watches his children after school and on weekends.

"License to Leave": Going Back and Forth

As immigrant parents and grandparents travel between the Dominican Republic and the United States and change residences, their influence over children and grandchildren is constantly being renegotiated because they spend long periods of time apart. These separations and disruptions can be difficult for children and grandchildren who come to depend on their parents and grandparents for different forms of support or, in some cases, have developed strategies to manage without such support.

When Teresa comes to stay in New York for several months, she complains that she often feels alone "entre los cuatro paredes" (between the four walls) or "encaramado en un apartamento" (high up in an apartment). Unlike some of her sisters who "have enlarged their knowledge of and access to the world beyond the household,"[38] Teresa often complains of feeling "ill at ease" and "homesick"[39] in New York. She asserts the moral superiority of small-town life over city life, invoking discourses of "homecoming"[40] based on the fear of urban crime and the perception that proper neighborly interaction is absent in the city.[41]

These concerns were common among Julia's daughters, and granted them what has been called "license to leave." The concept, discussed by Baldassar,[42] suggests something akin to "legitimacy of purpose."[43] More specifically, "license to leave" refers to whether migration and travel (between the United States and the Dominican Republic) are seen as appropriate.

Other difficulties in family relations encourage return and grant a "license to leave." Aging immigrants find their influence or authority contested by children and grandchildren who are more "American" in their views. Teresa and her sisters often complain, after being in the United States for a short time, that their children and grandchildren (now mostly teenagers or young adults) are less receptive to the kinds of care that they can provide. The opportunities for getting together (with grandparents) are limited by the pressures of a "modern" lifestyle and the difficulty of travel in large cities.[44] The grandchildren's behavior and attitudes, shaped in part by the urban surroundings in which they have been raised, reflect their social distance from their grandparents' world.

Teresa notices that her grandchildren in the United States are less respectful of her than Dominican customs dictate, calling her by her nickname instead of *abuela* (grandmother). Language barriers affect relations with grandchildren in the United States as well. Although most of the Castillo grandchildren speak Spanish, they lack the proficiency of their parents, and many prefer to speak English. This can create misunderstandings and tension, contributing to what Luis Guarnizo describes as the distress of immigrant parents who experience the incompatibility between their own cultural identity and the one their grandchildren acquire in New York.[45]

"License to leave" helps to explain how Teresa and her sisters manage the emotional strain of moving back and forth between the United States and the Dominican Republic, despite being reluctant to leave their children and grandchildren behind in the United States. The needs of other family members in the Dominican Republic and their views of aging help to justify their return. Teresa has a complex family network in the Dominican Republic, including two sons, several grandchildren (one of whom Teresa raised like a daughter), and a great-great-grandson.[46] Several of these family members rely on her for care. Teresa is especially attached to her granddaughter, whom she counts on to care for her when she is "old."

Teresa's sisters are drawn back to other family members living in the Dominican Republic, particularly to their elderly mother, Julia. Intergenerational ties have come full circle, as Zena and Mariana help to care for Julia when they are in Mao. Teresa's sisters and their husbands also see themselves as better off in the Dominican Republic and, despite the absence of children and grandchildren, anticipate that they will be better cared for in Mao as they age.

The contested nature of welfare, particularly as manifested in the 1996 Welfare Reform Act, has complicated the way some aging immigrants think about return. Sending-state initiatives such as dual citizenship have also contributed to changing sentiments surrounding life in the United States and the Dominican Republic. These developments have pushed some older immigrants to reclaim their sense of "home" in the Dominican Republic and reject U.S.-based retirement while at the same time seeking out U.S. citizenship as a form of insurance that guarantees access to "social rights."[47] After the welfare reform legislation of 1996, Teresa and Pedro, like many immigrants, became concerned about their standing in the United States as legal permanent residents.[48] Although Teresa and Pedro did not become U.S. citizens, all of Teresa's U.S.-resident sisters and their husbands naturalized. U.S. citizenship secured their access to basic social rights and also facilitated their travel abroad. Since the Dominican Republic now allows dual citizenship, they could retain their Dominican citizenship as well.

Aware that immigrants in the United States are often seen as undeserving recipients of welfare, Teresa and her sisters have responded in a number of ways. Teresa distances herself from notions of "undeservingness" by saying that she would like to have worked in the United States but was unable to do so owing to a variety of medical conditions. She claims that she never received benefits in the United States, although she has accessed some, including food stamps and Medicaid-funded health services for short periods of time. She says that her husband and children have worked in the United States. Moreover, Teresa claims her identity as a "Dominican" by reaffirming her preference for living in the Dominican Republic.

The elderly's autonomy, facilitated by their receipt of state aid, can sometimes create tensions with children and grandchildren, and again evokes the notion of "license to leave." For example, some of Teresa's children feel that since their parents are now "old," they should no longer be traveling back and forth so frequently, which they see as a waste of money. Others complain about the burden of accommodating parents when they are in the United States. Loading her bulging suitcases in the car before leaving for the airport, one of Teresa's sons remarked: "Mamá no hace nada aquí; gasta cuarto en el viaje" ("Mama doesn't do anything except spend money on the trip"). Moreover, adult children cannot rely on their mothers' child care in the Dominican Republic during the summer if they have gone to spend time in the United States. Rafaela, Teresa's daughter, has a different perspective, complaining that her mother should stay longer in the United States to help with her children.

Julia's Grandchildren: Knitting and Unknitting Family Networks

Four of Teresa's five children who migrated to the United States continue to reside in New York City. Over time, and in the absence of her parents, one of Teresa's daughters, Rafaela, has come to act as the head of the extended family (that is, her brothers and sisters and their children) in the United States. Rafaela, like her mother, is deeply invested in a caring identity. She is married to a Guyanese man, has three children, and does not work outside of the home. In 2002, Rafaela's husband bought a home in a suburban area of the Bronx. They have raised their children in what Annette Lareau calls the "natural growth" model, keeping them strongly integrated into the Guyanese and Dominican extended families.[49]

The capital that Rafaela has acquired through her marriage, her relationship to her in-laws, and her continuous residence in the United States have helped to legitimize her role as the head of the family. She performs a great deal of kin work, hosting family parties and get-togethers and keeping in contact with members of the extended family in both the United States and the Dominican Republic through telephone calls and visits. Kin work among her family members in New York City has increased Rafaela's influence, while her mother's has declined. As Micaela Di Leonardo[50] notes, taking on or ceding domestic tasks is clearly related to acquiring or divesting oneself of power within kin networks.

Teresa's declining influence on her U.S.-based family is part of the underlying basis for her struggles with her children. Generational clashes over the conduct of family life characterize some of the struggles between mothers and their children, particularly daughters. As might be expected, Teresa and her sisters are concerned about how their grandchildren are faring in the United States. Teresa makes critical comments when meals are bought from restaurants or stores rather than cooked, when mothers are not home to receive children after school, or when children are cared for by strangers. Depicting herself as a devoted and selfless mother, Teresa criticizes her daughters or (more commonly) her daughters-in-law if they focus more on themselves through spending time on their hair, clothing, and socializing rather than dedicating themselves to family. In close-knit immigrant communities, women often use notions of "good mothering" and chaste sexuality as a way to discipline other women;[51] gossip is a potent means of enforcing these notions.[52]

Despite these tensions, Rafaela still maintains a close relationship with her parents through phone calls and visits. She views her parents as a source of emotional support and a resource for her children. Although Rafaela generally gets along well with her in-laws, she feels marginalized in her husband's extended Guyanese family, in part because "Dominicans" are seen as inferior. Moreover, Rafaela worries about who will take care of her parents in the Dominican Republic, especially now that they have more health problems. Similar to what Baldassar[53] discusses in the case of Italian immigrants in Australia, Rafaela feels guilty about the perceived inability to meet family obligations due to her residence in the United States.

Other children have sought to break away from the family, and the attempt to do so reflects, at least in part, gendered struggles over the nature of family life. Some children, such as Zena's daughter Adela and Josefina's son Alejandro, have made a definitive split with their families by moving far away. Several others remain in New York City but do not actively socialize with extended family members, often to evade the social controls inherent in the family network.

Isabel's eldest daughter, Ivana, has reluctantly acted as the head of her family since she moved to Connecticut with her brother seven years ago. Moving accomplished several goals, including extracting herself from the orbit of her husband and improving her quality of life. Ivana's relationship with her husband had deteriorated over the years, and she was able to definitively cut ties with him once she left the city. Also, she objected to the way that the family catered to one of her sisters (Conchita), who was irresponsible and did not look after her children.

Since the move, Ivana has struggled with the expectation that she take on much of the caring labor and kin work in her extended family. Ivana has been called upon to host family gatherings and to assume a surrogate parent role with her sister's children. She took in Conchita's two daughters for a year after she first moved to Connecticut and later had them on weekends. She also helped look after Nicola's daughter after Nicola moved to Connecticut.

Ivana's situation represents the complexity of extended family relations. Ivana has attempted to carve out more space for herself and her daughters by distancing herself from her mother and sisters. However, to do so, she had to rely on her brother, who helped her purchase the Connecticut home. Her sisters, who are both raising their children without husbands, have maintained their families through reliance on extended family members.[54]

Mostly due to her economic situation, Ivana cannot completely disengage from her family obligations. She would like to sell the house and live on her own with her two daughters, but her brother does not have the money to buy her out of her half of the house. He was recently laid off from his job and has incurred debt from a failed business investment. Despite working two jobs, Ivana has acquired more than $8,000 in credit card debt over the past decade.

Mariana's two daughters have also struggled to separate from their extended family. Evelyn went abroad to marry, rejecting Dominican men as too macho. She married a Venezuelan man, but the family reacted to him poorly, claiming that he was addicted to drugs, which he took when suffering from depression. Evelyn and her husband, who later committed suicide, only rarely socialized with the extended family. Evelyn's sister married and moved out of her family's home. Although both sisters maintain close relationships with their mother, they each have full-time jobs, utilize non-family sources of childcare (i.e., after-school programs), and socialize outside the larger family circle.

Julia's Great Grandchildren: Maintaining Transnational Ties

A focus on Teresa's children and grandchildren demonstrates a range of intergenerational and transnational relationships within a segment of the Castillo family and shows how relationships between grandparents, adult children, and grandchildren develop over time and space. Children and grandchildren who emigrated at older ages and who have parents with stronger ties to the Dominican Republic have maintained active linkages to their country of origin.

Teresa played a crucial role in the care and socialization of many of her grandchildren, both when she was living in the Dominican Republic and during extended periods of residence in New York. She has worked to maintain relationships among various family members, through kin work and caring labor. Grandchildren born in Mao—for example, the children of Ernesto and Jaime, who were in their early thirties when they migrated in 1991— illustrate cross-border relationships. Not only did Teresa help care for these grandchildren as infants in the Dominican Republic, she also helped care for them after they and their parents moved to New York. Once the children arrived in New York, both Jaime and Ernesto relied on family members, including Teresa and her husband, to help care for their children there. Moreover, some of Teresa's grandchildren have traveled back and forth—for example, Jaime's son lived in Mao for the better part of his adolescence, in pursuit of his dream of becoming a professional baseball player. His residence in the Dominican Republic was facilitated by extended family there, including Teresa and his maternal grandmother, and transnational baseball networks.

Teresa also maintained contact with her U.S.-born grandchildren, through intensive contacts while visiting the United States or during their visits to Mao. Her relationships with her eldest son Joaquin's children became stronger when the children were older and were sent back to Mao. Joaquin, who obtained legal residence in 1977 through his wife, was not as close to Teresa, partly due to conflicts between Teresa and his wife and partly because he grew up with his grandmother Julia. Moreover, in New York City, Joaquin lived in Brooklyn, visiting other family members in the Bronx infrequently. Yet Teresa and her husband have been instrumental in maintaining Joaquin and his son's continued ties to the Dominican Republic. Joaquin and his wife built a large home in Mao. Concerns about the dangerous and corrupting influence of "the street" in New York neighborhoods and, in some cases, the availability of educational opportunities in the Dominican Republic have helped to construct life in Mao not only as a "safe space" but also as a place of opportunity for children, particularly boys and young men.[55] Joaquin's sons returned every summer and spent several years going to school in Mao; his younger son is currently pursuing a four-year university degree in Santiago and visits with Teresa frequently.

Rafaela relied heavily on her parents and siblings for support, particularly when her eldest daughter was born. At that point, she was not yet married to the father of her child. Over time, as her relationship with her children's father stabilized, their three children became more strongly integrated into their father's extended family network. However, they maintain strong ties to Teresa due to Rafaela's close relationship to her parents and the kin work Teresa performs.

The durable cross-border ties of Teresa's grandchildren reflect a variety of factors, including the relatively late age of migration of Teresa's children and grandchildren, Teresa's established middle-class position in Mao, and the resources and social capital that she and her family have amassed there. An interesting contrast is that of Dolores, the only child of Julia's to be denied a visa and who subsequently never left the Dominican Republic. Dolores has three children in the United States, all of whom were petitioned for by a spouse.[56] Yet she is unable to draw her children back, and her children are unwilling to petition for her to go to the United States. Having been left behind by her children, and abandoned by her husband, Dolores has had to rely on family members, including her mother, for help. She has little social and economic capital to attract her children and grandchildren in the United States to her.

Two other sisters of Teresa, Mariana and Isabel, arrived with younger children, whom they raised in the United States, and have led more settled lives there. As a result, they and their children have developed deeper ties to the United States. Although they lack the deep social ties in Mao that Teresa and her husband have accrued, they all own homes in Mao, and as they have aged they have spent more time there. Several have pulled some of their children and grandchildren back with them. Another of Teresa's sisters, Zena, now lives most of the year in Mao, helping to care for Julia. Zena's eldest son died last year; he is buried in Mao. Her remaining son, who has a son living in Mao, returns there frequently from New York. Two of Mariana's sons have begun returning more frequently to Mao, where they have invested in land with their father.[57] Isabel recently spent several months in Mao to observe the one-year anniversary of her husband's death. She took her two granddaughters with her, enrolling them in school there.

Conclusion

Many "young old" Dominicans, particularly women, are embedded in a web of close and interdependent relationships with children and grandchildren. The continued importance of grandparents in the lives of Dominican adult children and grandchildren reflects the nature of incorporation of immigrants into low-wage labor markets in the United States and the context of settlement in ethnic, transnationalized communities. Young-old Dominican women's embeddedness in family life, and the care they provide, including care from a distance, are central to understanding the nature of family dynamics.

As Julia's daughters have aged, they have struggled with the contradictory demands of maintaining relationships and performing caring labor for husbands, adult children, and grandchildren in the United States as well as the social forces that channel them back to their community of origin. Immigrant grandparents' access to state resources in the United States has given them a degree of power and autonomy vis-à-vis their children and grandchildren. It has allowed aging immigrants, especially women, to exert greater control over their domestic and caring labor and claim more leisure through travel to the Dominican Republic and independent living in the United States. State assistance has also allowed them to help their children and grandchildren and has, in effect, subsidized the incorporation of younger generations into the United States.

Robust ties to the Dominican Republic, however, have resulted in long periods of absence of the "young-old" grandparents from the United States. To a certain extent, and depending on adult children's economic and social capital, some adult daughters have stepped into the breach—recreating the kinds of kinship networks and performing the caring labor that their own mothers provided.[58] Larger families (those of Mariana, Teresa, and Isabel) are better able to provide support and care for children and grandchildren in the United States. Not surprisingly, when adult children rely especially heavily on siblings and parents for assistance, there is more conflict between and within generations over caregiving.

Some grandparents have pulled some of their children and grandchildren back with them to the Dominican Republic, reshifting the locus of family activity there and helping to maintain transnational family relations among the younger generations. Although most of Julia's great grandchildren are settled in the United States, their connections to the Dominican Republic are facilitated by their grandparents' residence there.

This chapter has focused on one extended family—and in one particular time period. Clearly, many different patterns and permutations develop over time that will, no doubt, be complicated further in the years to come as a growing number in yet another generation—the great-grandchildren of many original migrants to the United States—come of age.

ACKNOWLEDGMENTS

The author gratefully acknowledges the contributions of Mary Powers, Jeanne Flavin, Nancy Foner, Rodolfo Soriano-Nunez, and Ruth Cullen.

NOTES

1. This term is used by Baldassar (2007).

2. Da 2003.

3. Smith 2002.

4. Baldassar 2007.

5. Plaza 2000.

6. Bengston 2001. See also Ruiz and Silverstein 2007.

7. According to Levitt (2007), the 2000 U.S. census reported that just over 50 percent of Dominican households in the United States are female headed.

8. He 2002.

9. Biggs and Powell 2004.

10. Mills 1998.

11. For studies that address different aspects of transnational family life among Dominicans, see, among others, Garrison and Weiss 1979; Guarnizo 1997; Levitt 2001; Pessar 1995; Sørensen 2005.

12. Parreñas 2001.

13. Baldassar 2007: 276.

14. Williams and Crooks 2008. According to Karin Weyland (2004), Dominican women see themselves as "pillars of social life and family stability"—a nineteenth-century view imposed by a strong Catholic and capitalist ideology.

15. Jasso 1997.

16. Garrison and Weiss 1979.

17. Overall the Castillos have somewhat higher levels of education than the foreign-born Dominican population in the United States; according to the 2000 U.S. census, 41 percent of all Dominicans had a high school diploma or more, compared with 53 percent of the Castillos.

18. Olwig 2002.

19. The family was described in Gilbertson and Singer 2003a. The description of the family has been slightly modified since publication of that essay due to changes in family composition.

20. According to Waldinger (1996), migration from the Dominican Republic increased significantly throughout the 1960s and 1970s. Between 1980 and 2000, the population of foreign-born Dominicans in the United States grew by 315 percent. In 2000, Dominicans represented 2.1 percent of the total U.S. Hispanic population and were the fourth largest Hispanic group (Levitt 2007).

21. Dominicans have relied heavily on family reunification for entry; in 2001, almost 99 percent of all immigration was composed of persons who entered through family reunification provisions (McKay 2003).

22. Dolores, one of Julia's daughters, was petitioned but was denied a visa due to supposed health problems.

23. I use the term *generation* here to refer to family generations, that is, Julia's children, grandchildren, great grandchildren, and so on.

24. Baldassar 2007.

25. Several members of the family have moved to Florida and Connecticut.

26. Tancer 1973.

27. Unlike other countries, second families were not limited to the lower classes in the Dominican Republic.

28. Hoffert 2003.

29. Ibid.

30. Plaza 2000: 99.

31. The daughters' residential patterns reflect a general preference for matrilocal marriage residence.

32. Bolak 1997.

33. Levitt 2001.

34. Hochschild 2000.

35. City of New York, Department of City Planning, 2004; Hernandez 2002; Levitt 2007.

36. Monroy 1999.

37. See Plaza 2000 for a discussion of this.

38. Pessar 1995: 81.

39. Mills 1998.

40. Markowitz and Stefansson 2004.

41. Mills 1998.

42. Baldassar 2007.

43. Discussed by Mason (1999) and cited in Baldassar 2007.

44. Plaza 2000.

45. Guarnizo 1997: 301.

46. Family-based migration chains often have been perceived to be like a migration tidal wave, pulling all eligible persons in its wake. But it should be emphasized in the Dominican case that not all eligible persons want to be petitioned for, nor is petitioning axiomatic. Teresa's eldest son, for example, has no need or desire for legal residency in the United States. For the Dominican elite, having a tourist visa rather than legal permanent residence is a sign of high status.

47. As originally passed, the Welfare Act rendered legal permanent residents—including those who were participating in the programs at the time the law became effective—ineligible for public assistance benefits. Since the enactment of the Welfare Act, the federal government has restored eligibility for some of the benefits from which immigrants were originally barred, and some states and localities have provided substitute benefits.

48. Teresa and Pedro did not naturalize, although her four sisters (and their husbands) in the United States did.

49. Lareau 2003.

50. Di Leonardo 1987.

51. See Brennan 2004: 174.

52. Monroy 1999; Brennan 2004.

53. Baldassar 2007.

54. Nicola, for example, whose daughter was six in 2005, married a younger man in the Dominican Republic and brought him to the United States; they do not live together, although he sees his daughter. Dedicating herself to paid employment and rejecting marriage, Nicola has more leisure time and income and fewer household responsibilities than if she was in a more conventional marriage.

55. The gendered nature of immigrant parents' regulation of children is discussed in Thorne et al. 2003.

56. Her three children have not formed a cohesive network in the United States due in part to the fact that they were petitioned by their spouses.

57. See Pessar 1995: 81, for a similar description.

58. See Young and Wilmott 1957 for a similar discussion.

REFERENCES

Baldassar, Loretta. 2007. "Transnational Families and Aged Care: The Mobility of Care and the Migrancy of Ageing." *Journal of Ethnic and Migration Studies* 33: 275–97.

Bauer, Elaine, and Paul Thompson. 2004. "She's Always the Person with a Very Global Vision: The Gender Dynamics of Migration, Narrative Interpretation and the Case of Jamaican Transnational Families." *Gender & History* 16: 334–75.

Bean, Frank, and Gillian Stevens. 2003. *America's Newcomers and the Dynamics of Diversity.* New York: Russell Sage Foundation.

Bengtson, Vern L. 2001. "Beyond the Nuclear Family: The Increasing Importance of Multigenerational Bonds." *Journal of Marriage and the Family* 63: 1–16.

Biggs, Simon, and Jason L. Powell. 2004. "A Foucauldian Analysis of Old Age and the Power of Social Welfare." *Journal of Aging and Social Policy* 12: 93–112.

Bolak, Hale Chin. 1997. "When Wives Are Major Providers." *Gender & Society* 11: 409–33.

Brennan, Denise. 2004. *What's Love Got to Do with It: Transnational Desires and Sex Tourism in the Dominican Republic.* Durham, NC: Duke University Press.

Chee, Mariana W. L. 2005. *Taiwanese American Transnational Families: Women and Kin Work.* New York: Routledge.

City of New York, Department of City Planning. 2004. *The Newest New Yorkers 2000: Immigrant New York in the New Millennium.*

Da, Wei Wei. 2003. "Transnational Grandparenting: Child Care Arrangements among Migrants from the People's Republic of China to Australia." *Journal of International Migration and Integration* 4: 79–103.

Derby, Laura. 2000. "The Dictator's Seduction: Gender and State Spectacle during the Trujillo Regime." *Calaloo* 23: 1112–46.

Di Leonardo, Micaela. 1987. "The Female World of Cards and Holidays: Women, Families and the Work of Kinship." *Signs* 12: 440–53.

Duany, Jorge. 1994. *Quisqueya on the Hudson: The Transnational Identity of Dominicans in Washington Heights*. Dominican Research Monographs. New York: CUNY Dominican Studies Institute.

Foner, Nancy. 2005. *In a New Land: A Comparative View of Immigration*. New York: New York University Press.

Fuentes, Norma. 2007. "The Immigrant Experiences of Dominican and Mexican Women in the 1990s: Cross Class, Racial and Gender Boundaries or Temporary Work Spaces in New York City." Pp. 95–120 in Caroline Brettell (ed.), *Constructing Borders/Crossing Boundaries: Race, Ethnicity and Immigration*. Lanham, MD: Lexington Books.

Garrison, Vivian, and Carol I. Weiss. 1979. "Dominican Family Networks and U.S. Immigration Policy: A Case Study." *International Migration Review* 12: 264–83.

Gilbertson, Greta, and Audrey Singer. 2003a. "Gender and the Social Process of Naturalization among Dominican Immigrants." Pp. 359–78 in Pierrette Hondagneu-Sotelo (ed.), *Gender and U.S. Immigration: Contemporary Trends*. Berkeley: University of California Press.

———. 2003b. "The Emergence of Protective Citizenship in the USA: Naturalization among Dominican Immigrants in the Post-1996 Welfare Reform Era." *Ethnic and Racial Studies* 26: 25–51.

Guarnizo, Luis. 1997. "The Emergence of a Transnational Social Formation and the Mirage of Return Migration among Dominican Transmigrants." *Identities* 4: 281–322.

He, Wan. *2002 U.S. Census Bureau, Current Population Reports, Series P23-211, The Older Foreign-born Population in the United States: 2000*. Washington, DC: U.S. Government Printing Office.

Hendricks, Glenn. 1974. *The Dominican Diaspora: From the Dominican Republic to New York City—Villagers in Transition*. New York: Teachers College Press.

Hernandez, Ramona. 2002. *The Mobility of Workers under Advanced Capitalism: Dominican Migration to the United States*. New York: Columbia University Press.

Hochschild, Arlie R. 2000. "Global Care Chains and Emotional Surplus Value." Pp. 130–46 in Anthony Giddens and W. Hutton (eds.), *On the Edge: Globalization in the New Millennium*. London: Sage Publications.

Hoffert, Sylvia. 2003. *A History of Gender in America*. New York: Prentice-Hall.

Hondagneu-Sotelo, Pierrette. 1994. *Gendered Transitions: The Mexican Experiences of Immigration*. Berkeley: University of California Press.

Hondagneu-Sotelo, Pierrette, and Ernestine Avila. 1997. "I'm Here But I'm There: The Meanings of Latina Transnational Motherhood." *Gender & Society* 11: 448–71.

Jasso, Guillermina. 1997. "Migration and the Dynamics of Family Phenomena." Pp. 47–62 in Alan Booth, Ann C. Crouter, and Nancy Landale (eds.), *Immigration and the Family: Research and Policy on U.S. Immigrants*. Mahwah, NJ: Lawrence Erlbaum Associates.

Kibria, Nazli. 1993. *Family Tightrope: The Changing Lives of Vietnamese Americans*. Princeton: Princeton University Press.

Landolt, Patricia, and Wei Wei Da. 2005. "The Spatially Ruptured Practices of Migrant Families: A Comparison of Immigrants from El Salvador and the People's Republic of China." *Current Sociology* 53: 625–53.

Lareau, Annette. 2003. *Unequal Childhoods: Class, Race, and Family Life*. Berkeley: University of California Press.

Levitt, Peggy. 2001. *The Transnational Villagers*. Berkeley: University of California Press.

———. 2007. "Dominican Republic." Pp. 399–411 in Mary Waters and Reed Ueda (eds.), *The New Americans: A Guide to Immigration Since 1965*. Cambridge: Harvard University Press.

Markowitz, Fran, and Anders H. Stefansson. 2004. *Homecomings: Unsettling Paths of Return*. Lanham, MD: Lexington Books.

Mason, Jennifer. 1999. "Living Away from Relatives: Kinship and Geographical Reasoning." Pp. 156–75 in Susan McRae (ed.), *Changing Britain: Families and Households in the 1990s*. Oxford: Oxford University Press.

McKay, Ramah. 2003. "Family Reunification." *Migration Information Source*. Accessed at http://www.migrationinformation.org.

Mills, Mary Beth, 1998. "Gendered Encounters with Modernity: Labor Migrants and Marriage Choices in Contemporary Thailand." *Identities: Global Studies in Culture and Power* 5: 301–34.

Monroy, Douglas. 1999. *Rebirth: Mexican Los Angeles from the Great Migration to the Great Depression*. Berkeley: University of California Press.

Olwig, Karen Fog. 2002. "A Respectable Livelihood: Mobility and Identity in a Caribbean Family." Pp. 85–105 in Ninna Sørensen and Karen Fog Olwig (eds.), *Work and Migration: Life and Livelihood in a Globalizing World*. London: Routledge.

Parreñas, Rhacel Salazar. 2001. "Mothering from a Distance: Emotions, Gender, and Intergenerational Relations in Filipino Transnational Families." *Feminist Studies* 27: 361–90.

Pessar, Patricia. 1995. *A Visa for a Dream: Dominicans in the United States*. Boston: Allyn and Bacon.

Plaza, Dwaine. 2000. "Transnational Grannies: The Changing Family Responsibilities of Elderly African Caribbean-Born Women Resident in Britain." *Social Indicators Research* 51: 75–105.

Ruiz, Sarah A., and Merril Silverstein. 2007. "Relationships with Grandparents and the Emotional Well-Being of Late Adolescent and Young Adult Grandchildren." *Journal of Social Issues* 63: 793–808.

Skeggs, Beverley. 1997. *Formations of Class and Gender: Becoming Respectable.* London: Sage Publications.

Smith, Margo. 1973. "Domestic Service as a Channel of Upward Mobility for the Lower-Class Woman: The Lima Case." Pp. 191–208 in Ann Pescatello (ed.), *Female and Male in Latin America: Essays.* Pittsburgh: University of Pittsburgh Press.

Smith, Robert C. 2002. "Social Location, Generation and Life Course as Social Processes Shaping Second Generation Transnational Life." Pp. 145–68 in Peggy Levitt and M. Waters (eds.), *The Changing Face of Home: The Transnational Lives of the Second Generation.* New York: Russell Sage Foundation.

Sørensen, Ninna Nyberg. 2005. "Transnational Family Life across the Atlantic: The Experience of Colombian and Dominican Immigrants in Europe." Paper presented at the International Conference on Migration and Domestic Work in a Global Perspective, Wassenar, The Netherlands, May 26–29.

Stack, Carol B., and John B. Cromartie. 1992. "The Journeys of Black Children: An Intergenerational Perspective." Pp. 363–83 in Patrick C. Jobes, William F. Stinner, and John M. Mardwell (eds.), *Community, Society and Migration: Noneconomic Migration in America.* Lanham, MD: University Press of America.

Tancer, Shoshana B. 1973. "The Dominican Woman, 1940–1970." Pp. 209–30 in Ann Pescatello (ed.), *Female and Male in Latin America: Essays.* Pittsburgh: University of Pittsburgh Press.

Thorne, Barrie, Marjorie Faulstich Orellana, Wan Shun Eva Lam, and Anna Chee. 2003. "Raising Children, and Growing Up, Across National Borders." Pp. 241–62 in Pierrette Hondagneu-Sotelo (ed.), *Gender and U.S. Immigration: Contemporary Trends.* Berkeley: University of California Press.

Waldinger, Roger. 1996. *Still the Promised City? African-Americans and New Immigrants in Postindustrial New York.* Cambridge: Harvard University Press.

Waters, Mary. 1999. *Black Identities: West Indian Immigrant Dreams and American Realities.* Cambridge: Harvard University Press.

Weyland, Karin. 2004. "Dominican Women 'Con un Pie Aquí y Otro Allá': Transnational Practices at the Crossroads of Local/Global Agendas." Pp. 154–76 in Ernesto Sagás and Sintia E. Molina (eds.), *Dominican Migration: Transnational Perspectives.* Gainesville: University Press of Florida.

Williams, Allison, and Valerie A. Crooks. 2008. "Introduction: Space, Place and the Geographies of Women's Caregiving Work." *Gender, Place and Culture* 15: 243–47.

Young, Michael, and Peter Willmott. 1957. *Family and Kinship in East London.* New York: Penguin Press.

7

Parents and Children across Borders

Legal Instability and Intergenerational Relations in Guatemalan and Salvadoran Families

Cecilia Menjívar and Leisy Abrego

During a solo performance in Los Angeles,[1] the Salvadoran artist Carolina Rivera portrayed a mother who migrated without her children. After years of separation, and despite tremendous sacrifices, she is most devastated when she no longer recognizes her sons in recent photographs. Half the audience—mainly second-generation Central Americans—was in tears. Rivera's performance resonated with them, evoking the profound emotional distress associated with family separation that is not uncommon among Central American immigrants.

After nine years of separation, the Salvadoran Cabrera family was reunited in the United States.[2] The two oldest children traveled from El Salvador to join their parents and youngest sister in Atlanta. Although the family had longed for years to be reunited, the local newspaper documented the jealousies and frustrations that only eventually led to more harmonious relationships among family members.

Rigoberto Palomo may soon be separated from his family.[3] A Guatemalan undocumented immigrant, he hopes that a judge will allow him to remain with his U.S.-born children and ailing immigrant wife in Los Angeles. He worries that his absence will bring insurmountable challenges for the rest of his family—all of whom reside legally in the United States.

Immigration laws and the legal statuses they confer on immigrants powerfully shape family life for Guatemalans and Salvadorans. To a great degree, laws induce lengthy separations across borders, notable adjustment periods following reunifications, and stratified access to resources for individual members who reside together in the United States. Each of these situations is fraught with difficult, often painful, challenges that add to the complexities of family life. In this chapter we offer a glimpse into this complicated picture, with a focus on dynamics between parents and children.

Families throughout the world are experiencing long-term separation across national borders. Limited economic opportunities along with human-made and natural catastrophes drive individuals in families to opt for migration, despite the financial, physical, and emotional risks involved in international movements. In many cases and for different reasons, parents must leave their children behind,[4] creating what have been called "binational" or "transnational" families, in which "core members are located in at least two or more nation-states."[5] In recent years, many receiving countries have implemented increasingly restrictive immigration policies that include tighter border controls, more temporary worker permits, and greater restrictions on the ability to acquire permanent residence. Arguably, family separation is built into these immigration policies.[6] Noteworthy, not only have immigration laws limited migration in multiple ways, but they also have constrained immigrants already in receiving countries, making it difficult for them to obtain legal residency and diminishing the possibility for family reunification. Even for those who are eligible, the policies have created long waiting periods that can stall family reunification for years, if not decades.[7] Therefore, long-term and indefinite separations are not the exception. Instead, they have become "normalized" in the context of contemporary migration regimes.

In the United States, immigration policies (that determine the number and the type of individuals admitted and are the purview of the federal government) intersect with immigrant policies (that shape immigrant incorporation, often through local government implementation) to affect immigrants and their families' lives. Specifically, these policies create multiple obstacles to stable employment and living wages for immigrants, thus reducing the chances for economic well-being for all immigrant families, whether they are separated across borders or residing together in the United States. With few opportunities to earn enough money to significantly improve their children's living conditions, immigrant parents and their children must negotiate intergenerational dynamics within the difficult context of legal and economic restrictions.

Several studies have explored families' arrangements and coping mechanisms to stay connected across borders.[8] As this scholarship matures, empirical work underscores complexity, nuances, and negative consequences of separations. Recent feminist research has shown,[9] for instance, the tremendous emotional and social costs associated with immigration-induced family separation. In this chapter we offer a more complicated picture, analyzing both positive and negative aspects of family separation and reunification. Especially in the context of increasingly tighter immigration laws at the federal level and a series of ordinances at the state and local levels in the United States, it is important to understand the effects of immigration policies on intergenerational dynamics, whether families reside together or across borders. Undoubtedly, the nature of ruptured family arrangements, often contentious reunifications, diverse legal statuses within families, and their associated social consequences will generate increasing interest not only among academics but also among policy makers, activists, and social service providers.

For all immigrant families, intergenerational relations are framed by complex and often difficult processes of assimilation.[10] Tensions arise when parents try to maintain the family's ethnic culture while children, more exposed to forces of socialization in the United States, learn English and adapt more rapidly than their parents.[11] If parents and children expect different kinds of support from each other, the negotiations can become difficult and painful.[12] The legal statuses of individual family members are also closely implicated in the dynamics of intergenerational relations. Lengthy separation, reunification after many years, and multiple legal and economic barriers add many layers of challenges, often aggravating tensions and negotiations between parents and children and posing new complications.

Guatemalans and Salvadorans, the focus of this chapter, face particularly lengthy family separations, usually owing to their unstable legal statuses resulting from a hostile context of reception. Often, at least some children are left behind when a parent (or parents) go to the United States. Many of these immigrants are neither completely undocumented nor documented, but must, instead, straddle both legal statuses.[13] In many ways, these immigrants can be thought of as the paradigmatic case of the consequences of new immigration regimes, close to an "ideal type" in the

Weberian sense, as their experiences vividly exemplify what it means to be separated from loved ones indefinitely.[14] These immigrants' situations are tenuous and tension-filled because the threat of deportation always looms, even once they reunite, or whether they have always resided together. However, despite instability and lack of resources, Guatemalan and Salvadoran immigrant parents strive to do their best to provide for their children.

Our findings demonstrate that legal uncertainty inevitably affects intergenerational relations. Children left behind try to make sense of the situation and look for cues from parents about what they hope is a continued commitment to them. The parents longingly hope to be reunited with their children. If they do reunite, families are likely to experience difficult adjustment periods. And if they have never been apart, immigrant families that include undocumented members or members in "in-between statuses" face the challenges of stratified access to resources. In most cases, parents work several jobs, attempt to secure permanent legal status for themselves and their children, and make Herculean efforts to provide a better future for their families. The parents' efforts, suspended lives, and deferred personal dreams represent a kind of generational sacrifice. In these contexts, the parents' relations with their children are not always smooth. Nor are they solely conflictive. They reflect the complexity of deeply connected lives that are not only powerfully framed by stiff and hostile immigration policies, but are also often spread apart in different physical and social locations.

The data on which this chapter is based come from several studies. Between June 2004 and September 2006, Abrego conducted 130 in-depth interviews with Salvadoran families in the midst of long-term separation, including interviews with 83 children of migrants in El Salvador and 47 parents (25 mothers and 22 fathers) in the United States (mostly in Los Angeles). The parents' average age was forty. She recruited adolescents and young adults for the study in public and private high schools and colleges in two sections of San Salvador. Their average age was eighteen. In the United States, she located migrant parents in businesses, churches, union halls, day labor sites, public parks, and community-based organizations. The average length of separation from their children was eleven years; among the children in El Salvador, the average length of separation from their parents was nine years. Abrego also carried out a 2001 study that focused on undocumented high school and college students in Los Angeles.[15] Although that study was concerned with access to higher education, she collected several compelling stories about mixed-status families that we highlight here.

Menjívar draws on a series of studies of Latin American–origin immigrants in the Phoenix metropolitan area that she conducted between 1998 and 2004. These studies used a purposive approach to identify potential study participants, relying on the expertise of key informants in churches, community organizations, and neighborhood shops and restaurants as a way to locate informants. The study participants were selected so that all were at least eighteen years old at the time they left their home countries and arrived in Phoenix in the 1990s. Informants chose the location of the interviews—usually their homes—which provided an opportunity to gain valuable insights into their lives. The studies included fourteen Guatemalans and twenty-two Salvadorans; at least half were re-interviewed one or more times. The women ranged in age from twenty to sixty-six and the men twenty-one to sixty-two. More than half arrived in Arizona from California and the rest came directly from their respective countries.[16]

The Legal Framework and Central Americans' Lives

A hallmark of Salvadorans' and Guatemalans' legal status has been its prolonged uncertainty. From the initial years of their massive migration to the United States in the early 1980s to the present, their legal reception has been ambivalent, qualified, and cold at best. They have faced being granted only temporary permits, seemingly interminable applications, reapplications, long waiting times for their applications to be processed, and the threat of imminent deportation. All the while, the recalcitrant government stand against recognizing many of them as victims of geopolitics in the Central American region makes them ineligible for some form of legal protection. The legal framework these Central Americans confront and the consequent ambiguity in their lives locate them in a situation of "permanent temporariness"[17] or "liminal legality."[18]

Salvadorans and Guatemalans, unfortunately, are not alone in their experiences. Many immigrants in the United States as well as in other major receiving countries have faced overwhelming obstacles in the quest to obtain permanent legal status. However, the experiences of many Guatemalans and Salvadorans bring this situation into sharp relief and capture analytically what it means to live in legal ambiguity. As Salvadoran cultural critic Ana Patricia Rodríguez argues,[19] Central American immigrants "personify the (un)sung heroes of legendary border crossing."

Throughout the 1980s, many thousands of Central American immigrants fled the danger and devastation of war-torn countries, but less than 3 percent of Salvadoran and Guatemalan applicants were granted political asylum. Immigrants' rights groups lobbied on their behalf, and eventually Congress granted Temporary Protected Status (TPS) from deportation to all Salvadorans who arrived prior to September 19, 1990, but Guatemalans were not extended this protection.[20] TPS allowed Salvadorans to live and work legally in the United States for a period of eighteen months; it was extended a few times and expired in December 1994, but was extended by President Clinton for an additional nine months until it ended for good in September 1995. Close to 200,000 Salvadorans applied for TPS, but fewer resubmitted applications for the successive extensions. Some had been able to change their status to permanent residents, but others missed deadlines or, lacking access to reliable information, found the application procedure for the extensions confusing. TPS was neither asylum nor refugee status, and the only privilege it bestowed was a work permit for the duration of the dispensation.

In 1990, as a result of the settlement of a class-action suit (*American Baptist Churches vs. Thornburgh*; hereafter, *ABC* settlement) that alleged discrimination against Guatemalans and Salvadorans on the part of the Immigration and Naturalization Service, Salvadorans and Guatemalans were allowed to resubmit asylum applications. In fiscal year 1992, the success rate for Salvadoran applications increased to 28 percent, and for Guatemalan applications it went up to 18 percent.[21] Another possible pathway to legal status—legalization under the provisions of the Immigration Reform and Control Act (IRCA) of 1986—was available to only a relatively small percentage of Salvadorans and Guatemalans who arrived in the United States prior to January 1, 1982.[22] The many thousands who arrived at the height of the political conflicts in their countries before that date were ineligible for amnesty under IRCA.

To add further complexity to the legal story, benefits of the 1997 Nicaraguan Adjustment and Central American Relief Act (NACARA) were extended to some Guatemalans and Salvadorans. Salvadorans who entered the country before September 19, 1990, and Guatemalans who entered before October 1, 1990, and who had registered under the *ABC* settlement (or filed an asylum application before April 1, 1990) could be granted a "cancellation of removal."[23] Salvadorans and Guatemalans who already had been placed in deportation procedures had to appear before an immigration judge to request a cancellation of removal, and if approved, were given permanent resident status after a probationary period. Since 1998 immigrant rights groups have lobbied Congress for Salvadorans and Guatemalans—like Nicaraguans and other nationals included in NACARA—to have their status adjusted to permanent residence without hearings on a case-by-case basis, but so far these lobbying efforts have not been successful.

Although the civil conflicts officially ended in 1992 in El Salvador and in 1997 in Guatemala, immigration from both countries has continued. The structures of inequality at the root of the civil conflicts—and of emigration—are still in place, and are now exacerbated by high rates of unemployment and underemployment, as well as by high levels of violence associated with "common crime."[24] Also, the social channels for Central American migration have expanded as more and more people have relatives and friends in the United States. Furthermore, El Salvador suffered two devastating earthquakes in early 2001 that worsened many of the social, political, and economic problems left by the years of civil war. Salvadorans who arrived after the earthquakes were originally granted TPS for a period of nine months. This TPS has been extended multiple times and at the time of this writing will expire on March 9, 2009, for those who successfully re-registered between August 21 and October 22, 2007. Once again, this is temporary, not permanent, status, as made all too clear by the multiple deadlines for application and re-registration. Guatemala also endured the destruction of Hurricane Stan in late 2005, but Guatemalans who arrived after this disaster were not granted TPS.

Guatemalan and Salvadoran immigrants' legal uncertainty has been aggravated by a generalized restrictive immigration regime at federal and state levels. Most notably, the 1996 Illegal Immigration Reform and Immigrant Responsibility Act (IIRIRA) has facilitated the "removal" of hundreds of thousands of immigrants for various criminal offenses.[25] Since the passage of IIRIRA, there have been 175,802 deportations each year (compared to 69,680 the year before it passed). Those deported between 1997 and 2005 included 42,862 Salvadorans and 54,250 Guatemalans.[26] These deportations, reported almost daily in both U.S. and Central American news media, are notorious for tearing many families apart.[27] In addition, in recent years, a barrage of local-level ordinances throughout the United States have targeted undocumented immigrants—from public ordinances penalizing city contractors for hiring them to attempts to bar landlords from renting to them.[28] This multi-level, multi-pronged approach to restricting immigration may not actually decrease levels of immigration, but it makes the lives of immigrants already in the country extremely difficult.

The key point is that a large proportion of Salvadoran and Guatemalan immigrants live in the United States in an uncertain legal status. According to the 2000 U.S. census,[29] one quarter of the nation's 1,011,000 Salvadorans and 575,000 Guatemalans were naturalized citizens.[30] However, 70 percent of Salvadorans and 75 percent of Guatemalans were foreign born,[31] and the Immigration and Naturalization Service (INS) estimated that close to 60 percent of them were undocumented or protected only by temporary status arrangements.[32] In a climate of insecurity and hostility to immigrants, particularly Latinos, those in unresolved statuses find it more difficult to travel back and forth to visit families in their home countries and to bring family members to the United States, and some have been forcibly separated from loved ones through deportation. It is within this legal context that we examine intergenerational relations of Central Americans.

Intergenerational Relations

Not surprisingly, Central Americans' legal statuses shape their experiences in multiple spheres, from access to education,[33] well-paid jobs, social services, and decent housing to their involvement in churches and forms of artistic expression.[34] Legal uncertainty also affects the composition, organization, and dynamics of their families, including relations between parents and children. Understanding the dynamics of family relations among Guatemalans and Salvadorans involves considering a complex web of factors, including the broader political and economic context and immigrants' social position. A central aspect is family separations, which are linked to unstable legal statuses and deportations and are also shaped by gender, life-course stage, and ethnicity.

Guatemalan and Salvadoran families have a multiplicity of forms that involve members in different countries and with different statuses. There are families in which one or more children are non-citizens (and find themselves in various legal statuses). In some families, children are in the United States but the parent or parents are in their countries of origin; in others, the pattern is reversed. And there are families in which all members have different legal statuses. Even Michael Fix and Wendy

Zimmerman's[35] otherwise useful notion of "mixed-status families" does not capture the wide variety of family forms among Central American immigrants because their mixed-status families are not contained solely on U.S. soil or in one location in the United States. Given this complexity, we are unable to capture the full range of experiences of intergenerational relations in this chapter. What we offer is a discussion of three common scenarios that highlight different types of family arrangements and bring out the central role of family members' legal and social position for parent-child relations.

Parents and Children Who Are Separated (and Still Live Apart)

Many Salvadorans and Guatemalans cannot obtain a U.S. visa, so they travel undocumented and by land. The journey across several national borders is dangerous and costly, and most prefer not to expose their children to such hardships, opting to leave them home instead. Over time, some parents eventually send for their children, but it becomes difficult and expensive to care for the children in the United States, particularly when they live in inner cities. Thus, some parents send children back to be cared for by (usually female) relatives in the home country.[36] Whether parents leave the children back home or send them back, the result is often a lengthy and painful separation.

Remittances represent tangible forms of care for the children back home. Research has found that when the parents and children remain separated, parents are more likely to remit and, when they do, to send more than if their children are with them.[37] Our observations indicate that structural conditions, including legal status and labor market opportunities, determine the sums and frequency of remittances migrants are able to send their children. For instance, Nelson, a Salvadoran undocumented immigrant parent in Los Angeles, earns less than the minimum wage for back-breaking work. As he explains:

> You see that without papers it is very difficult to be hired just anywhere. So my brother-in-law found me a job with some Chinese owners of a company where the trailer trucks come and you pack them and unpack them. That is hard work because they don't care if one is tired, if one needs to rest, or if [the weather is] too hot or too cold. And so, since they didn't even let us rest, I messed up my back and when I told them, they pretended not to hear me, they didn't do anything. I kept complaining and in the end they

told me that if I couldn't do the work anymore, I should look for another job because they needed someone who could stay on schedule. And after that I still had to fight with them to get my last paycheck because they were saying that I worked too slowly. Until now, I still can't carry anything too heavy, so I haven't been able to find a steady job.

Because of his undocumented status, Nelson was afraid to apply for worker's compensation or to denounce the employer who fired him when he complained of back pain. Since losing the steady job, he spends most of his time at a day labor site, trying to get short-term jobs. However, this unstable employment does not generate sufficient wages to support his family in El Salvador.[38] Unfortunately, Nelson's is not an isolated case, and several immigrant parents in our studies cited similar reasons for no longer being able to work and send remittances.[39]

In El Salvador and Guatemala, children rely on remittances for their daily survival and during long-term absences from parents, and they often come to associate these sums with love. As Viviana Zelizer[40] observes, remittances not only provide vital resources for survival but also serve to mitigate the trials and uncertainty of long-term separations between parents and children. When parents are able to remit large and consistent sums of money, their children experience improved living conditions, greater access to education, and sometimes notable upward mobility in socioeconomic status. Despite the pain of separation, they are likely to appreciate their parents' sacrifices and maintain strong, positive contact with their parents. Sixteen-year-old Marisa, whose mother migrated four years earlier, describes the improvements in her life in El Salvador since her mother left with a tourist visa to join her stepfather in the United States:

Yes, you could say that we are living better now. I stopped going to public school because there were always fights there and my parents told my sister [the caregiver] to sign me up for this private school. And although I still have a hole in my heart because I miss my mother, because nothing can replace a mother, I remember how much she worked here, selling drinks at the outdoor market, and I am grateful that things are better.

Like others who benefit consistently from their parents' remittances, Marisa justifies the separation through the obvious life improvements that resulted.

Those who receive regular sums, whose life improvements are visible and tangible—through luxury items in the home or greater access to education—have *proof* that their parents continue to be committed to the family. This became apparent for Menjívar during fieldwork in Guatemala, when locals would gauge whether a woman and her children were at risk of being abandoned by a partner in the United States by looking at their expenditures on clothing, toys, and even vitamins.[41]

Children who receive few or no remittances express an intense sense of abandonment and resentment. When migrants face obstacles in the labor market and are unable to send money, children have nothing to show for their parents' absence. The prolonged separation, in these cases, seems unjustified and the impoverished conditions of the family in El Salvador or Guatemala become evidence of the parents' failed commitment to the family. This is due, in part, to unrealistic expectations that many non-migrants have about migrants' living conditions and opportunities for success in the United States. In reality, immigrants who find themselves in unstable legal statuses generally earn less and have less stable jobs than legal immigrants,[42] so they may not be able to afford to send money and gifts as often as the children would like—if at all. This leads to family tensions.

Sandra, in El Salvador, describes the relationship she and her brother have with their father, who, in spite of qualifying for TPS, was unable to renew it when he lost track of the deadlines and re-registration procedures. In turn, he only rarely sends remittances:

> We would talk to him, ask him for things and he would agree to everything. And then we never saw anything of it. So it was uncomfortable to be in that position and you end up opting to not know anything about him instead and just not call him. Of course you always want to know something, at least know if he's still alive, but I opted not to call him anymore. And now, I don't care if he calls or not. He didn't care about us.

Their father, who is undocumented in Los Angeles, admits that he does not send money consistently:

> I don't have an exact date to send them money, nothing on the calendar forcing me to do it. I simply send it to them when there is a need. That's why I say that [my children] are good people, because they don't expect me to be sending them money for everything they want. . . . The truth is, I couldn't tell you how much I usually send per year. Sometimes, I know there have been years when I didn't send anything.

From his perspective, his children are "good people" because they do not demand money he cannot send. Although the father believes he has a positive relationship with his children because he sends them money for emergencies, his children experience the relationship negatively. He interprets their silence as a positive sign when, in fact, they are attempting to break ties with him in response to his failure to remit consistently.

Or consider Patricia, an undocumented mother in Los Angeles, who sobs as she describes her relationship with her three children in El Salvador. She has been in the United States for eight years and lives with a five-year-old son who was born after she migrated. She provides for her children in El Salvador, but also has to cover living expenses for her youngest son in Los Angeles, thereby adding to her economic burden. With her meager wages in the informal sector, she has difficulty making ends meet and cannot always send money to her children in El Salvador. Her sense of guilt about not doing more for her family in El Salvador is made more acute by her children's angry complaints.[43] In her words:

> I wish I could say that I did the right thing in coming. Sometimes I think it was the right decision. But when you have your kids yelling at you, being so angry that you left them, it just makes you sad. (Crying.) But there's nothing I can do. I barely make enough for rent and bills here. I don't always have enough left over to send to them, but I do try. And they tell me, "Mami, but things are more expensive now," but they don't understand that it's also expensive here.

Our years of fieldwork among Central Americans in different cities in the United States reveal the central role of the *image* of family in determining how immigrants frame their sacrifices, their ups and downs in life, and their dreams and plans.[44] Indeed, it is the *idea* of family and perceived obligations back home (in spite of time and distance), together with weakened economies and increasing inequality in the home countries, that are the engine behind the huge volume of remittances that immigrants send to their loved ones.[45] Parents feel they are doing their best, under difficult circumstances, to send money. The children, however, often reproach the parents for "abandoning" them. Thus, many children opt for migrating on their own to be with their parent or parents in the United States. Indeed, the great majority of unaccompanied children entering the United States through the southern border are Central Americans.[46]

Remittance practices, although largely dependent on the labor market options and migratory status of immigrants, are also gendered. For example, men sometimes stop remitting to their children when their partners in the origin country begin (or are rumored to begin) new relationships. In Los Angeles, several Salvadoran immigrant men interviewed said they were uncomfortable sending money to a household that now includes another male. Similarly, a few Salvadoran immigrant men who formed new unions in Los Angeles stopped remitting in an effort to avoid problems with their new partners. Unfortunately for the children, some fathers equate parental responsibilities with marital responsibilities, and when the latter end they stop sending money to the children.

Immigrant women, in contrast, rarely stop remitting, even if their partners back home form new unions. Moreover, unlike men, several immigrant mothers described how they *increased* remittances when they formed new unions in the United States. Juana, an undocumented Salvadoran mother in Los Angeles, explained that she was able to increase the monthly sum she sends to her children in El Salvador by sharing household expenses with her new partner:

> Since both of us work, we split the expenses and I am able to send my daughters more money now. The money that I used to spend on rent and bills, that's only half now, because my husband pays the rent every month. That leaves me with a lot of money, and I'm happy that it can go to my daughters.

Her daughters have benefited from the increased sums. They have been able to attend private school in El Salvador, and emotionally, they feel their mother has not "abandoned" them. Despite her new relationship, she has continued to give their well-being priority.

Because immigrant women typically earn less than their male counterparts, they must make greater sacrifices to remit consistently to their children. Esperanza, who had recently filed for legal residency through marriage to a U.S. citizen in Los Angeles, described the hardships she faced to ensure her family's economic well-being in El Salvador, particularly when she was undocumented:

> I've always sent $300 [monthly] to my mother and I would get paid $100 weekly [working as a live-in nanny]. I would end up with $90 because I also had to pay the fee to wire the money. . . . It was horrible because I had to live the entire month with $100, with $90, because $310 was for my

family. Each week I would buy a dozen ramen noodle soups that I don't even want to see anymore, really. I would think, you're supposed to enjoy the weekend here, no? At least go out to eat. For me, it meant a ramen noodle soup three times a day because since I had the day off, I couldn't eat [my employers' food]. I had to eat my own food and so my food was the ramen noodle soup. But I was the happiest woman in the world because my daughter had something to eat!

In El Salvador, Esperanza's daughter, Raquel, is grateful for her mother's continued support. Although she is sad about the separation, she recognizes her mother's efforts to improve her life and is content with their ability to maintain a close relationship despite the distance.

Children in El Salvador and Guatemala express great sorrow about their family's separation, but their narratives reveal greater suffering and more emotional language if it is the mother, as opposed to father, who has migrated. This was true regardless of the family's economic situation. Alondra is a forty-seven-year-old Salvadoran mother of three. She went to the United States when her husband, who had previously migrated, stopped remitting altogether. In Los Angeles, she has worked in the garment industry where wages fluctuate and jobs are unstable. Despite her many sacrifices to send money to her children, they grew up resenting her, and rebelling in response:

ALONDRA: I would call them on the phone and not understand why they had so much anger toward me. The boy, he wouldn't ask, he *demanded* that I send him money. . . . He tells me that he looks forward to the day, because he has all those emotions, he just waits for the day to come and tell me in my face, to create a war against me, so that I can feel all the pain he felt when I left. And he already has vices, he drinks. So when he's drunk, he likes to mistreat me, he tells me so many things.

LA: Does he feel the same way toward his father?

ALONDRA: No . . . his response is that the man can do as he pleases, but the woman can't. . . . He still says that it would have been better for me to be there and to eat rice and beans, but to have someone there. But the resentment is only toward me, not his father.

That Alondra's eighteen-year-old son in El Salvador, who suffered emotional distress from the absence of both parents, expresses his anger and resentment toward his mother is painful for her since she made many sacrifices, all in the name of the children who are now so hostile toward her. Although both parents migrated, her son directs his anger and resentment only toward his mother, with the gendered justification that "the man can do as he pleases."

Parents and Children Who Are Reunited after Long Separations

Then there are the difficulties that develop around family reunification. Although many parents and children look forward to being reunited, the process does not always go smoothly.[47] It usually involves re-acquaintance, accommodation, and generally learning to fit into a family that is different from the one imagined. Economic readjustment adds further complications when the gifts previously remitted must stop because life becomes more expensive when the children arrive.

Leigh Leslie[48] notes that family reunification for Central Americans can be problematic due to unrealistic expectations that parents and children have of each other. For instance, Eduardo, a young man in Phoenix who is half Salvadoran and half Guatemalan, felt "robbed" of a sense of family because he had been sent back from the United States to be raised by his maternal grandmother in El Salvador, "with comforts and everything I wanted materially, but without my parents." His parents spent almost a decade and a half regularizing their statuses, had two more children in the United States, and finally brought Eduardo back to this country when he obtained his permanent legal residence. Afraid that they would jeopardize their chances for permanent residence, the parents did not travel to see their son during the waiting time, and their reunification has been difficult. As Eduardo explained:

> What do you think is worse, to share poverty here with my half-siblings and mother and father, or not having learned how to love them because I never saw them? What would I have given for a goodnight kiss from my mother, for instance, or even for a fight with a sibling! You know? That's what makes a family a family. But instead, I don't know who these people are! I am sorry if you feel I'm an ingrate because you're Salvadoran and you and everyone else think my parents are great and you're going to tell me about their sacrifice and blah blah blah. I know the story (smiles). And I'm sure you'd side with my mother because, oh, she's such a hard worker [rolling his eyes] and loves me and all that. But I am not and will not be grateful to them for having sent me back.

Leticia, his mother, said that Eduardo has had a hard time accommodating to his new family and that he reproaches them for having "abandoned" him—which has been very hurtful. Leticia and her husband have explained that they sent him back because they only wanted the best for him. In her words:

> Do you know how much it hurts that he thinks I abandoned him, when all I did was kill myself working three jobs, yes, three jobs, Cecilia, so that he could have a good education there, away from all the bad things here? I wanted the best for him; I'm his mother, not a stranger. I have asked him to stop reproaching me because it is too painful (voice quivering, teary eyes). . . . During all those years he was there [in El Salvador] I used to miss him so much, I used to cry at night, but I kept thinking, no, this is good for him and as a mother I only want the best for him. And then look what he says to me now! Look at how he's paying me back! Is this fair?

Leticia admits that she often gets upset at Eduardo and even wonders if it was a good idea for him to return to the United States:

> Sometimes I say, God forgive me, but maybe it would have been better to leave him there, or to not have let him go. When we sent him we didn't know it would be so difficult, that it would take so long to get him back, that we would have to wait so long. It was only going to be for some time, but with immigration problems then it became years. One thinks only to do the best for one's children, but you never know, right?

Lengthy separations can also lead to estrangement between parents and children because they are exposed to different environments during their separation. Virginia and her two sons spent almost sixteen years separated from her husband, Mario, after he left El Salvador for the United States. During the separation Mario never traveled to visit his family because he was waiting for his "papers." Like many others in a similar situation, Virginia described the difficulties of adjustment when they reunited in Phoenix because Mario had been physically absent for nearly the entire childhood of his sons. When Mario went to pick them up from the airport, he did not recognize the children and they saw him as a stranger.

> It was like having arrived to a complete stranger! My sons and my husband really didn't know each other, he didn't know what his sons looked like, and

they didn't know what their father looked like. They were about three and four when he left to come here. When we came here, the boys were already young men, about 19 or 20. . . . So it's like forcing them to create a family. . . . Oh, there are many things, like how you like your food, the music you like. My husband got used to living alone, so he didn't know adolescents like loud music, those big clothes, you know. Ay, they couldn't agree and my husband says that I spoiled them because they're boys. He thinks that I spent all that he sent us [remittances] on spoiling them.

Virginia commented that Mario was unpleasantly surprised to discover that, when his sons were in El Salvador, they had adopted the lifestyles and tastes of youngsters in the United States. The youngsters, for their part, could not understand why their father, having lived in the United States for almost two decades, was unfamiliar with the styles among the young. In this case, generational location trumped geographical location.[49] In Virginia's words:

At the beginning, he was upset because the boys liked all that music that you hear here, they wanted to wear those earphones in the house and he would talk to them and they wouldn't hear him! (laughing). . . And the clothes. Ay, the clothes! [There were] fights for those clothes. He would get so angry! I would tell him, "Look, they are of the new generation, you are the one who is antiquated." I think it's because he never saw them grow up and develop new interests, but I did. So I knew them better, right? And the kids could not understand how their father didn't know anything about these new fashions even if he had been living here all those years. They thought he just wanted to bug them. Yes, this created tensions. But one gets used to it, we adjust.

Also, the long wait for their eventual reunification had negative consequences for the sons' legal status. Apparently, "He [Mario] put in the papers when they were still minors, but because they turned eighteen with the papers still in process, they haven't gotten their papers [permanent resident status] yet. We worry about the older one who's going to be twenty-one soon; the younger one still has some years that he can wait because the wait is long." Virginia is concerned that because her sons will soon be twenty-one, their process toward legal resident status will be greatly slowed down as stipulated by family reunification laws. In effect, they are at risk of being left undocumented for reasons completely beyond their control, a situation closely tied to the context of liminal legality. Sometimes, the sons reproach their father in a mix of generational rebellion, a lingering resentment over their sense of abandonment, and the frustration of possibly remaining undocumented indefinitely.

Reunifications can be bittersweet, leading to moments of happiness, as well as tension and disappointment. As Zelizer[50] aptly notes, close family members support and help each other, but they can hurt each other as well. For instance, Josefina and her husband, Ricardo, brought their three sons, Manuel, Edwin, and Antonio, one by one, from El Salvador to Phoenix in the 1990s. A few years later, one of Edwin's teenage daughters wanted to migrate, and her father financed her trip with loans from the rest of the family. To everyone's surprise (and disappointment), Carolina, the girl, was pregnant when she arrived. She has been living in a multi-generational household with her grandmother, her father, and the baby—a situation ripe for conflict but also for cooperation and joy.

In Josefina's and Edwin's eyes, Carolina does not behave like a responsible mother because she does not properly wash the baby's bottles and in general does not seem to be as "loving as a mother should be." Josefina has even considered formally requesting custody of the baby. Edwin and his brother, Manuel, would like to adopt the baby as well. However, only Josefina is a permanent legal resident; Edwin has had TPS and Manuel is still waiting, after nine years, for his NACARA application to be approved. What this means, Josefina explains, is that she is the only one eligible to adopt the baby, and since she is in her fifties, she feels "too old" to start raising another child. Josefina explained how furious she was one day when Carolina came home past midnight, after having gone out with her new boyfriend after work. Legal status plays a central role in their relations.

> You see how irresponsible she is? Yes, we're all there to care for the baby, but she has to realize that her priority is her baby and not going to parties. The next day I was so angry at her that I slapped her once . . . and told her that I would buy her a plane ticket back to El Salvador and would keep her baby with us. I wouldn't have her deported—although I could, and sometimes I really would like to—but I don't think I could do that. The baby was born here, so he's a U.S. citizen and can stay without a problem.

Apparently, Carolina apologized and promised to be more responsible. Because Carolina is such a hard worker, Josefina has agreed to pick up the baby from the sitter's house everyday and watch him until Carolina gets home from work. A few moments later, in the same conversation, Josefina described with delight the surprise birthday party that her granddaughter had organized for her.

> Can you imagine, after having slapped her the week before, she organized a party for me? She invited people, bought balloons and a big cake, made a sign, "Happy Birthday, Abuelita," and prepared a barbecue and cooked all sorts of things. And she dressed up the baby especially for the occasion. I said to myself, the poor girl is trying. Sometimes she gets me so angry that I feel I'll lose it, but at the same time, I feel sorry for her. So we just go on like that.

The ups and downs in this multigenerational family are cast against constant reminders of imminent deportations, differentiated legal statuses, and waiting indefinitely for the elusive "papers."

Parents and Children in the United States: Shared Precarious and Mixed-Status Families

It is already clear that Guatemalans and Salvadorans in the United States are often in "mixed-status families," that is, they include various combinations of U.S. citizens, permanent legal residents, undocumented immigrants, and individuals in gray areas of legal limbo. Furthermore, the family's legal composition does not remain static, as members go from being undocumented to temporary workers, permanent legal residents to citizens, or holders of temporary statuses to undocumented immigrants.[51]

The complexity and fluidity of their legal statuses influence opportunities and resources, thereby affecting intergenerational relations and individuals' perceptions of their place in their families. For instance, Mario is a sixteen-year-old Guatemalan undocumented immigrant who lives in Los Angeles. His younger brother was born in the United States, making him the only member of the family with U.S. citizenship. In the following excerpt, Mario describes, sometimes in a sarcastic tone, resentments that have arisen owing to the mixed statuses in his family:

> Well, basically, I don't have medical insurance. My younger brother, whenever he's sick, they always take him to the hospital, and stuff like that, because the government pays for him. . . . My mom takes him to the dentist

yearly, to the doctor, you know, but if I feel really sick, like I have to be dying to go to the hospital. But then, you know, my brother, he feels a stomach ache, "Let's go to the hospital." (laughs)

As Mario's comments indicate, stratified access to health care may lead to preferential treatment of some children owing to their legal status.[52] Despite understanding that his brother had legal access to more resources, Mario harbored resentment toward his mother for what he experienced as limited concern for his well-being. In general, the fact that U.S. citizens and legal residents in the same household have greater access to resources than liminally legal or undocumented members of the same family can lead to tension across and within generations.

But this is only part of the story. Mixed status in Guatemalan and Salvadoran families does not always lead to tension and resentment. For example, Alisa, a nineteen-year-old Guatemalan undocumented college student in Los Angeles, is thankful that her entire family can benefit from the fact that her younger twin sisters are U.S. citizens. Because her sisters were born in the United States, they are eligible for government assistance, including public housing that is more spacious than what the family—all the rest of whom are undocumented—could otherwise afford.

We moved over here because of the twins. I have two smaller twin sisters, they were born here, but when they were five months old, they got epilepsy, both of them, so it damaged their brains. . . . Because of them we moved over here, because of the housing. We used to live in a smaller apartment so they gave us a larger apartment for them, because of them, so they could have more room to walk around and stuff. . . . This is not in a nice neighborhood, but from the inside, it's nicer than a lot of my friends' apartments.

Although her younger sisters' severe developmental disabilities have taken a physical and emotional toll on the family, Alisa is grateful that as U.S. citizens, her sisters have access to health care and housing. She is aware of the benefits the entire family receives as a result of the twins' legal status. In this case, intergenerational relations are mediated by the benefits accorded to the U.S. citizens in the family.

Other unintended consequences of mixed statuses in Guatemalan and Salvadoran families affect intergenerational relations. Because U.S.-born children can travel to their parents' countries of origin without problems, while their Guatemalan- or Salvadoran-born siblings who lack documents (or are in legal limbo) cannot, the U.S.-born children can help maintain relations with grandparents back home.[53] Adela, a Salvadoran woman in Phoenix, explained this added benefit of her daughter's citizenship:

> I can send my daughter, the one born here, to my mom every summer. I don't do it all the time because of money, you know, it's expensive. But when I send her she takes things for my mom that she needs over there, and I feel more at ease because my mom is *solita* [alone] over there. So while I can't go because [I'm waiting for] my papers, I say to myself, at least I send my daughter so my mom doesn't feel completely forgotten.

In this case, the daughter's U.S. citizenship helps to sustain links between generations across borders.

In some cases, all members of a family living together share the same legal status. When all are undocumented, tensions can arise due to the different meanings that children and parents attach to their undocumented status. Undocumented parents often feel less stigmatized by their status than youth raised in the United States, who have a stronger desire to fit in and may face intense harassment and marginalization at school on account of being unauthorized. The parents may not understand their children's discomfort, while the children may be annoyed by what they view as their parents' acquiescent attitude. Moreover, when the children are socialized in the United States, they develop different aspirations than their parents, although their legal status limits them to what they regard as undesirable jobs.[54] The children are much more resentful than their parents of the low-level jobs available to them—and reluctant to accept them. For example, for Central American women who migrate as adults, domestic jobs are common and even desirable;[55] young women who were largely raised and educated in the United States do not share this view and often reject these positions.[56]

Compounding the difficulties, the children sometimes do not make an effort in school or drop out because they are aware that, with tenuous legal statuses, more schooling will not provide the rewards they desire. Parents are frustrated that the children do not seem to want to reap the benefits of access to education in the United States, and clashes may well ensue.[57] The mother of Jovani, a sixteen-year-old undocumented Guatemalan high school student in Los Angeles, is a part-time nanny and active volunteer at his school. She expects Jovani to be a focused, successful student, but he has been influenced by his older, also undocumented cousin's inability to attend college despite great effort. Jovani's mother has requested advice from school staff to help her son pursue higher education, but Jovani, who feels an acute sense of stigma associated with his unauthorized status, prefers to avoid authorities and is inclined to give up. Instead of working hard, he is enrolled in the tenth grade for the second year in a row after failing all of his classes.

Discussion and Conclusion

Most migratory movements today involve family separation accompanied by publicized images of its detrimental effects. Our analysis underscores the complexity involved in family separation, which is seldom perceived as dissolution by those involved, particularly the parents in the United States. We also have emphasized the central role of immigration laws—expressions of the political power of the nation state in demarcating borders—in establishing the contours of family dynamics among Guatemalan and Salvadoran immigrants. The case of Guatemalan and Salvadoran immigrants who have migrated to the United States within the past two decades is paradigmatic in this respect. The liminal legality that shapes their lives has affected intergenerational relations, including among family members who reunite after long periods of separation, as well as among members who remain separated by geographical distance.

Guatemalan and Salvadoran immigrants' fragile legal statuses translate into a diversity of mixed-status families. Within these families, intergenerational relations can be fraught with tension as members face divided fates where competition can arise. At the same time, family members cooperate, work through complicated relations upon reunification, and learn to interpret and express love in multiple ways during long and uncertain separations. Our research shows that the initial trauma of separation is often repeated during reunification, as parents and children find strangers in each other and face multiple challenges in accommodating to living together again. Children must cope with the triple burden of dealing with adolescence, entering a new society, and learning their place in new and reconstituted families.

Intergenerational dynamics are also mediated by the social location of the parents and children, by gender ideologies and conceptions of motherhood and parenthood, and by the socioeconomic and cultural resources available to parents and children by virtue of their physical and social locations. Consequently, relations between parents and children in these families defy easy classification. During the long and uncertain separations, parents and children hold onto ideals of a family that keep them hoping for and dreaming of an eventual reunification. Such idealized images find expression in the form of remittances and gifts that parents send from the United States, as well as in the assurances of continued affection on the part of both parents and children. These exchanges reveal that transactions between intimates have important economic consequences and take their meaning from long-term social ties.[58] When the parents and children are reunited, however, many expectations go unfulfilled and tension can develop. At the same time, reunifications in the United States offer new opportunities for parents and children to be reacquainted, to recognize each other's sacrifices, and to face together the many challenges that the new context offers.

The cases discussed here make clear that the dynamics of intergenerational relations in immigrant families cannot be understood by focusing only on individual members. Such relations are embedded within broader forces and intricately shaped by the macrostructural contexts in which family members live, as well as by their social positions and the sociocultural ideologies that guide their attitudes and behaviors. In this regard, it is important to keep in mind that political decisions embodied in immigration law determine, to put it in Kim-Puri's[59] terms, "who is a subject and therefore has access to social resources, who is made invisible and therefore denied, who is seen as a victim and therefore in need of protection." As immigrant-receiving countries around the globe pursue temporary statuses and guest-worker programs to regulate and control immigrants,[60] we should expect these new and complex forms of generational relations to flourish. Social service providers, for example, are already taking note. At a mandatory meeting for teachers and other school personnel of the Miami-Dade County Public Schools,[61] medical researchers inform them of the psychological and behavioral manifestations resulting from family separation and reunification among Latino students. Meanwhile, in Phoenix, a psychologist who hosts a radio show to assist Latino families receives regular calls from Latino children who experience very high levels of anxiety related to family separation and reunification. Indeed, in a conversation with Menjívar he mentioned that Latino children tend to experience the highest levels of anxiety, which to him is related to the looming uncertainty of family separation as a result of deportation. The emotional severity of these separations is even finding artistic expression—as evident in Reyna Grande's novel *Across a Hundred Mountains* and the film *La Misma Luna* (Under the Same Moon). The experiences of Salvadoran and Guatemalan immigrants in this chapter thus begin to capture the nuances and dynamics that will undoubtedly play out just as vividly for other immigrant groups.

ACKNOWLEDGEMENTS

The authors wish to thank Nancy Foner for the insightful comments and careful editing and Nestor Rodriguez for sharing some of the data he has collected as soon as we asked.

NOTES

1. Carolina Rivera performed her piece, entitled "Prosperity," as part of a show with various acts collectively entitled *Epicentrico: Rico Epicentro*, directed by Raquel Gutierrez, 2003.

2. Pérez 2006.

3. Durán 2006.

4. Families across borders (or transnational families) include a host of possible combinations of migrants and non-migrants. In highly skilled migration streams where families seek to further increase their cultural and economic capital, children may migrate while parents stay behind, or only one parent may stay behind to work while the other parent migrates with the children (see Chee 2005; Wong 1998; Yeoh, Huang, and Lam 2005). In our work, we focus on poor families in which parents pursue migration and family separation as a last resort in the face of serious woes resulting from a host of structural dislocations.

5. Parreñas 1998: 144.

6. Bernhard, Landolt, and Goldring forthcoming.

7. Menjívar 2006a; Menjívar 2006b.

8. López Castro 1986; Massey et al. 1987.

9. Bernhard, Landolt, and Goldring forthcoming; Hondagneu-Sotelo and Avila 1997; Parreñas 2005.

10. Kwak 2003.

11. Menjívar 2000; Portes and Rumbaut 2001.

12. Pyke 2000.

13. Menjívar 2006b.

14. Guatemalans and Salvadorans seem to feel the effects of stiffer laws more

directly than other groups. For instance, one study in New Jersey found that among Latin American–origin immigrants, Guatemalans rank at the bottom in a system of stratification based on legal status (Adler 2006). This is especially true because Immigration and Customs Enforcement agents' raids disproportionately target Guatemalans and therefore other Latinos avoid being associated with them. Another study in Dallas and Fort Worth, Texas, found that compared to other immigrant groups in the region, Salvadorans were more likely to prioritize not being harassed by *la migra* as a reason for seeking naturalization (Brettell 2006: 86).

15. Abrego 2006.

16. Figures from the 2000 U.S. census reveal the generally low socioeconomic status of Salvadorans and Guatemalans. For example, 62.3 percent of Guatemalans and 64.6 percent of Salvadorans in the United States have less than a high school education; 31.4 percent of Guatemalans and 30 percent of Salvadorans are high school graduates; and only 6.3 percent of Guatemalans and 5.1 percent of Salvadorans have completed college. The median household income for Guatemalans in the United States is $41,100; for Salvadorans it is $42,000.

17. Bailey et al. 2002.

18. Menjívar 2006b.

19. Rodríguez 2001: 387.

20. This temporary amnesty was not extended to Guatemalans because U.S. officials argued that they did not deserve protection, even though the U.S. State Department had noted on several occasions the Guatemalan government's atrocious human rights record.

21. National Asylum Study Project 1992.

22. Menjívar 2000.

23. Menjívar 2006a.

24. Ibid.

25. Rodriguez and Hagan 2004.

26. See DHS Statistical Yearbook 2005, Table 41, "Aliens removed by criminal status and region and country of nationality: Fiscal years 1998 to 2005—continued"; and DHS Statistical Yearbook 2000, Table 66, "Aliens removed by criminal status and region and country of nationality, fiscal years 1993–2000."

27. Since IIRIRA was passed, many of those deported were lawful permanent residents and refugees; they left behind at least 1.6 million spouses and children, many of whom are U.S. citizens (Human Rights Watch 2007; Menjívar and Rumbaut 2008). Although we do not have specific figures for deportation-induced family separations among Guatemalans and Salvadorans, given their deportation rates, we expect many have been affected.

28. Some of these ordinances are largely symbolic since they seek to bar undocumented immigrants from accessing services that were not available to them in the first place.

29. Cresce and Ramirez 2003.

30. There is no consensus on the number of Salvadorans and Guatemalans in the United States. Given the large numbers of immigrants in precarious legal statuses, even re-estimated figures may fail to account for the actual size of these populations. See, for example, the discussion about Salvadorans in PNUD 2005: 37.

31. Logan 2001.

32. Immigration and Naturalization Service 1997.

33. Abrego 2006.

34. Menjívar 2006b; Rodríguez 2005.

35. Fix and Zimmerman 2001.

36. See also Ho 1993; Levitt 2001; Menjívar 2002; Miller Matthei and Smith 1998.

37. Menjívar et al. 1998.

38. Cf. Valenzuela 2002.

39. See also Walter, Bourgois, and Loinaz 2004.

40. Zelizer 2007.

41. Menjívar and Agadjanian 2007.

42. Fortuny, Capps, and Passel 2007.

43. This sense of guilt seems to be common among mothers who are unable to remit regularly or even to bring their children to live with them (see also Bernhard, Landolt, and Goldring forthcoming).

44. PNUD 2005.

45. Menjívar 2006a.

46. Howley 2005.

47. See also Suárez-Orozco, Todorova, and Louie 2002.

48. Leslie 1993.

49. Guatemalan indigenous parents seemed to be particularly upset when the young people opted for U.S. fashions and lifestyles and shunned Mayan customs, clothes, and other cultural manifestations (Menjívar 2002).

50. Zelizer 2007.

51. Fix and Zimmerman 2001.

52. Indeed, many eligible citizen children do not participate in social service programs because the non-citizen parents are unaware of their children's eligibility or are afraid that receiving these benefits may eventually hurt their own chances for legalization (Hagan, Rodriguez, and Nika 2003).

53. Menjívar 2002.

54. Abrego 2006.

55. Hondagneu-Sotelo 2001.

56. Abrego 2006.

57. Menjívar 2000.

58. Zelizer 2005.

59. Kim-Puri 2005: 151.
60. Cf. Mountz et al. 2002.
61. Accessed at http://www.cfs.med.miami.edu/.

REFERENCES

Abrego, Leisy J. 2006. "'I Can't Go to College Because I Don't Have Papers': Incorporation Patterns of Latino Undocumented Youth." *Latino Studies* 4(3): 212–31.

Adler, Rachel H. 2006. "'But They Claimed to Be Police, Not *La Migra!*': The Interaction of Residency Status, Class, and Ethnicity in a (Post-PATRIOT Act) New Jersey Neighborhood." *American Behavioral Scientist* 50(1): 48–69.

Bailey, Adrian, Richard Wright, Alison Mountz, and Inés Miyares. 2002. "(Re)producing Salvadoran Transnational Geographies." *Annals of the Association of American Geographers* 92(1): 125–44.

Bernhard, Judith K., Patricia Landolt, and Luin Goldring. Forthcoming. "Transnationalizing Families: Canadian Immigration Policy and the Spatial Fragmentation of Care-giving among Latin American Newcomers." *International Migration*.

Brettell, Caroline B. 2006. "Political Belonging and Cultural Belonging: Immigration Status, Citizenship, and Identity among Four Immigrant Populations in a Southwestern City." *American Behavioral Scientist* 50(1): 70–99.

Chee, Maria W. L. 2005. *Taiwanese American Transnational Families: Women and Kin Work*. New York: Routledge.

Cresce, Arthur R., and Roberto R. Ramirez. 2003. "Analysis of General Hispanic Responses in Census 2000." Washington, DC: U.S. Census Bureau.

Durán, Agustín. 2006. "En las garras del infortunio." *La Opinión*, September 2, p. 2A.

Fix, Michael, and Wendy Zimmerman. 2001. "All under One Roof: Mixed-Status Families in an Era of Reform." *International Migration Review* 35(2): 397–419.

Fortuny, Karina, Randy Capps, and Jeffrey Passel. 2007. "The Characteristics of Unauthorized Immigrants in California, Los Angeles County, and the United States." Washington, DC: The Urban Institute.

Hagan, Jacqueline, Nestor Rodriguez, and Nika Kabiri. 2003. "The Effects of Recent Welfare and Immigration Reforms on Immigrants' Access to Health Care." *International Migration Review* 37(2): 444–63.

Ho, Christine. 1993. "The Internationalization of Kinship and the Feminization of Caribbean Migration: The Case of Afro-Trinidadian Immigrants in Los Angeles." *Human Organization* 25(1): 32–40.

Hondagneu-Sotelo, Pierrette. 2001. *Doméstica: Immigrant Workers Cleaning and Caring in the Shadows of Affluence*. Berkeley: University of California Press.

Hondagneu-Sotelo, Pierrette, and Ernestine Avila. 1997. "'I'm Here, But I'm There': The Meanings of Latina Transnational Motherhood." *Gender & Society* 11(5): 548–70.

Howley, Chris. 2005. "Young Migrants Crossing All Alone." *The Arizona Republic*, January 19, p. A-1.

Human Rights Watch. 2007. "Forced Apart: Families Separated and Immigrants Harmed by United States Deportation Policy." Washington, DC: Human Rights Watch.

Immigration and Naturalization Service. 1997. *INS Releases Updated Estimates of U.S. Illegal Population*. News Release, 7 February. Washington, D.C.: U.S. Department of Justice.

Kim-Puri, H. J. 2005. "Conceptualizing Gender-Sexuality-State-Nation: An Introduction." *Gender & Society* 19(2): 137–59.

Kwak, Kyunghwa. 2003. "Adolescents and Their Parents: A Review of Intergenerational Family Relations for Immigrant and Non-Immigrant Families." *Human Development* 46(2–3): 115–36.

Leslie, Leigh A. 1993. "Families Fleeing War: The Case of Central Americans." *Marriage and Family Review* 19: 193–205.

Levitt, Peggy. 2001. *The Transnational Villagers*. Berkeley: University of California Press.

Logan, John R. 2001. "The New Latinos: Who They Are, Where They Are." Albany, NY: Lewis Mumford Center for Comparative Urban and Regional Research.

López Castro, Gustavo. 1986. *La casa dividida: Un estudio de caso sobre la migración a Estados Unidos en un pueblo michoacano*. Zamora, Michoacán: Colegio de Michoacán y Asociación Mexicana de Población.

Massey, Douglas, Rafael Alarcon, Jorge Durand, and Humberto González. 1987. *Return to Aztlan: The Social Process of Migration from Western Mexico*. Berkeley: University of California Press.

Menjívar, Cecilia. 2000. *Fragmented Ties: Salvadoran Immigrant Networks in America*. Berkeley: University of California Press.

———. 2002. "Living in Two Worlds? Guatemalan-Origin Children in the United States and Emerging Transnationalism." *Journal of Ethnic and Migration Studies* 28(3): 531–53.

———. 2006a. "Family Reorganization in a Context of Legal Uncertainty: Guatemalan and Salvadoran Immigrants in the United States." *International Journal of Sociology of the Family* 32(2): 223–45.

———. 2006b. "Liminal Legality: Salvadoran and Guatemalan Immigrants' Lives in the United States." *American Journal of Sociology* 111(4): 999–1037.

Menjívar, Cecilia, and Victor Agadjanian. 2007. "Men's Migration and Women's Lives: Views from Rural Armenia and Guatemala." *Social Science Quarterly* 88(5): 1243–62.

Menjívar, Cecilia, Julie DaVanzo, Lisa Greenwell, and R. Burciaga Valdez. 1998. "Remittance Behavior among Salvadoran and Filipino Immigrants in Los Angeles." *International Migration Review* 32(1): 97–126.

Menjívar, Cecilia, and Rubén G. Rumbaut. 2008. "Rights of Racial and Ethnic Minorities and Migrants: Between Rhetoric and Reality." Pp. 60–74 in Judith Blau et al. (eds.), *The Leading Rogue State: The United States and Human Rights*. Boulder, CO: Paradigm Publishers.

Miller Matthei, Linda, and David A. Smith. 1998. "'Belizean 'Boyz 'n the 'Hood'? Garifuna Labor Migration and Transnational Identity." Pp. 270–90 in Michael P. Smith and Luis E. Guarnizo (eds.), *Transnationalism from Below*. New Brunswick, NJ: Transaction Publishers.

Mountz, Alison, Richard Wright, Inés Miyares, and Adrian Bailey. 2002. "Lives in Limbo: Temporary Protected Status and Immigrant Identities." *Global Networks* 2(4): 335–56.

Parreñas, Rhacel Salazar. 1998. "The Global Servants: (Im)Migrant Filipina Domestic Workers in Rome and Los Angeles." Ph.D. dissertation, Department of Ethnic Studies, University of California, Berkeley.

———. 2005. *Children of Global Migration: Transnational Families and Gendered Woes*. Stanford: Stanford University Press.

Pérez, Linda Carolina. 2006. "Tan cerca y tan lejos: el sufrimiento de una familia." *Mundo Hispanico*, January 26–February 1, p. A4.

Portes, Alejandro, and Rubén G. Rumbaut. 2001. *Legacies: The Story of the Immigrant Second Generation*. Berkeley: University of California Press; New York: Russell Sage Foundation.

Programa de Naciones Unidas para el Desarrollo. 2005. "Informe sobre desarrollo humano de El Salvador 2005: Una mirada al nuevo nosotros, Impacto de las migraciones." San Salvador, El Salvador. United Nations Development Program.

Pyke, Karen. 2000. "'The Normal American Family' as an Interpretive Structure of Family Life among Grown Children of Korean and Vietnamese Immigrants." *Journal of Marriage and the Family* 62: 240–55.

Rodríguez, Ana Patricia. 2001. "Refugees of the South: Central Americans in the U.S. Latino Imagery." *American Literature* 73(2): 387–412.

———. 2005. "'Departamento 15': Cultural Narratives of Salvadoran Transnational Migration." *Latino Studies* 3(1): 19–41.

Rodriguez, Nestor, and Jacqueline Maria Hagan. 2004. "Fractured Families and Communities: Effects of Immigration Reform in Texas, Mexico, and El Salvador." *Latino Studies* 2(3): 328–51.

Suárez-Orozco, Carola, Irina L. G. Todorova, and Josephine Louie. 2002. "Making Up for Lost Time: The Experiences of Separation and Reunification among Immigrant Families." *Family Process* 41(4): 625–43.

Valenzuela, Abel, Jr. 2002. "Working on the Margins in Metropolitan Los Angeles: Immigrants in Day-Labor Work." *Migraciones Internacionales* 1(2): 6–28.

Walter, Nicholas, Philippe Bourgois, and H. Margarita Loinaz. 2004. "Masculinity and Undocumented Labor Migration: Injured Latino Day Laborers in San Francisco." *Social Science & Medicine* 59: 1159–68.

Wong, Bernard P. 1998. "Transnationalism and New Chinese Immigrant Families in the United States." Pp. 158–73 in Carol A. Mortland (ed.), *Diasporic Identity: Selected Papers on Refugees and Immigrants*. Washington, DC: American Anthropological Association.

Yeoh, Brenda S. A., Shirlena Huang, and Theodora Lam. 2005. "Transnationalizing the 'Asian' family: Imaginaries, Intimacies and Strategic Intents." *Global Networks* 5(4): 307–15.

Zelizer, Viviana. 2005. *The Purchase of Intimacy*. Princeton, NJ: Princeton University Press.

———. 2007. "Culture and Uncertainty." Presented at the Conference on the work of Robert K. Merton, Columbia University.

8

|||||||||||||||||||||||||||||||||||||||||||||||||||||||||

Negotiating Work and
Parenting over the Life Course
Mexican Family Dynamics in a Binational Context

Joanna Dreby

Every year, more than 500,000 Mexicans migrate to the United States.[1] Tens of thousands leave children behind in Mexico when they do.[2] These migrants make an unusual, but common, parenting decision. Taking advantage of the economic disparities between the United States and Mexico, parents move to places, where they can earn more for their human labor, while their children remain in hometowns in Mexico, where the cost of living is low. In this sense, migration is a gamble; by leaving children behind, migrant parents hope to better provide for their children. Their migration represents a sacrifice of the present for the future.

In some ways, Mexican migrant parents' strategy is not so different from those of other working parents in the United States. Like many American working parents, Mexican migrants put in long hours on the job and entrust the care of their children to others.[3] They expect that through continued labor force participation, they will be able to enhance their children's opportunities. They feel conflicted about their decisions over how to balance work and home life.[4] Yet transnational parents work thousands of miles away from their children. Unable to see their children at the end of every day, these parents make an enormous sacrifice in their work-family life balance.

This chapter describes how Mexican migrants, both mothers and fathers, reconcile the demands of their work life with those of parenting their children from a distance. In what follows, I briefly review the differences between the sacrifices made by mothers and fathers. I then consider how social conditions, changes in family composition over time, and the sharing of parental roles with children's caregivers affect parents' relationships with their children and the gendered expectations of parents' migrations. In doing so I focus on how migrant men and women seek to achieve a work-family life balance over time, in accordance with their—and their children's—changing needs.

Past Patterns

Mexican fathers' decisions to migrate without their children are not new. What scholars previously termed "split-family migration" was common a century ago for, among others, Chinese, Polish, Jewish, and Italian immigrants to the United States.[5] From 1870 to 1920, more than two-thirds of Italian migrants were men; the majority supported wives and children in Italy with remittances.[6] Male Chinese immigrants outnumbered women 18 to 1 in 1860 and 26 to 1 in 1890, and more than half left wives at home in China.[7] Many men gradually brought their family members to the United States when possible, although return migration rates were also high; between 1900 and 1920, more than a third of immigrants to the United States returned home.[8]

Unlike Chinese and Italian immigrants, at the turn of the twentieth century Mexican families generally migrated together. Indeed, for most of the nineteenth century— even after the Mexican-American War (1846–48), when the United States took more than 500,000 square miles of land previously belonging to Mexico—the U.S.–Mexican border was much more porous than it is today.[9] In fact, family migration grew considerably during the upheaval of the Mexican Revolution (1913–20).[10] Yet with the economic turmoil of the Great Depression of the 1930s, entire families were sent back to Mexico during deportation campaigns.[11] By 1940, the Mexican American population was just half what it had been only ten years earlier.[12]

Not until the mid-twentieth century did typical Mexican migrants begin to look more like those from Europe and Asia years earlier. After labor shortages during World War II, the United States instituted the Bracero

Program (1942–64), which allowed Mexican men, but not women, to mi-grate on temporary labor contracts.[13] Unlike immigrants from other coun-tries, who generally settled in the cities, *braceros* worked in agriculture, returning to Mexico at the end of the growing season.[14] The Bracero Pro-gram was instrumental in establishing an entrenched pattern of male-led temporary migration between Mexico and the United States. Ever since, many Mexican communities—and families—have come to depend on some of their members seeking employment north of the border.[15]

The migration pattern in which men worked abroad and women stayed in the home community and tended to children conforms, in many ways, to the gender division of labor in families. Such a balance between work and family was not without problems. The women and men in these fam-ilies were divided between what William I. Thomas and Florian Znaniecki described as "old" and "new world" values.[16] Ensuing conflicts between women and men led, they suggested, to wider levels of social disorganiza-tion in both the communities of origin where women lived and urban im-migrant communities in the United States, which were mostly inhabited by men.[17] Particularly during the early twentieth century, social workers and other reformers in the United States defined the problem of immigra-tion as one of "family disorganization."[18] Although Mexican men's migra-tion patterns were typically more circular than those of European immi-grants, fathers' periodic absences did not go unnoted. These absent fathers were often criticized, as the popular expression goes, for being "padres de cheque no mas" [fathers only by virtue of a check].[19]

New Patterns: Migrant Mothers

Today, a new migration pattern in which mothers leave their children to work abroad marks a major shift in the ways families balance work and family via migration. Pierrette Hondagneu-Sotelo and Ernestina Avila have labeled this phenomenon "transnational motherhood."[20] Although some migrant mothers left their children behind in earlier periods, such cases appear to have been unusual.[21] A study of family separation among U.S. immigrants in 1910 found that only 7 percent of immigrant women across ethnic groups had left their children in their home country when they came to the United States.[22] By the end of the twentieth century, transnational mothering spanned the globe, from Turkish women in Germany to Colombians in Spain and Filipinas in Canada, Hong Kong, and Italy.[23] The growing presence of women in migration streams and the increased frequency of female-led migration suggest that contemporary families are meeting productive and consumptive needs through migration in distinctly different ways than in times past, when men were the primary movers in families. When mothers from poorer countries such as Mexico migrate to more industrialized nations, they fill what Barbara Ehrenreich and Arlie Hochschild call the "care deficit" that emerges when women enter the workforce in wealthier nations. In effect, they pass on the "care deficit" to the children they leave behind, reproducing global inequalities within their families.[24]

Although rates of male migration still outpace those of females among Mexicans, in the past ten to twenty years, many characteristics of Mexican migration have changed. For one, the destinations of Mexican migrants have become increasingly diversified. Labor demands throughout the forty-eight continental United States have meant that Mexicans now seek work outside of the Southwest in rural, urban, and suburban areas that have not seen sizable immigrant populations in the past.[25] Moreover, since the debt crisis in the mid-1980s, migration to the United States has become common throughout Mexico. Today, nearly every Mexican state has a significant number of migrants in the United States; they leave both rural and urban areas and come from areas where indigenous languages, not Spanish, are spoken.[26] More importantly, the past twenty years have seen a marked increase in female migration rates. Not only are men of all socioeconomic backgrounds migrating from all areas of Mexico as never before, but so are their wives and children.[27] A considerable number of single women, including many divorced and widowed mothers, have begun to seek employment in the United States as a means for survival.[28] Estimates suggest that 38 percent of Mexican fathers and 15 percent of Mexican mothers living in the United States have left children back in Mexico.[29]

The increasingly diverse Mexican migrant population confronts an ever more hostile environment in the United States. Since the early 1990s, many policies restricting immigration to the United States have been implemented.[30] Such measures, aimed at reducing unregulated Mexican migration, have had a number of unintended consequences.[31] The undocumented crossing of the U.S.–Mexican border has become more dangerous—especially for women—and death rates have soared.[32] The costs of migration have also risen considerably. Consequently, Mexicans are more likely than in times past to settle in new destinations further away from the border.[33] As it has become ever more difficult for migrants to move back and forth between their homes in Mexico and their workplaces in the United States, they are staying longer.[34] In other words, Mexican families continue to depend on U.S. employment as a labor strategy, but they must endure longer family separations to do so. Immigration policy has created the conditions under which Mexicans working in the United States, and particularly mothers, must remain apart from their children.[35]

Today's Mexican migrant mothers, as well as fathers, face a series of strains and stressors that, though they at times echo concerns voiced by reformers in the early twentieth century, are unique to their generation of migrants.[36] Transnational parents are caught in an increasingly complex web of migratory laws in both "sending" and "receiving" nations.[37] Legal statuses within migrant families often vary, with some siblings having U.S. citizenship rights while others remain undocumented.[38] Moreover, new technologies facilitate more frequent contact between family members abroad and those back home.[39] Parents can speak to their children on the phone and often do on a daily basis.[40] Money is easily sent to Mexico, and parents can travel back home rather quickly in response to any immediate crisis, such as when a child is ill. More immediate and frequent means of communicating with children back at home may make mothers more willing to leave them when they migrate. Yet prolonged separation is accompanied by a new set of problems, particularly for women. When mothers migrate, expectations of women's roles at home lag behind their contributions as family wage-earners.[41] Mothers often feel guiltier than fathers about having left their children behind.[42] Families lament that love becomes a commodity when it is only expressed through gifts parents send back home to their children.[43] In summary, the balance between work and family in a transnational context is complicated by both changing gendered expectations in the family and by Mexicans' social status as migrant workers in the United States.

Methodology

The analysis in this chapter draws on a *multi-sited ethnography*[44] in the United States and Mexico. Between 2003 and 2006 I conducted participant observation as well as interviews with 142 members of Mexican transnational families residing in and around a new destination of Mexican migration in central New Jersey and in south-central Mexico.[45]

In a city in central New Jersey, I interviewed forty-five migrant parents (twenty-two mothers and twenty-three fathers) between 2003 and 2004 and conducted participant observation in the Mexican immigrant community.[46] The migrant mothers I interviewed generally worked in local fast-food restaurants and factories, the fathers in landscaping, construction, and private restaurants. All but three of the men and women interviewed were undocumented, and nearly all came from the three-state region of Oaxaca, Guerrero, and Puebla. In Mexico, the men had been farmers (eight), government administrators (three), electricians (two), a police officer, and an accountant. Most mothers had not been regularly employed outside of the home in Mexico. I used various personal contacts to identify parents for the interviews. Indeed, the fact that my young son's father is a Mexican immigrant and part of the city's Mexican immigrant community helped pave the way for informal conversations and observations.

In south-central Mexico, between 2004 and 2005, I interviewed sixty children of migrant parents, ages five through nineteen, as well as thirty-seven of their caregivers, mostly grandmothers. Most of the people interviewed lived in a community in the lower Mixtec region of Oaxaca, which I call San Angel. (All personal names used in the chapter are also pseudonyms.) Because I spent seven months in San Angel, I was also able to observe, at close range, how migration permeated everyday experiences. Surveys I carried out at the local middle school made clear how common it was for children to have close relatives in the United States: 65 percent of the students had members of their nuclear family (parents and/ or siblings) in the United States and 28 percent had one or both parents there. Four of the families I focused on in San Angel were closely related to parents I had previously interviewed in New Jersey; I also made trips to other parts of the region to interview children and their caregivers in eight families whose parents had been part of the study in New Jersey.

Parent–Child Relationships

When Mexican parents and children live apart, three aspects of migrants' experiences shape how they manage the balance between work and family life and, ultimately, relationships with their children. First, parents' experiences as low-wage, undocumented workers in the United States influence their ability to fulfill parental obligations from a distance and often lengthen family separations. Second, events related to parents' changing relations with their family members, especially marital conflicts and the birth of children in the United States, cause tensions in relationships with children back at home. Third, parental struggles to negotiate their roles with children's caregivers, particularly in terms of feelings of jealousy and exerting authority over their children, affect their experiences as transnational parents.

Undocumented, Low-Wage Workers

Parents often did not anticipate the difficulties they would face when they decided to leave home. In San Angel, for example, return migrants sported fancy clothes, brought nice gifts for their relatives, and invited friends and others to parties during the holiday season. Not having lived as minority immigrant workers in the United States, few of San Angel's residents understood the psychological importance for return migrants of saving enough money to be able to show off their economic prosperity. Those in San Angel believed that anyone who works hard in *el norte* can be successful.[47] Migrants who did not send money home regularly were considered lazy or suspected of spending money on vices such as alcohol or drugs. One migrant father in New Jersey said:

> I would say 75 percent of the people come fooled by this country. They are fooled by us immigrants who go back. We get a nice pair of shoes, good clothes and we say, "I earn so much and I have a car." . . . Everyone thinks that by coming they will make money quickly. They think coming here is living well.

Migrants arriving in New Jersey faced a stark reality. Work was not always easy to obtain; most migrants initially used temporary employment agencies that offered irregular jobs and deducted fees for their services, including transportation, from workers' salaries.[48] Even when they were better established and able to obtain jobs directly from employers, migrants were frequently unemployed. Many Mexican women worked in factories that depended on a floating labor force and provided them no benefits or job security. One mother I interviewed had held a steady job for more than two years at a factory but was fired when she took time off to care for a family member diagnosed with AIDS. Ever since, she has moved from job to job, part of the temporary workforce. Work is irregular in construction and landscaping, common jobs for Mexican men in central New Jersey. While jobs may be plentiful during the summer, and some men I interviewed at times worked up to sixty hours a week at ten to fifteen dollars per hour, when it rained and during the winter they did not work at all.

Mexican workers also did not expect that health problems, coupled with lack of health insurance, would affect their ability to work. One mother, for example, had to leave her job when she underwent an emergency kidney stone operation. Others stopped working during and after pregnancies. A father, Armando, had health problems when he first arrived in the United States and landed a job in landscaping with his brothers. He told me:

> I didn't think it would be so hard here. My brother gave me the impression that there was money to be made everywhere. . . . I first worked mowing lawns. But I didn't last because my health wasn't good when I got here. . . . I couldn't last at that job. Instead, I went to work in a factory.

Because factory work pays less than landscaping, the move meant a lower salary than Armando had originally anticipated. Work-related accidents were also a problem for the fathers I interviewed. Mexican men are employed in some of the most dangerous workplaces in the United States.[49] Even though workplace accidents are covered under worker's compensation (regardless of immigrant status), they affected migrants' ability to save money and send funds home.

Given these problems, migrants generally found they had to adjust their economic goals. José, who had worked steadily at a pizzeria for over three years, explained, "My plan initially was to stay here for two, maybe three, years in order to save enough money just to fix up my house. I calculated pretty carefully that it would take me this long to earn the money I needed." When I expressed surprise that he knew how much he would make before coming to the United States, José said, "Well, [I didn't know] exactly (pause). But based on what they told me people earn, I thought I would work approximately this many hours a week at this salary and I thought it would take me two years to reach my goal." José was already past the two-year mark when I first met him and was not sure when he would be able to go back to Mexico. He had made little progress toward his original goals.

One option was to simply return to Mexico. Some parents did. When I met Armando, he was frustrated by the difficulties he faced after his marriage fell apart (in New Jersey) and planned to go back to his three children in Mexico. "I was going to leave now, but my siblings convinced me to stay to December and save up some more money before leaving." True to plan, he returned home that Christmas. Such a return home requires parents to work long enough in the United States to pay off the debts accrued from their migration or, as in Armando's case, accrued at home during their absence. The result is that a return home is often delayed much longer than desired.

Many parents adjusted their economic strategies by sending for their children—although, like so much in the migrants' lives, bringing children to the United States is fraught with complications related to undocumented status. Generally, it took years to arrange, since it is considerably more dangerous and costly for unaccompanied children to cross the border.[50] One mother, for example, decided to send for her teenage son after he dropped out of the university, but she had to wait until her boyfriend went back for a vacation and could accompany her son across the border. José eventually decided to bring his eighteen-year-old son (who was twelve when he first left) to New Jersey, but for the past three years has been figuring out how to do this.

I found that many children—particularly young children—resisted parents' efforts to send for them and preferred to stay in Mexico.[51] In the face of such resistance—as well as the difficulty of meeting their economic goals in the United States—parents often resigned themselves to making family separation a more permanent arrangement than they had originally planned. At times, parents dealt with prolonged separation by returning to visit their children whenever possible. Return visits were again complicated by parents' legal status. A return visit required saving up significant money for the trip, making arrangements for the return passage to the United States, and securing time off or new employment upon their return.

Migrant mothers and fathers had different attitudes about these lengthy separations. Fathers were more likely to prefer that their children remain in Mexico. As one father said, "I am not the kind of person who likes this life for my children. Here there is too much freedom for them. It is not really a safe environment. I prefer that they stay in Mexico where they can receive a good education." Mothers hoped to be reunited with their children more quickly. Their return visits were generally motivated by the thought that if they saw their children in person, they could convince the children to migrate. Such visits were infrequent, however. Undocumented crossing is particularly perilous for women.[52] In fact, I only interviewed three mothers who had been home to visit their children. One of these mothers, Zelia, explained how women manage the crossing:

> You know what we do? We look for someone from town to go with. So then when you are going to wash up, you say to them, watch out for us, and they say, oh sure, and since they know us, they watch out for us. . . . Alone, I wouldn't come.

Although fathers also described the undocumented crossing as dangerous, particularly as compared to years past, this did not prevent them from going home to visit their families. Indeed, thirteen of the twenty-three fathers I interviewed had made a return trip multiple times.

No matter how parents adjusted their economic goals after they came to the United States, the end result was almost always a longer separation from children than originally planned. Social status as low-wage, undocumented workers in the United States put parents in a bind. Once having left their children behind, reunification was almost always more difficult and costly than parents anticipated.

The Changing Composition of Families

Transnational parents not only face challenges at work, they also must deal with shifting family dynamics that may lead to strains. Changing relations with marital partners often lead to tensions with children in Mexico. Marital discord frequently arises in immigrant families as couples find they must adjust their relationships to the U.S. context.[53]

For men who migrated without wives, accusations of infidelity affected relationships with children in Mexico.[54] One migrant father said his relationship with his oldest daughter was damaged by false rumors that he had had a baby with his sister-in-law. When this daughter migrated as a young adult, she refused to live with him; he complained that to this day she does not trust or respect his fatherly advice. A father of four teens told me that his wife suspected he had another wife in the United States. When he last went home, "My two older boys came to me together and they said: 'Dad, if you have another wife, we don't want you here. You can leave.'" At times such accusations were based on rumors; at other times men I interviewed did have new partners in the United States, although they still maintained ties to their wives and children in Mexico.

For women who migrated on their own, communication with children could be problematic when they had to deal with difficult ex-husbands. One mother, for example, left home when she found out her husband was living with another woman. For three years she had little contact with her three boys; she only occasionally spoke to the oldest when a neighbor helped arrange it. Another was unable to talk to her two children living with her ex-husband, who was remarried. He would not even accept the gifts that she sent the children. She was infuriated when she learned that the children were selling candy. "When I was there we were poor, but at least they weren't out on the streets."

It was fairly common for divorced or widowed migrant mothers who came on their own to remarry once in the United States. Relationships with step-fathers could be very difficult for children in Mexico to accept.[55] Moreover, new partners did not always recognize the women's children back in Mexico as part of their new family. Occasionally, I heard criticism of mothers who had lost touch with their children in Mexico (although there were very few such mothers in my sample). I was told that they had remarried and that the new husband was unwilling to provide for children from a former partner. One woman I interviewed praised her new husband for not being like others; he had accepted her two daughters back home as his own. "My girls even call him *papi*."

Couples migrating together were not immune from marital problems.[56] Many divorced or separated once in the United States—and gendered expectations of mothers and fathers affected their relationships with children back home.

Consider the case of José and Elsa. José was the first to migrate, leaving twelve-year-old Brian and ten-year-old Tina behind; he sent for his wife, Elsa, after she allegedly had an affair while he was away. After attempting to fix their marital problems, they subsequently separated. Over time, both found new partners in the United States. Back in Mexico, Brian and Tina felt more abandoned by their mother than by their father. According to Tina at age thirteen, "[My mom] now lives somewhere else [not with my dad], but she calls us every month. She rarely calls us. And, if she calls, it is a really quick conversation." When I first met Brian, then fifteen, he preferred talking to his mother on the phone. "When he [dad] calls it is like hello. And when my mom calls it is like, hey, it is so good that you called, how are you and all that. Like there is a different type of communication between mother and son." A year later, I spoke with him after he had learned of his mother's boyfriend:

J D : Do you love your mom?

B R I A N : Little, just a little bit.

J D : Do you feel like she loves you?

B R I A N : Uh, uh. No.

J D : Do you love your dad?

B R I A N : Yes.

J D : Do you feel like your dad loves you?

B R I A N : Sometimes I say—that no, but, well, yes. He is the only one who supports us.

The expectation that mothers should continue to act as primary caregivers meant that children were extremely distraught by their mothers' boyfriends.[57] They felt that their mothers' love and devotion were impossible to share with new partners in the United States.[58]

It is also hard for children in Mexico to share their parents, particularly their mothers, with step-siblings born abroad. A consistent theme in interviews with parents and children was how the birth of children in the United States threatened parents' relationships with children left behind. One father, for example, wondered whether his two children in Mexico would accept his newborn son, but then decided "they are young enough to grow attached to him." Another explained that his daughters in Mexico are jealous of his U.S.-born child: "Once one of the girls asked me to go home because [she worries that] if I don't I am going to love the one that was born here more than them." A mother who joined her husband two years earlier left two daughters with her sister-in-law and subsequently had a baby boy in the United States. She complained that on the phone "the girls reproach me. They are jealous, extremely jealous, the younger one more than the older one."

Children in Mexico described U.S.-born children as a potential threat. Younger children, in particular, feared that U.S.-born siblings or half-siblings would compete more successfully for their parents' love and attention since they lived with the parents. Fatima's mother, for example, had a baby in New York City, brought the baby back to Mexico to live with Fatima and her grandmother in San Angel, and then returned north. Fatima—age eleven at the time—said, "Sometimes I think my mom loves my little sister more because she was born there with her. I feel like she gives her more love. When she arrived I didn't like her." A sixteen-year-old whose father had a U.S.-born child told me, "I don't understand—it is so ignorant. If he cannot make it with us, how can he with another one." In effect, U.S.-born children not only compete with children in Mexico for scarce parental resources, they also undermine parents' statements that migration to the United States was undertaken for the sake of their children back in Mexico.

Children's fears were not entirely unfounded. For mothers, the pain of separation was so great that having a new child in the United States made them feel better. According to one mother, who had a daughter in Mexico and two U.S.-born children, "It is like you carry the weight of all the love that you have been holding in and then you put it on them [U.S.-born children]." Fathers were often much more involved with the care of U.S.-born children than they had been with children in Mexico; when both partners work in the United States, they tend to share child-care, and many men migrated while their Mexican-born children were still infants or sometimes before they were born.[59] A father who returned to San Angel with his U.S.-born daughter and his wife to be reunited with the couple's oldest son, said his son is not close to him and thinks that he loves his daughter more. The father insisted he loves his son, but he admitted that it is not the same. "I also feel different [toward them]. I raised my daughter since she was born. I bathed her, I changed her diapers, I prepared her bottles. I never did that for my son because I was away working in the north when he was little."

Of course, conflicts related to step-parents and step-siblings are common in the general American population.[60] Yet in many American families, the passage of time helps parents and children adjust to the changes in family composition and eventually accept new routines and new family members.[61] In contrast, for Mexican transnational families, parents and children have few, if any, opportunities to work out their differences in daily interactions. Over time, the likelihood of marital conflict, new partners, and U.S.-born children increases. The strains that the changes in family composition cause are likely to intensify or remain unresolved in the transnational context.

Parents and Caregivers

Children are not the only ones to experience jealousy while parents are away. Parents are also upset about being away from their children, and many are jealous of those in Mexico who live with and care for their children. Fathers who migrated without their wives lamented that their children grew closer to their wives during their absences. Armando said, "Right after I left for the United States, they [children] were more distanced from me, like they didn't miss me much." He suspected that his wife said bad things about him to the children, telling them that he was irresponsible.

When mothers migrate, feelings of jealousy toward those caring for their children are counterbalanced by the fact that they also feel grateful to have people they trust in this role. The most common caregivers for children when both parents (or mothers on their own) migrate are grandparents. Migrants are most at ease leaving their children with their own parents, who have a biological tie to their children (*por la sangre*) and will raise them with values similar to the parents' own. According to one mother, "I wouldn't have done it [if it weren't for my mother]. With my mother I know that they are okay." Migrants feel assured that their remittances are fulfilling economic obligations to both their children and their parents. Moreover, grandparents generally do not question biological parents' primary rights to their children, exemplified by one grandmother's comment: "I know it is not the same to be with your grandparents as to be with your parents. I am always conscious of this."

Despite the agreement by all parties that this is the best arrangement possible, tensions between migrant parents and grandparents over children's loyalties do arise. Children often emphasized affections for grandparents when they were upset by a mother's absence—calling their grandmothers "mami" or "mama," for example, which was acceptable to migrant mothers except when children subsequently stopped calling them mother. Migrant mother Sandra explained why she disliked telephoning her nine-year-old daughter:

> When I call I ask to speak with my daughter and, although they are not talking to me, I overhear a conversation that goes something like this: They say, "Come, Raquel, your mom is calling." And she answers, "Who? Who wants to talk to me?" "Your mom." "Oh, Sandra" [name drawn out] she says before coming to talk to me on the phone.

Nydia also was upset when her son Kevin did not want to talk to her over the phone. "The only thing that makes me feel badly is when he doesn't want to talk to me. Sometimes there is a little distance between us and he doesn't want to talk. When I was there, he was a little closer to me."

Grandparents often tried to smooth relations between the children and their migrant parents by highlighting parents' sacrifices to their grandchildren. They did not question parents' rights over the children. And they typically did not flaunt their own close relations with the children. Yet they did feel quite close to their grandchildren, something that did not escape migrant parents' observations. Many migrants, in fact, were worried about taking their children away from grandparents. Nydia said that one reason she did not send for four-year-old Kevin was that her parents would be upset if she took him away. Her mother, Doña Ana, told me how important Kevin was to her and her husband; Doña Ana feared that if Kevin left, her husband would become ill. "He is very close to the boy because he has always lived with him and he helped take care of Kevin since he was only forty days old. Once [before she migrated] Nydia took Kevin to visit his other grandparents for a week and Nydia's father was sick with worry the whole time."

Unable to bear being apart from Kevin any longer, Nydia and her husband decided to return to Mexico. Once back with her family, however, Nydia's husband was unhappy; he was uncomfortable living with his in-laws. He left Nydia and moved in with his own parents. Nydia explained the separation from her husband by saying that she refused to leave Kevin again and could not take the boy away from her parents. "The first time, I left my son for my husband [to migrate to the United States]. This time I will stay with my son." In the end, tensions over Kevin's loyalties led not to a fight between mother and daughter, but rather to an irreconcilable conflict between husband and wife.

Parents not only had trouble coping with children's loyalties toward caregivers, they also often felt frustrated by their inability to exert authority over children from a distance. Although migrant parents (and caregivers) considered that the parents' rights over their children remained intact, young children in Mexico generally asked caregivers for permission to do things.[62] For example, an eleven-year-old girl whose parents recently returned from the United States told me, "I ask my parents for permission only because that is what my grandmother told me I should do." Before returning to Mexico Nydia said, "Maybe if I correct him he listens to me and sometimes he doesn't. But with my parents, no. There is more respect for them."

When children ignored parents' attempts to exert authority from a distance, parents felt badly that they were away. Children's deference to their primary caregivers in Mexico was especially hurtful for fathers, who consider authority in Mexican families to be ultimately theirs.[63] Gabriela cared for her children in Mexico while her husband worked in New Jersey. When I spoke with her, he had recently come to Mexico to visit during the holidays. She said: "The kids always come to me for permission and with their problems. My husband has even commented to them, 'Am I not worth anything here?' Once he told them, 'I am going to leave because you don't respect me.'" Her husband, Angelo, explained that when he visited Mexico, his eight-year-old son "comes into the house and walks by me looking for his mother to ask if he can go play. I stop him and say, 'What's this, *¿y yo qué?*' What about me?"

Whether intentional or subconsciously, by overlooking their migrant parents and ceding authority to the caregivers who raise them, children signal the importance of the primary caregiver in their lives. Migrant parents may laugh it off but later shake their heads and wonder, as Angelo did, What about me? When children ignore parents' authority, they underscore the emotional costs of parental absences. In response, parents often make significant efforts to adjust their economic strategies, usually by making arrangements to send for their children, which, as I have already indicated, involve substantial economic resources for low-wage workers in the United States. In this way, young children's emotional reactions to their parents' absences often have significant economic repercussions.[64] They affect the ways parents evaluate their decision about how to manage the work-family life balance.

Gendered Expectations

In some ways, the transnational context presents similar challenges to both women and men who parent children from afar. Mexican mothers and fathers working in the United States face legal constraints owing to their immigration status; it is estimated that 80 to 85 percent of Mexicans arriving in the United States between 1995 and 2005 were undocumented.[65] The migrant mothers and fathers I interviewed lived apart from their children mainly because financial and legal constraints prevented the family from migrating together. Nonetheless, Mexican mothers' and fathers' experiences differ in important ways that highlight the gendered expectations involved in parenting. They also underscore how gender inequality plays a critical role in the way men and women negotiate a work-family life balance during international migration.

In general, women faced greater difficulties visiting their children in Mexico than men did. They felt more at risk crossing the border to go home for visits.[66] Their work patterns also played a role. Although migrant women often experienced spells of unemployment, they had greater job stability than the men I interviewed. Many men worked in seasonal occupations, like landscaping and construction, so that there was a regular time of the year when they had fewer obligations in the United States and could easily contemplate a visit home. Women, in contrast, worked year-round, for lower wages than men. Their regular labor-force participation was important to the family income. Among couples living together, many men depended on their wives' employment during the winter months to pay the bills—and wives, as a result, had less freedom to return home to see their children.

Fathers' visits home were often as unpredictable as their employment was volatile, which was not always a positive experience for their children. Some children had spent most of their childhood in Mexico living without fathers. Many in San Angel described their fathers as popping in and out of their lives; fathers' departures were a source of anxiety.[67] One twenty-five-year-old looked back on her father's perpetual absences: "I felt like the U.S. robbed my father from me."

Mothers planned their separations more carefully than fathers did and, at least initially, anticipated being reunited with their children quickly. Although they visited Mexico less frequently than fathers, the mothers I interviewed averaged fewer years apart from their children. During separation, the migrant mothers felt more distraught than did fathers about maintaining communication with children whom they rarely saw. More so than fathers, their goal in saving money was to be reunited with their children. Although many mothers hoped to retire to Mexico, the burden of living apart from their children often became too much to bear. Many ended up reuniting with their children in the United States. Referring to her children's imminent arrival in New York City, Nicandra explained, "This was not my plan. . . . I always thought I would work until I could go back there. But now I guess that all of us will end up here." Fathers' separations from their children, in contrast, were often more longstanding.

Changes in family composition in the United States also shaped mothers' and fathers' relationships with children in different ways. Because fathers were evaluated as family providers, the fathers' new partners or children in the United States only became problematic for children in Mexico when fathers' economic resources were strained as a result. While fathers' economic support was enough to demonstrate love, children expected mothers to express greater concern and devotion. Fifteen-year-old Brian, for example, was quite resentful of his mother for divorcing his father in New Jersey and moving in with another man. He said he didn't feel like he loved his mother or that she loved him. "Because if she loved us really, she would call. Or not even, that she doesn't send (money), because that doesn't matter. But at least she has to call." In contrast, Brian said he loves his father, who also had remarried in New Jersey. Children were likely to question the devotion of their mothers when they became involved with new partners and had new children abroad.

The gendered double standard during migration is also evident in parents' conflicting emotions at being separated from their children. Both mothers and fathers worried about children's loyalties and were frustrated when children did not acknowledge them or their authority. Yet fathers described such tensions as unavoidable side-effects of the migratory experience, something they just had to deal with. They generally minimized the emotional costs of family separation—perhaps owing to men's efforts to distance themselves from "direct manifestations of sadness."[68] Mothers, in contrast, expressed great remorse over the decision to work in the United States. Fourteen mothers said that they cried for months upon arrival in the United States, lacked appetite, and became physically ill, and a number said they were severely depressed. One mother told me, "I cried for two months when I first arrived. . . . I was nervous all the time and made lots of mistakes when I first started to work." Another complained that before her husband went back for her son, "I didn't work well. I didn't sleep well. I didn't eat well." A mother in San Angel told me she returned to Mexico because "I suffered a lot . . . without my son, especially when we had first arrived. When we would go out to the stores and I saw the children with their parents, I would start to cry."

Fathers rarely said they felt guilty about having left their children in Mexico. For example, a father of three, who called and sent money weekly to his children in Mexico, explained: "No, [I don't feel guilty]. I think I would feel bad if I knew the children were suffering, and that they wouldn't suffer if I was there with them. But they aren't, so I don't." He considered his responsibility to be for his children's economic well-being. His children suffered less economically because he worked abroad and sent money home regularly, thereby making his sacrifice guilt-free.

In contrast, mothers often said they felt guilty about leaving their children behind.[69] Nicandra, whose teenage sons lived in Mexico, told me,

"I often feel guilty. When things aren't going well I feel guilty. When my son wasn't doing well, it was like I wasn't on top of things. I mean, one feels guilty for not giving them the attention they need." Like many other migrant women, Nicandra felt that her children's emotional well-being was her responsibility. Even though the children's father (her ex-husband) lived near them in Mexico, Nicandra felt that because she was unable to meet her son's emotional needs from abroad she was failing to live up to her role as a mother.

Changing Dynamics over Time

Today's Mexican families are achieving a work-family life balance in new ways. Women are now joining men and using international migration without their children as a means to better provide for their children's future. In a number of ways, women's and men's experiences are similar. As low-wage, undocumented workers, mothers and fathers find they are unable to meet their migration goals as quickly as they originally anticipated. A combination of constraints related to their legal and labor statuses tends to prolong separation from their children. While in the United States, events like the birth of a new child or marital conflict affect the types of relationships both mothers and fathers are able to maintain with children back in Mexico. Mothers and fathers struggle to exert their authority from a distance over children who are dubious and at times resentful of their parents' decisions to migrate. Mothers as well as fathers often feel jealous of their children's primary caregivers in Mexico.

Yet women and men ultimately have different experiences as transnational parents. Mothers cannot visit their children as easily as fathers. Mothers' absences are seen as more upsetting to children and the "family order" than those of fathers; mothers' attentions towards new family members in the United States are considered more disruptive to relationships with children in Mexico. Mothers also feel guiltier than fathers about their difficulties in parenting from a distance. In the end, what these differences make clear is that gendered expectations are of great significance in the transnational context. Comparing the experiences of Mexican mothers and fathers reveals that mothers' sacrifices are viewed more harshly, both by children and mothers themselves, than those of fathers.

Mexican mothers' and fathers' own evaluations of their sacrifices are also shaped by their children's reactions to separation. Because parents care about their children, they are generally responsive to their children's needs. When children refuse to migrate, for example, parents attempt to persuade them otherwise through return trips home. Children's reactions also make both mothers and fathers feel badly about being away. Parents, especially mothers, may reconsider their migration decisions, and even alter the family migration strategy, based on their children's reactions to separation. It may well be that American working parents are as influenced by children's emotions as the Mexican migrants I interviewed.[70] Yet when parents and children live together, they interact frequently and more readily adjust to each other's changing needs. Children's influence over parents' work life is perhaps more evident in the transnational context, when physical separation heightens parents', and particularly mothers', sense of sacrifice as a result of employment.

The uncertainty inherent in managing relationships as intimate as those between parents and children from a distance means that intergenerational dynamics in many migrant families have distinctive features. When parents and children do not live in the same country, share in the same routines, or experience similar opportunities and constraints, intergenerational relationships are constantly in flux. During periods of separation, parents and children must constantly adapt to each other's changing needs. They do so based on the little information they can glean through weekly phone conversations, second-hand accounts from caregivers, and neighbors' gossip.[71] Lack of contact increases insecurity and intensifies emotions. The effects of changes in family composition are harder to adjust to. And, over time, the work and legal conditions that both shape and restrict parents' choices about how to manage work and family life make the sacrifice inherent in international migration all the more difficult.

NOTES

1. Pew Hispanic Center 2007.

2. A Pew Hispanic Center survey of immigrants at Mexican consulates throughout the United States found that 18 percent of all immigrants surveyed and more than one in four parents had one or more children in Mexico. Most were fathers, but a significant proportion of mothers also had children in Mexico. See Suro 2005.

3. Of the nearly 10 million working mothers in the United States, 79 percent leave children with someone besides a parent while they are at work. See Johnson 2005.

4. For descriptions of parents' struggles to achieve a work-life balance, see Hochschild 1997; Schneider and Waite 2005; Stone 2007.

5. Foner 2000; Gabaccia 2001; Nakano Glenn 1983; Thomas and Znaniecki 1927.

6. Gabaccia 2001.

7. Nakano Glenn 1983.

8. Foner 2000: 172.

9. For an excellent description of the racial dynamics during this period in Arizona, see Gordon 1999.

10. See Hondagneu-Sotelo 1994; Martin 1998; Massey et al. 1987.

11. Sanchez 1993.

12. Hondagneu-Sotelo 1994.

13. Today we know that return migration rates were also high among earlier immigrants and that many Mexicans outstayed their *bracero* visas and settled in the United States. However, the specific regulations of the Bracero program, and the proximity of Mexico to the United States, meant Mexicans' migrations were generally much more temporary in nature than those of people traveling from Europe or Asia.

14. During this period, as some *braceros* left their contracts and sent for their families and others moved north without ever participating in the program, Mexican communities began to grow, primarily in the U.S. Southwest. See Cohen 2004; Hondagneu-Sotelo 1994; Martin 1998; Massey et al. 1987.

15. See Massey et al. 1987.

16. Thomas and Znaniecki 1927.

17. See also Gabaccia 2001; Piore 1979.

18. Gordon 1988; Irving 2000; Sanchez 1993.

19. For more on the lives of Mexican women whose husbands have migrated, see D'Aubeterre 2000, 2002; Fagetti 2000; Hondagneu-Sotelo 1994; Marroni 2000; Mummert 1988.

20. Hondagneu-Sotelo and Avila 1997. For discussions of transnationalism as a theoretical perspective for understanding new patterns of migration, see Portes, Guarnizo, and Landolt 1999; Schiller, Basch, and Blanc 1998; Schiller and Fouron 1999; Smith 2000, 2006; Smith and Guarnizo 1999.

21. West Indian women, for example, have been leaving children with grandmothers to work in New York City since the 1920s. Wet nurses in eighteenth-century Spain left their infants with their husbands to work in the city of Madrid. See Sarasüa 2001; Watkins-Owens 2001.

22. Robles and Watkins 1993.

23. Chang 2000; Cohen 2000; Constable 1999; Ehrenreich and Hochschild 2002; Erel 2002; Hondagneu-Sotelo 2001; Lan 2003; Salazar Parreñas 2001; Schmalzbauer 2005a; Sørenson 2005.

24. Ehrenreich and Hochschild 2002: 8.

25. Durand, Massey, and Capoferro 2005; Hirsch 2003; Zuñiga and Hernandez-Leon 2005.

26. Cornelius 1991; Escobar Latapi and Gonzalez de la Rocha 1995; Stephen 2007.

27. Cornelius 1991; Donato 1993.

28. Kanaiaupuni 2000.

29. Dreby forthcoming.

30. After an amnesty program in 1986, efforts were redoubled to restrict undocumented migration. Border enforcement was heightened and, more importantly, concentrated in areas considered to be the "main gates" of illegal entry on the U.S.-Mexican border, making crossing the border increasingly dangerous. Immigration reform in 1996 implemented greater penalties for the undocumented who had illegally crossed the border (read Mexicans), and social benefits to the families of immigrants were curtailed under the Welfare Reform Act of the same year. See Chang 2000; Cornelius 2001.

31. Massey, Durand, and Malone 2002.

32. Cornelius 2001.

33. See Cornelius 2001; Massey 2006; Passel 2005.

34. Massey 2006; Massey, Durand, and Malone 2002.

35. See also Dreby forthcoming.

36. Echoing complaints waged nearly one hundred years earlier, today many journalists and social workers have pointed out the deleterious effects of migration on children left behind by their mothers. According to Salazar Parreñas (2005), who has studied Filipino transnational families extensively: "Much academic and newspaper writing on transnational families assumes that children growing up in the Philippines without their parents, particularly their mothers, are prone to delinquency and declining moral values, particularly materialism" (p. 39). For examples of such journalistic approaches, see Garcia-Navarro 2006; Hansen 2003; Nazario 2006.

37. For examples of the different ways states may regulate migratory flows, see Menjívar 2006; Sadiq 2005; Tyner 1999.

38. See Passel 2006.

39. Mahler 2001.

40. Dreby 2006.

41. Dreby 2006; Salazar Parreñas 2005.

42. Dreby 2006, forthcoming.

43. Hondagneu-Sotelo and Avila 1997; Salazar Parreñas 2001.

44. Marcus 1998.

45. For more details on the methods used and characteristics of the samples, see Dreby forthcoming.

46. In this city of about 50,000 residents, the Mexican immigrant population went from 1.3 percent in 1990 to 12.6 percent in 2000. I should note that I lived

in this city for ten years starting in 1997 and had previously worked in four different social service agencies, including as an ESL teacher, where I came to know many Mexican families (U.S. Census Bureau n.d.).

47. See also Chavez 1992; Malkin 2004; Schmalzbauer 2005b.

48. See Ortega 2006.

49. Pritchard 2004.

50. Marizco 2004; Nazario 2006.

51. Dreby 2007.

52. See Amnesty International 1998; Chavez 1992.

53. Reanne Frank (2005) has shown rates of marital dissolution to be higher among Mexican migrants than their non-migrant counterparts. See also Kibria 1993; Min 1998; Smith 2006.

54. For more on transnational gossip, see Dreby 2008; Menjívar and Agadjanian 2007.

55. See also Chinchilla and Zentgraf 2007.

56. See Hirsch 2003; Smith 2006.

57. Dreby 2006.

58. For more on step-parents, see Ahrons 2004; Furstenberg and Cherlin 1994; Wallerstein and Blakeslee 1989.

59. Levitt 2001.

60. Furstenberg and Cherlin 1994; Jensen and McKee 2003.

61. Furstenberg and Cherlin 1994.

62. Dreby 2007.

63. See Esteinou 2004.

64. Dreby 2007.

65. Passel 2006.

66. Dreby forthcoming.

67. See Dreby 2009.

68. Riessman 1990: 155.

69. See also Dreby 2006.

70. See Galinsky 1999.

71. For more on these families' experiences with gossip, see Dreby 2009.

REFERENCES

Ahrons, Constance. 2004. *We're Still Family: What Grown Children Have to Say about Their Parents' Divorce.* New York: Harper Collins.

Amnesty International. 1998. "Human Rights Concerns in the Border Region with Mexico" (AMR 51/03/98 May 20). Washington, DC: Amnesty International. Accessed September 16, 2005 at http://web.amnesty.org/library/Index/engAMR510031998.

Chang, Grace. 2000. *Disposable Domestics: Immigrant Women Workers in the Global Economy.* Cambridge, MA: South End Press.

Chavez, Leo R. 1992. *Shadowed Lives: Undocumented Immigrants in American Society.* Case Studies in Cultural Anthropology. Fort Worth, TX: Harcourt Brace Jovanovich.

Chinchilla, Norma, and Kristine Zentgraf. 2007. "Immigrant Children's Views of Family Separation and Reunification." Paper presented at the Latin American Studies Conference in Montreal, September.

Cohen, Jeffrey H. 2004. *The Culture of Migration in Southern Mexico.* Austin: University of Texas Press.

Cohen, Rina. 2000. "'Mom Is a Stranger': The Negative Impact of Immigration Policies on the Family Life of Filipina Domestic Workers." *Canadian Ethnic Studies* 32: 76–89.

Constable, Nicole. 1999. "'At Home But Not at Home': Filipina Narratives of Ambivalent Returns." *Cultural Anthropology* 14: 203–28.

Cornelius, Wayne. 1991. "Los Migrantes de la Crisis: The Changing Profile of Mexican Migration to the United States." Pp. 155–94 in M. Gonzalez de la Rocha and A. Escobar Latapi (eds.), *Social Responses to Mexico's Economic Crisis of the 1980s.* San Diego: University of California, Center for U.S. Mexican Studies.

———. 2001. "Death at the Border: Efficacy and Unintended Consequences of U.S. Immigration Control Policy." *Population and Development Review* 27: 661–85.

D'Aubeterre, Maria Eugenia. 2000. "Mujeres y espacio social transnacional: maniobras para renegociar el vinculo conyugal." Pp. 63–85 in D. Barrera and C. Oehmichen (eds.), *Migración y relacciones de género en México.* Mexico City: GIMTRAP and UNAM, Instituto de Investigaciones Antropológicas.

———. 2002. "Genero, parentesco y redes migratorias femeninas." *Alteridades* 12: 51–60.

Donato, Katharine M. 1993. "Current Trends and Patterns of Female Migration: Evidence from Mexico." *International Migration Review* 27: 748–68.

Dreby, Joanna. 2006. "Honor and Virtue: Mexican Parenting in the Transnational Context." *Gender & Society* 20: 32–59.

———. 2007. "Children and Power in Mexican Transnational Families." *Journal of Marriage and Family* 69: 1050–64.

———. 2009. "Gender and Transnational Gossip." *Qualitative Sociology,* forthcoming.

———. Forthcoming. *Divided by Borders: Mexican Migrants and Their Children.* Berkeley: University of California Press.

Durand, Jorge, Douglas S. Massey, and Chiara Capoferro. 2005. "The New Geography of Mexican Immigration." Pp. 1–20 in Victor Zuniga and Ruben Hernandez-Leon (eds.), *New Destinations: Mexican Immigration in the United States.* New York: Russell Sage Foundation.

Ehrenreich, Barbara, and Arlie R. Hochschild. 2002. *Global Woman: Nannies, Maids and Sex Workers in the New Economy.* New York: Metropolitan/Owl Books.

Erel, Umet. 2002. "Reconceptualizing Motherhood: Experiences of Migrant Women from Turkey Living in Germany." Pp. 127–45 in D. Bryceson and U. Vuorela (eds.), *The Transnational Family: New European Frontiers and Global Networks.* Oxford: Berg.

Escobar Latapi, Agustin, and Mercedes Gonzalez de la Rocha. 1995. "Crisis, Restructuring and Urban Poverty in Mexico." *Environment and Urbanization* 7: 57–76.

Esteinou, Rosario. 2004. "Parenting in Mexican Society." *Marriage and Family Review* 36: 7–29.

Fagetti, Antonella. 2000. "Mujeres abandonadas: Desafios y vivencias." In D. Barrera and C. Oehmichen (eds.), *Migración y relacciones de género en México.* Mexico City: GIMTRAP and UNAM, Instituto de Investigaciones Antropológicas.

Foner, Nancy. 2000. *From Ellis Island to JFK: New York's Two Great Waves of Immigration.* New Haven: Yale University Press.

Frank, Reanne. 2005. "The Grass Widows of Mexico: Migration and Union Dissolution in a Binational Context." *Social Forces* 83: 919–47.

Furstenberg, Frank F., and Andrew Cherlin. 1994. *Divided Families: What Happens to Children When Parents Part.* Cambridge: Harvard University Press.

Gabaccia, Donna. 2001. "When the Migrants Are Men: Italy's Women and Transnationalism as a Working Class Way of Life." Pp. 190–208 in P. Sharpe (ed.), *Women, Gender and Labour Migration: Historical and Global Perspectives.* London: Routledge.

Galinsky, Ellen. 1999. *Ask the Children: What America's Children Really Think about Working Parents.* New York: William Morrow.

Garcia-Navarro, Lourdes. 2006. "Mexican Migrants Leave Kids, Problems Back Home." National Public Radio, Morning Edition: May 9, 2006. Accessed July 27, 2006, at http://www.npr.org/templates/story/story.php?storyId=5392227.

Gordon, Linda. 1988. *Heroes of Their Own Lives: The History and Politics of Family Violence.* New York: Penguin Books.

———. 1999. *The Great Arizona Orphan Abduction.* Cambridge: Harvard University Press.

Hansen, Gerry. 2003. Morning Edition. National Public Radio. June 23. Accessed on July 27, 2006, at http://www.npr.org/templates/story/story.php?storyId=1307611.

Hirsch, Jennifer S. 2003. *A Courtship after Marriage: Sexuality and Love in Mexican Transnational Families.* Berkeley: University of California Press.

Hochschild, Arlie R. 1997. *The Time Bind.* New York: Metropolitan Books.

Hondagneu-Sotelo, Pierrette. 1994. *Gendered Transitions: Mexican Experiences of Immigration.* Berkeley: University of California Press.

———. 2001. *Doméstica: Immigrant Workers Cleaning and Caring in the Shadows of Affluence.* Berkeley: University of California Press.

Hondagneu-Sotelo, Pierrette, and Ernestine Avila. 1997. "'I'm Here But I'm There': The Meanings of Latina Transnational Motherhood." *Gender & Society* 11: 548–60.

Irving, Katrina. 2000. *Immigrant Mothers: Narratives of Race and Maternity, 1890–1925.* Urbana: University of Illinois Press.

Jensen, An-Margritt, and Lorna McKee. 2003. *Children and the Changing Family: Between Transformation and Negotiation.* London: Routledge Falmer.

Johnson, Julia Overturf. 2005. *Who's Minding the Kids? Child Care Arrangements: Winter 2002.* Washington, D.C.: U.S. Census Bureau. Accessed August 28, 2005 at http://www.census.gov/prod/2005pubs/p70-101.pdf.

Kanaiaupuni, Shawn Malia. 2000. "Reframing the Migration Question: An Analysis of Men, Women and Gender in Mexico." *Social Forces* 78: 1311–42.

Kibria, Nazli. 1993. *Family Tightrope: The Changing Lives of Vietnamese Americans.* Princeton: Princeton University Press.

Lan, Pei-Chia. 2003. "Maid or Madam? Filipina Migrant Workers and the Continuity of Domestic Labor." *Gender & Society* 17: 187–208.

Levitt, Peggy. 2001. *The Transnational Villagers.* Berkeley: University of California Press.

Mahler, Sarah. 2001. "Transnational Relationships: The Struggle to Communicate across Borders." *Identities* 7: 583–619.

Malkin, Victoria. 2004. "'We Go to Get Ahead': Gender and Status in Two Mexican Migrant Communities." *Latin American Perspectives* 31: 75–99.

Marcus, George E. 1998. *Ethnography through Thick and Thin.* Princeton: Princeton University Press.

Marizco, Michael. 2004. "Smuggling Children." *Arizona Daily Star,* November 21. Accessed November 4, 2005, at http://www.azstarnet.com/sn/border/49066.

Marroni, Maria da Gloria. 2000. "'El siempre me ha dejado con los chiquitos y se ha llevado a los grandes . . .' Ajustes y desbarajustes familiares de la migración." Pp. 15–44 in D. Barrera and C. Oehmichen (eds.), *Migración y Relaciones de Género en México.* Mexico City: GIMTRAP and UNAM, Instituto de Investigaciones Antropológicas.

Martin, Philip. 1998. "Guest Workers: Past and Present." *Mexico-United States Binational Study,* vol. 3. Accessed September 21, 2005, at www.utexas.edu/lbj/uscir/binpapers/v3a-3martin.pdf.

Massey, Douglas. 2006. "Borderline Madness." *Chronicle of Higher Education,* June 30, p. B11.

Massey, Douglas, Rafael Alarcon, Jorge Durand and Humberto Gonzalez. 1987. *Return to Aztlan: The Social Process of International Migration from Western Mexico.* Berkeley: University of California Press.

Massey, Douglas, Jorge Durand, and Nolan Malone. 2002. *Beyond Smoke and Mirrors: Mexican Immigration in an Era of Economic Integration.* New York: Russell Sage Foundation.

Menjívar, Cecilia. 2006. "Liminal Legality: Salvadoran and Guatemalan Immigrants' Lives in the United States." *American Journal of Sociology* 111: 999–1037.

Menjívar, Cecilia, and Victor Agadjanian. 2007. "Men's Migration and Women's Lives: Views from Rural Armenia and Guatemala." *Social Science Quarterly* 88: 1243–62.

Min, Pyong Gap. 1998. *Changes and Conflicts: Korean Immigrant Families in New York*. Boston: Allyn and Bacon.

Mummert, Gail. 1988. "Mujeres de Migrantes y Mujeres Migrantes de Michoacon: Nuevo papeles para las que se quedan y las que se van." Pp 281–95 in T. Calvo and G. Lopez (eds.), *Movimientos de población en el occidente de México*. Mexico City and Zamora, Michoacán: Centre d'Estudes Mexicaines et Centramericaines and El Colegio de México.

Nakano Glenn, E. 1983. "Split Household, Small Producer and Dual Wage Earner: An Analysis of Chinese-American Family Strategies." *Journal of Marriage and the Family* 45: 35–46.

Nazario, Sonia. 2006. *La Travesía de Enrique*. New York: Random House.

Ortega, Ralph R. 2006. "No Papers? No Problem." *Newark Star Ledger*, July 23.

Passel, Jeffrey. 2005. "Unauthorized Migrants: Size and Characteristics." Pew Hispanic Center, Washington, DC. Accessed August 8, 2005, at http://pewhispanic.org/files/reports/44.pdf.

———. 2006. "The Size and Characteristics of the Unauthorized Migrant Population in the US." Pew Hispanic Center, Washington, DC. Accessed April 7, 2006, at http://pewhispanic.org/files/reports/61.pdf.

Pew Hispanic Center. 2007. *Factsheet: Indicators of Recent Migration Flows from Mexico*. Washington, DC, May 30. Accessed August 28, 2007, at http://pewhispanic.org/files/factsheets/33.pdf.

Piore, Michael J. 1979. *Birds of Passage: Migrant Labor and Industrial Societies*. Cambridge: Cambridge University Press.

Portes, Alejandro, Luis Guarnizo, and Patricia Landolt. 1999. "The Study of Transnationalism: Pitfalls and Promise of an Emergent Research Field." *Ethnic and Racial Studies* 22: 217–37.

Pritchard, Justin. 2004. "One Mexican Worker Dying a Day." *Associated Press*, March 13. Accessed March 23, 2006, at http://fmmac2.mm.ap.org/polk_awards_dying_to_work_html/DyingtoWork.html.

Riessman, Catherine Kohler. 1990. *Divorce Talk: Women and Men Make Sense of Personal Relationships*. New Brunswick, NJ: Rutgers University Press.

Robles, Arodys, and Susan Cott Watkins. 1993. "Immigration and Family Separation in the U.S. at the Turn of the Twentieth Century." *Journal of Family History* 18: 191–211.

Sadiq, Kamal. 2005. "When States Prefer Non-Citizens over Citizens: Conflict Over Illegal Immigration into Malaysia." *International Studies Quarterly* 49: 101–22.

Salazar Parreñas, Rhacel. 2001. *Servants of Globalization: Women, Migration and Domestic Work*. Stanford: Stanford University Press.

———. 2005. *Children of Global Migration: Transnational Families and Gender Woes*. Stanford: Stanford University Press.

Sanchez, George J. 1993. *Becoming Mexican American: Ethnicity, Culture and Identity in Chicano Los Angeles, 1900–1945*. New York: Oxford University Press.

Sarasüa, Carmen. 2001. "Leaving Home to Help the Family? Male and Female Temporary Migrants in Eighteenth- and Nineteenth-Century Spain." Pp. 29–59 in P. Sharpe (ed.), *Women, Gender and Labour Migration: Historical and Global Perspectives*. London: Routledge.

Schiller, Nina, Linda Basch, and Cristina Szanton Blanc. 1998. "Transnationalism: A New Analytic Framework for Understanding Migration." Pp. 26–59 in Steven Vertovec (ed.), *Migration, Diasporas and Transnationalism*. Cheltenham, UK: Edward Elgar.

Schiller, Nina, and Georges Fouron. 1999. "Terrains of Blood and Nation: Haitians Transnational Social Fields." *Ethnic and Racial Studies* 22: 340–66.

Schmalzbauer, Leah. 2005a. "Searching for Wages and Mothering from Afar: The Case of Honduran Transnational Families." *Journal of Marriage and Family* 66: 1317–31.

———. 2005b. "Transamerican Dreamers: The Relationship of Honduran Transmigrants to the Ideology of the American Dream and Consumer Society." *Berkeley Journal of Sociology* 49: 3–31.

Schneider, Barbara, and Linda Waite. 2005. *Being Together, Working Apart: Dual-Career Families and the Work-Life Balance*. Cambridge: Cambridge University Press.

Smith, Michael P., and Luis Eduardo Guarnizo (eds.). 1999. *Transnationalism from Below*. New Brunswick, NJ: Transaction Publishers.

Smith, Robert C. 2000. "How Durable and New Is Transnational Life? Historical Retrieval through Local Comparison." *Diaspora* 9: 203–33.

———. 2006. *Mexican New York: Transnational Lives of New Immigrants*. Berkeley: University of California Press.

Sørensen, Ninna Nyberg. 2005. "Transnational Family Life across the Atlantic: The Experience of Colombian and Dominican Migrants in Europe." Paper presented at the International Conference on Migration and Domestic Work in a Global Perspective, Wassenar, The Netherlands. Accessed November 4, 2005, at http://www.nias.knaw.nl/en/news_forthcoming_activities/lutz/new_3/sorensen.pdf.

Stephen, Lynn. 2007. *Transborder Lives: Indigenous Oaxacans in Mexico, California, and Oregon*. Durham, NC: Duke University Press.

Stone, Pamela. 2007. *Opting Out? Why Women Really Quit Careers and Head Home*. Berkeley: University of California Press.

Suro, Roberto. 2005. "Survey of Mexican Migrants Part 1: Attitudes about Immigration and Major Demographic Characteristics." Washington, D.C., Pew Hispanic Center. Accessed February 5, 2007, at http://pewhispanic.org/files/reports/41.pdf.

Thomas, William I., and Florian Znaniecki. 1927. *The Polish Peasant in Europe and America*. New York: Alfred A. Knopf.

Tyner, James A. 1999. "The Global Context of Gendered Labor Migration from the Philippines." *American Behavioral Scientist* 42: 671–89.

U.S. Census Bureau. n.d. *2000 Census of Population and Housing Summary File 3*. Accessed May 2, 2005, at http://www.factfinder.census.gov.

Wallerstein, Judith, and Sandra Blakeslee. 1989. *Second Chances: Men, Women and Children a Decade after Divorce*. New York: Ticknor and Fields.

Watkins-Owens, Irma. 2001. "Early Twentieth Century Caribbean Women: Migration and Social Networks in New York City." Pp. 25–51 in Nancy Foner (ed.), *Islands in the City: West Indian Migration to New York*. Berkeley: University of California Press.

Zuñiga, Victor, and Ramon Hernández-Leon (eds.). 2005. *New Destinations: Mexican Immigration in the United States*. New York: Russell Sage Foundation.

III

About the Contributors

LEISY ABREGO is Postdoctoral Fellow at the University of California, Irvine. Her research interests include international migration, the effects of legal status on the well-being of immigrants and their families, gender, and the sociology of law. She has published articles in *Latino Studies* and *Law & Social Inquiry* about undocumented students' access to higher education. She recently completed her dissertation in Sociology at UCLA on the effects of migrant parents' legal status and gender on Salvadoran transnational families.

JOANN D'ALISERA is Associate Professor of Anthropology at the University of Arkansas. Her research interests include transnational communities and identities, material culture, sacred space, Sierra Leone, and Islam. She is the author of *An Imagined Geography: Sierra Leonean Muslims in America* (University of Pennsylvania Press, 2004).

JOANNA DREBY is Assistant Professor of Sociology at Kent State University. Her research on Mexican migrant families has been published in *Gender & Society*, the *Journal of Marriage and Family*, and *Qualitative Sociology*. She has also coauthored publications on child-care safety in the *American Sociological Review*, *Contexts*, and *Teaching Sociology*. Her book *Divided by Borders: Mexican Migrants and Their Children* is forthcoming from the University of California Press.

YEN LE ESPIRITU is Professor of Ethnic Studies at the University of California, San Diego. Her latest book, *Home Bound: Filipino American Lives across Cultures, Communities, and Countries* (University of California Press, 2003), received two national book awards. Her current research projects explore "rememorations" of the Vietnam War and Vietnamese and Vietnamese American transnational lives.

NANCY FONER is Distinguished Professor of Sociology at Hunter College and the Graduate Center of the City University of New York. She is the author or editor of more than a dozen books, including *In a New Land: A Comparative View of Immigration* (New York University Press, 2005); *Not Just Black and White: Historical and Contemporary Perspectives on Immigration, Race, and Ethnicity in the United States* (edited with George Fredrickson; Russell Sage Foundation, 2004); *Islands in the City: West Indian Migration to New York* (University of California Press, 2001); *New Immigrants in New* York (rev. ed., Columbia University Press, 2001); and *From Ellis Island to JFK: New York's Two Great Waves of Immigration* (Yale University Press, 2000).

GRETA GILBERTSON is Associate Professor in the Department of Sociology and Anthropology at Fordham University. Her interests include immigration, citizenship, and gender. Her work has appeared in journals such as *Ethnic and Racial Studies, International Migration Review,* and *Sociological Perspectives.* She is currently working on a book on the dynamics of caregiving in Dominican immigrant families.

NAZLI KIBRIA is Associate Professor of Sociology and Director of Graduate Programs in Sociology at Boston University, where she teaches courses on immigration, contemporary South Asia, and the sociology of family and childhood. She was born in Bangladesh and received her undergraduate degree from Wellesley College and her Ph.D. from the University of Pennsylvania. She is the author of numerous publications, including *Family Tightrope: The Changing Lives of Vietnamese Americans* (Princeton University Press, 1993) and *Becoming Asian American: Identities of Second-Generation Chinese and Korean Americans* (Johns Hopkins University Press, 2002). She is currently at work on a book on the lives of Bangladeshis around the world.

CECILIA MENJÍVAR is the Cowden Distinguished Professor of Sociology in the School of Social and Family Dynamics at Arizona State University. Her research interests focus on the intersection between larger political and economic structures and the everyday lives of individuals. Within this general rubric, she has examined social processes of migration from Central America to the United States within specific legal and historical contexts. Her publications include *Fragmented Ties: Salvadoran Immigrant Networks in America* (University of California Press, 2000) and several edited volumes, and her work has appeared in the *American Journal of Sociology, International Migration Review, Social Problems, Ethnic and Racial Studies,* among other journals.

JENNIFER E. SYKES is a Ph.D. candidate in Sociology and Social Policy at Harvard University. Her research interests include social stratification, poverty and inequality, and child and family welfare. She has published in the area of child protection and is currently doing research on child-rearing strategies among immigrant and non-immigrant working poor in Boston.

MARY C. WATERS is the M. E. Zukerman Professor of Sociology at Harvard University, where she has taught since 1986. She studies immigration, racial and ethnic identities, and intergroup relations. She is the author, co-author, or editor of numerous books and articles, including *Inheriting the City: The Children of Immigrants Come of Age* (Harvard University Press, 2008); *The New Americans: A Guide to Immigration since 1965* (Harvard University Press, 2007); and *Black Identities: West Indian Immigrant Dreams and American Realities* (Harvard University Press, 1999).

MIN ZHOU is Professor of Sociology and the Founding Chair of the Department of Asian American Studies at the University of California, Los Angeles. Her main areas of research are immigration and immigrant adaptation, immigrant youths, Asian Americans, ethnic and racial relations, ethnic entrepreneurship and enclave economies, and urban sociology. She is the author of *Chinatown: The Socioeconomic Potential of an Urban Enclave* (Temple University Press, 1992) and *The Transformation of Chinese America* (Sanlian Publishers, 2006); coauthor of *Growing Up American: How Vietnamese Children Adapt to Life in the United States* (Russell Sage Foundation, 1998); and coeditor of *Contemporary Asian America* (New York University Press, 2000; 2d ed., 2007) and *Asian American Youth: Culture, Identity, and Ethnicity* (Routledge, 2004).

Index

acculturation: Chinese language schools, 13, 33–36; "consonant acculturation," 8

Across a Hundred Mountains (Grande), 183

Africa: Western images of, 114–116, 118–121, 129; Western images of, challenges to, 126–128

African Americans: corporal punishment in child-rearing, 77–78; second generation Sierra Leoneans and West Indians, 132n29

Africans, fears of contagion spread by, 117–118, 120–121, 125

American Baptist Churches vs. Thornburgh (*ABC* settlement), 165–166

American Community Survey (2004), 23, 48

Americanization, fears of, 22, 31

American Son: A Novel (Roley), 51

Appadurai, Arjun, 123

arranged marriages, 6

Asian immigrants: conspicuous consumption, 56; panethnic consciousness, 14; sexualization of Asian women in United States, 12, 64

authoritarian parenting, 86–89, 92–93

Avila, Ernestina, 192

Baldassar, Loretta, 135, 136, 145, 149

Bangladeshi immigrants, 98–113; Diversity Visa Lottery Program, 100, 112n7; downward class mobility after migrating, 101; family-based social capital, 103–104; family trips to the homeland, 107–111; "good family" notion, 103; "hometown" associations, 101; household income, 112n11; intergenerational conflict, 7, 98; intergenerational cooperation and caring, 8; involvement with Muslim and South Asian communities, 105–106, 112; marriage of U.S.-born and/or -raised children, 102–107, 111; parental pressure to marry within the ethnic group, 6; population growth, 100–101; poverty rate, 112n11; racial marginality in the United States, 107, 112; sample studied, 102, 113n14; second generation, 16, 101–102, 105–107, 109–111, 112; socioeconomic status, 101; transnational reproduction, 98–111; transnational ties and obligations, 16, 101, 105–106, 108–111, 112

Bangladeshis, middle-class, 103, 107–108

Barbadian immigrants, child-rearing practices, 84

Bashi, Vilna, 99